The Soul's Brain

The Soul's Brain

The Neurology and Logic of Your Intuition

Dr. Catherine Wilkins

HAY
HOUSE

Design by Rhett Nacson
Typeset by Bookhouse, Sydney
Edited by Margie Tubbs

ISBN: 978-1-4019-5467-3
E-book ISBN: 978-1-4019-5081-1

10 9 8 7 6 5 4 3 2 1
1ˢᵗ Edition, February 2018

Printed in the United States of America

Extract from *Awakening Osiris* © 1988 by Normandi Ellis, used with permission from Phanes Press c/o
Red Wheel Weiser, LLC, Newbury Port, MA 01950 www.redwheelweiser.com

This book is dedicated to my father,
who taught me to never be afraid to ask questions,
even if he didn't like the answers I found.

Contents

SECOND TRIANGLE   Strength

THIRD TRIANGLE   Sovereignty

GET READY

· · · · · · · · · · · · · · · ·

Intuition is a skill

....

Astonishing stories of intuition abound. In the dream that saves your life, alerting you early enough to a threatening illness. In the impulse that leads you to attend a function where you meet your life partner. In that flash of insight that gets you in touch with your life's work. Intuition appears as a source of magic in our lives. But then, all things were magic before we understood them.

Would you like to be a magician? Learn to use your intuition as easily, reliably and confidently as you do anything else. Then you'll be an everyday magician. But intuition can be tricky.

How do you know what you're thinking is intuition? What if it's just your imagination? How can you tell the difference? Isn't intuition just random and unreliable? What told my dad to suddenly slow to a crawl when driving on the highway? He drove round that blind corner at a walking pace. If he hadn't, he would've driven over the motorbiking couple who'd skidded out and were lying on the road.

Intuition's what told you to call your friend in distress. It's what told me to call a friend to give them the news that a mutual friend's father had passed. I did that even though I knew she was among the first people he'd call. Later we learned he'd been so thrown that he'd called her fax number rather than her mobile when he left her the message. Through my intuition, his message got through anyway. Intuition also enables messages from someone who's passed to get through. Or your irresistible impulse to change travel arrangements, which kept you from joining those who had a fatal accident.

Society is consumed with figuring out intuition. Does it only happen when you take drugs like *Lucy*? Are you an alien if you have it, as in *I am Number Four*? Or did you inherit intuition like *Beautiful Creatures*? Is it a gift you have little control over, as in *Frozen* or *The Medium*? Or do you get intuition from esoteric knowledge and study, similar to *Dr. Strange*? We're all fascinated by intuition; the power of its mysterious allure offers our life greater meaning and insight.

Intuition gives us hope and is linked to our drive to understand ourselves. Through understanding ourselves we understand the universe. However, to master our intuition we need a deeper awareness of ourselves. Especially the way our neurology works. Most profoundly, we have to move beyond our compartmentalized view of ourselves and our world. We need to know how we're connected internally to Who We Truly Are and externally to the physical substance of our lives. We have to work with **both sides of our brain**.

For our intuition to be consistent, we need to understand the principles involved. Musicians understand frequency, chords and rhythm. Carpenters understand alignment and proportion. Artists understand perspective and color theory. Physicists understand quantum effects and higher mathematics.

These principles allow us to operate consistently. Without an understanding of the principles of intuition, life is completely random. Amazing people such as Edgar Cayce, Esther Hicks and Caroline Myss produce consistent results with their intuition, by working powerfully with the principles of intuition. You can do this too. Work at these principles and your intuition will become an everyday skill that can deliver extraordinary results over and over.

Like any skill, there are a number of steps to mastery. For intuitive mastery there are nine steps for you to work through. So hold onto your hat and take your first step. Your life is about to change.

. . . .

Nine steps to mastering your intuition
Journey to shared value
....

From your first flash of intuition or yearning for a more expansive life, there are nine steps to intuitive mastery. Powerful intuition can deliver an abundant expansive life. These nine precious steps will take you from that intuitive knowing of an internal truth to a practical skill such as driving your car or working your laptop. Mastering your intuition is like walking from left foot to right foot and back again. When you take the nine steps to intuitive mastery, you do it from left brain to right brain and back again.

Your nine-step journey has three stages, each involving three steps. Why not visualize these steps as a triangle, each step reinforcing and supporting the others.

The three stages are:

1. building a stable foundation
2. growing strength
3. creating true authority, through the logic of your intuition and the workings of your neurology

This true authority is your sovereignty. Together these three phases make up the 'triangle of triangles' of the nine-step journey. We'll fill in the details of our intuition 'triangle of triangles' as we go.

The first triangle is all about stability, about building ourselves a stable intuitive foundation. Step One involves learning to complete our life cycles, to stop our energy going round and round in pointless, exhausting loops. Are you caught up in endless loops right now? Thoughts going round and round in your head? Taking up all your headspace? Draining your energy? That's an incomplete cycle. As soon as the cycle's complete, your head goes quiet. Then you can use your energy for more useful things. The more complete you get, the more energy you'll have flowing through your system.

In Step Two, you'll learn how to handle your increasing energy. The key to that is keeping yourself balanced. Just like a good work-life balance, you'll need to keep your energy balanced to keep stress at a minimum.

With increasing and balanced energy, the next step is to get to know your own energy. To recognize and understand your own unique voice. This is your own intuitive language. Getting to know your unique inner voice is Step Three, the final step in the first triangle that brings your life stability. Once you know your own intuitive language, you're ready for a wider intuitive understanding. You start to become aware of the importance of contrast, just as you understand 'soft' because it's different when compared to 'hard'. You learn intuitive skills in a similar way. Here though, you'll compare the external world with its myriad energies to your own energy. This means getting clear and precise about your own energy.

Once you've completed the first triangle, you'll have a stable foundation and be ready to build some walls. In intuitive terms, you're ready to get stronger. The second phase in developing your intuition is in getting true strength, so you're energetically fit. Have you noticed how you work and feel better when you're physically fit? Your intuition works the same way.

Step Four continues working with your own energy to build its incredible power, so you can send a clear signal out to the universe, like a radio station. If you're to achieve this, your signal needs to be clear and strong, so it won't get lost or drowned out. If you're streaming a movie or webinar, it's really annoying when your movie keeps stopping and starting. The same is true of your energetic signal. A powerful energetic signal means you can do some energetic 'heavy lifting', manifest what you want and influence matters of concern to you in the world with far greater ease.

Getting energetically fit gives you stronger intuitive 'muscles'. Your intuitive muscles are your focus and intention. That's what Step Five will help you develop. Then you can use your intuitive muscles, your focus and intention to move your energy and create your goals.

Getting a stronger, clearer focus enables you to use your energy with greater precision and effectiveness.

By Step Six you'll have developed considerable power, enough to begin to transform yourself and the world. Understanding the patterns of transformation helps this process go with far greater ease and grace, getting you ready for the huge expansion to come. Transformation is never easy, whether it's going from school to college or university, or going from being single to being in a committed relationship. The more you understand just **how** you transform, the easier and more graceful this process will be. Once you've developed the wisdom of guided transformation, you've completed the second triangle.

Now you have a stable foundation and strong intuitive walls, you're ready for the roof—living within an intuitive life with clarity and purpose. This sovereignty enables you to step into your true authority, with your own resonant pattern and the unique resonances of others. With a complete intuitive 'house', you can create a whole new way of life for yourself.

In Step Seven, you learn how to expand your ability to work with patterns. You learn how to work with multiple patterns, alongside the integrity patterns of others in the same moment. This skill is the key to true co-creation and a source of consistent expansion and joy. Some life patterns don't serve you, such as saying 'yes' to things that don't work for you. Other patterns do serve you, but how do you know when to say 'yes' and when to say 'no'? In Step Seven, you'll learn which patterns to work with and how to let go of those you don't want.

Step Eight uses the patterns that create positive expansion. With more energy and abundance in your life, it's important to ensure that everyone you invite in strengthens your pattern. That way your intuition will continue to strengthen. This is important as you don't want energy leaks. Did you know that only 10 percent of people who win the lottery keep and grow the money they won? The rest are broke after a few years. You want to be one of those people who can grow energetic abundance, until your expansion reaches critical mass. That is the point at which its growth just continues, whether you're working on your energy consciously or not.

Step Nine completes the final triangle and is the key to true co-creation with the universe. It enables you to operate in the way the universe operates. You'll learn how to enrich your own resonance with harmonics. Your energy can grow from a single note to a melody, one as rich as an orchestra. A ham sandwich is good. But it's so much better with mayonnaise or a bit of salad. Staying centered in your own energy and pattern, while enriching it, will take you to a very different way of operating. This new way creates a richness of life for yourself and others, a richness you can't currently imagine. This creates a life of constant, joyful, mutual expansion for you.

These nine steps take your intuition from a random wonderful mystery to an everyday reliable skill. Your intuition is meant to be a part of your life, a part that enables you to grow with ease and grace. But in order for you to understand it, you're going to need a new type of logic than the one you've used until now.

. . . .

Linear versus pattern-based logic
Intuition has its own logic

T he key to coordinating your science brain and intuition brain is understanding the logic of your right brain with your left brain. You learned the logic of your left brain in school. It goes 1+1 = 2, 1+2 = 3, and so on. This logic is familiar. It works from known details. But you probably weren't taught pattern-based logic at school, unless you were taught how to do IQ tests.

The gold standard of pattern-based logic is fractal-based logic. This is the key to coordinating both sides of your brain. You may not know the word, but you do know what a fractal is. Fractals are patterns that repeat over and over to build up more complex patterns. Snowflakes, trees, mountain ranges, nautilus shells and some vegetables are clear fractals. Break off a twig and what's it look like? A miniature tree!

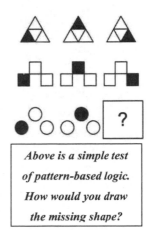

Above is a simple test of pattern-based logic. How would you draw the missing shape?

There are fractals in your body. Your lungs look like miniature trees or fractals. So too does your nervous system. Your DNA uses fractals to construct your body. Your brain works with information along fractal lines. Your heart beats in a fractal pattern; it's not so much a regular as a regularly irregular pattern. Your heartbeat's a dynamic, moving fractal. The fractal part of the beat is so important that if your heartbeat loses its timing, a heart attack can be reliably predicted.

On the next page is a snapshot of another moving fractal: a Lorenz attractor. It's the path of a moving system. A Lorenz attractor comes from studying the fluid circulation of temperature when it's heated below and cooled from above. The butterfly shape comes from the exchange between those two sources of energy. Lorenz attractors are important for your body, because your body's made up of so much fluid. You also have to keep your temperature balanced.

Notice how similar that pattern looks to the pattern of your two brain hemispheres connecting. Interestingly, the same pattern also looks like colliding galaxies. Fractals are significant to us, our intuition and the entire universe.

In society and business, we get details we can study and agree on from the linear logic of our left brain. If we didn't all agree to stop on a red light and drive on the same side of the road we'd be in trouble. We trust and act on how much gold is worth per ounce, because it's easy to tell if other people agree with our assessment of gold's value on a particular day. If they disagree, the price of gold will go up or down until we reach a new agreement.The problem is that our intuitive truths are more personal. This makes it difficult to trust our inner knowing or intuition the same way, unless we can translate the truths of our right brain into the kind of external truths others can agree on, or not. That's what pattern-based or fractal logic can do.

Lorenz attractor

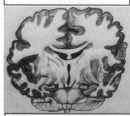

Connection between the two hemispheres of the brain

Until now, the unique character of individual intuition has been hard to understand. Fractals help us join the dots. Our intuition works as uniquely as a snowflake's creation. Snow crystals are formed with tiny differences in mineral concentration, freezing rates, wind, humidity and other factors. That gives each snowflake a unique fractal variation on a six-point star.

Everyone's intuition works slightly differently. Your nervous system also had a

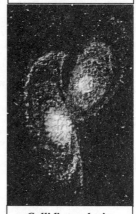

Colliding galaxies

unique start. It too is a unique fractal variant of a general pattern. You receive intuition or internal truths and teachings in a form unique to you. Even if a roomful of people are getting intuitive information on the same subject, it'll be communicated differently to each person. You may get a sound, an image, a symbol, an intense feeling or something else. In a very real sense, each of us has our own intuitive language.

Because of the unique nature of our neurology, our intuition will work differently from others, even though it's telling us about the same universe we all live in.

What we need is a translation system that lets us convert our unique, right-brained, intuitive information into a left-brained piece of data that others can understand. This is what *The Soul's Brain* will give you. A way to get a good flow from one side of your brain to the other, so you can use your intuition to create a more joyful, abundant life for yourself. Then others can understand and agree with your intuition, as clearly as we agree that chloroplasts in leaves make energy from sunlight. With conscious intuition and an integrated left/right brain process, you can move through the nine steps and develop conscious intuition. Then you'll be able to translate your internal truths into external truths with significant value. You can then work with your intuition as normally and readily as you read street signs or check your bank balance. A coordinated whole brain expands your life more than either half of your brain can do on its own.

. . . .

A whole brain is better than half
Left-right-left-right-left-right

· ·

Intuition has two major problems. The first happens if you have it. The second happens if you don't. Sounds confusing? Not for long. You'll need to handle both of these concepts before you can claim true intuitive mastery.

The first problem of intuition is due to the rise in energy and sensitivity that intuition brings. This can be so overwhelming it's hard to stay grounded or operate in day-to-day life. It seems your intuition is controlling you, rather than the other way around. Some people feel so out of control they're driven to take refuge in the countryside, turn to abstemious diets, or take up time-consuming meditation regimes. Images of those with vast awareness but chaotic lives give intuition a bad rap. Indeed, one of the oldest words for an intuitive is a 'sensitive'. Such people have an extraordinary ability to detect or be affected by things the rest of us aren't immediately aware of.

Nicola first came to me for help in getting her energy more stable. She was so sensitive and so affected by everything around her, and found it hard to maintain her focus. This created stress in her physical system, manifesting as irritable bowel symptoms. She also had learning difficulties. The energy of whatever she read affected her so much she found it hard to pick up a book. After I'd worked with her for a while, her energy became more stable. Yet it wasn't until she started to understand and use the principles of a whole-brained approach that her health and ability to learn really took a turn for the better.

Once she understood how her system integrated the wisdom of her left and right brain, she could use her intuitive sensitivity for her own benefit. She overcame her learning difficulties. She also got a right-brained clarity on her path in life with left-brained understanding. She knew how her path looked in everyday terms. With that certainty, she found the inspiration to complete some years of study that previously would have been completely daunting.

Nicola's life is now very different. Her health is good. She's has a great career as a registered nurse. She's mastered her sensitivity to the point where she works in intensive care. She's also a Fractology Practitioner, the system I developed to teach people the principles of their intuition. Learning those principles enabled her to create a life of greater opportunity and abundance. Her physical life is now a mirror of her spiritual life, with all the wonderful satisfaction that flows from her deep, clear, spiritual awareness.

The second problem with intuition comes from living in a world in love with science. Science has brought huge benefits but comes at a psychological cost. We've come to believe only the things we can analyze and understand have value. Our intuition appears irrational, leading us to ignore it, shut it down or deny its existence, depriving us of untold benefits in our careers, wellbeing and relationships.

Russell's a brilliant psychiatrist. Ask him anything you like about mental health. He'll give you a clear precise answer. Like many others, he's so strong logically; Russell relies on his left brain completely. As a consequence and despite his thriving practice, a lot of his life didn't work for him. His relationships were draining. His work-load was exhausting. He was stressed but saw no way out. His logic told him doing what he'd always done brought him success. But he needed his intuition to help him find a new path in life. That's what I helped him do.

When I was working with Russell, he was constantly astonished at my ability to show him new perspectives, new ways of working with what he already knew. New options for a truly satisfying life opened up. Of course, the true changes came when his intuition kicked in. He no longer had to rely on my insight. Russell could then find the logical path forwards and refine it into the path that worked for him. Once his logical mind was supported and guided by his intuition, his life began to work for him as well as all his clients.

The problems of intuition are actually a left-brain/right-brain communication issue. Consider a tree and you'll understand what I mean. Look at a tree with your left brain. You focus on tiny details such as the chloroplasts, those clever little chlorophyll factories for converting sunlight into food in the cells. Or how a cell uses energy, forms a leaf with other cells or is affected by each season. Bit by bit, fact by fact, your left brain builds a science-type picture of a tree.

On the other hand, your right brain connects to the **whole** tree in one glance. Then it goes deeper to find the pattern that underlies its structure. That's how you know how well a tree is doing, even if you're not a botanist. Where the tree's health is strong, the pattern is clear. Where it's got a problem, the pattern is broken or distorted. You can even tell if another tree is the same type, as they've got the same pattern.

Being able to track the pattern of anything and draw conclusions from that is pattern-based logic. We can reach a deep understanding of the world by knowing what aligns to the **underlying pattern**. We can appreciate what works and what doesn't by how well or badly that alignment is held.

This intuitive understanding helps us in our lives, improves our health, relationships and careers. It empowers our levels of abundance and life satisfaction. It also helps us deal better with other people and our environment. Your left-brain details are aligned by your right brain into a complete healthy whole. Your right brain takes you to new and amazing places, but it's your left brain that figures out how you got there. Only then can you go back whenever you want or ground what you've learned into your finances and everyday life.

If you're using only half your brain, you end up knowing a lot of stuff but the facts won't take you where you want to go. Or you'll have the most amazing vision of what could be, without any ability to get physical reality to match it.

Most of us are taught to use only the fact-based details of our left brain. That means we're only using half our brain. We don't know how to use our right brain or intuition. The two sides are meant to work together. A whole brain is better than half. When we work with our whole brain, our capacity to see through the complexities of life to the simple patterns that underlie it is vastly increased.

. . . .

The truth is always simple

Pattern-based logic—the logic of your right brain—is different to the logic you're used to. In school or at home you were taught to do things in a specific way, even if it didn't feel right to you. You were taught a set of rules. You weren't taught how to find the **underlying** pattern of things and to ensure you strengthened that pattern. That's why sometimes you did all the right things but it didn't turn out too well. Like doing a painting with perfect perspective and following all the rules of composition but it was somehow uninspiring. Following the rules won't find the pattern underlying any creation.

Operating with pattern-based logic means learning to be careful of **how** we do things, not just **what** we do. Operating from alignment to each pattern is new for many of us. Getting used to new ways of thinking may be uncomfortable. It takes time and sometimes angst to change our ideas. Think back to the last time you had to let go of a cherished belief, such as being the center of the universe. You probably felt that as a kid. A few centuries ago everyone believed it. Changing that belief may not have been easy.

In Ancient Greece, the masters of logic and mathematics studied the world with their senses. Without technology, they realized the earth was a sphere and everything was built from atoms. But they also believed everything, even the sun, revolved round the earth. Then along came Galileo with his ability to grind lenses. That let him make better telescopes. He saw the planetary paths clearly enough to see they weren't moving as they should. So how to hold onto the belief that the earth was at the center of all things? Aha! Planets must travel in epicycles.

Did you ever play with a spirograph? That neat toy draws smaller circles as your pen travels round a bigger one. That's an epicycle. Turning through smaller circles while traveling around a bigger circle is what creates an epicycle. Clever, yet just a way to hang onto old beliefs.

We hang onto old ideas by forcing new observations to fit them. That complicates things. It slows down our expansion. And expansion is the primary purpose of our intuition.

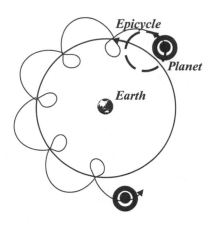

When we start to tell ourselves complicated stories in order to convince ourselves our old beliefs still work, we're using metaphorical epicycles. You're living a classic example of that if you tell yourself you have to be practical because you can't make a living from your own creativity or passion. Like writing. If you continue to think in that kind of epicycle, you'll never get to know the joy of living from your own self-expression. The more strongly we hold onto our old beliefs, the more we'll complicate things and the more metaphorical epicycles we'll create.

The better the telescopes became, the more epicycles astronomers needed. At its height, they had as many as 42! Maybe that's why 42 is the answer to life, the universe and everything, as Douglas Adams said in *The Hitchhiker's Guide to the Galaxy.* The more complicated something is, the further away from the truth it probably is. Occam's razor, the principle that the more assumptions we make the less likely it is to be true, supports this. Occam's is a mental razor, to cut ideas down to essentials. If we stop assuming we're the center of everything, the solar system is suddenly much simpler. No need for epicycles.

You can apply Occam's razor to your own self-understanding. When we live by right-wrong rules, we have to make many assumptions to make our lives work. When we let go of the rules, things get simpler. When we live by aligning ourselves to the integrity

geocentric system
(earth at the center)

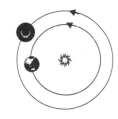

heliocentric system
(sun at the center)

of our own beingness, things get expansive. Our intuition operates by aligning us to the pattern of our integrity.

In our everyday lives, Occam's razor gets distilled into the common wisdom that the simpler something is, the closer it's likely to be to the truth. Think of all your relationships. Each person you know, whether a family member, a spouse or partner, a friend or colleague, has different 'rules'. Every person thinks your relationship should work a particular way. When you attempt to keep all of these rules or assumptions about relationships in mind, you end up juggling a whole lot of different pieces of data. Let go of all of that. Focus on the simple fact that healthy relationships are based on love and respect. Especially self-love and self-respect. Then things get simpler. And easier.

Occam's razor also works in business. When there are a lot of complicated procedures and rules to observe, corporations waste a lot of time, money and energy on compliance. The excellent companies have very few rules. That enables them to focus on what matters. They simplify their business to make sure what they do works for their team and their clients.

These days the most advanced telescope tech is in orbit. This has simplified the process of observation, as the telescopes are away from atmospheric interference and have brought us to another level of understanding. A new opportunity to test our beliefs. At first, scientists expected not to find any planets beyond our solar system, because ours is so special. Then they found planets around other stars called exoplanets. The first ones were massive enough to wobble their star. Such planets are unlikely to support life. With new tech, scientists could detect the faint shift in light caused by planets passing between their sun and ours, which led to the discovery of earth-like exoplanets. Some are even in the Goldilocks zone (not too hot and not too cold). These may contain life.

Not feeling quite so special? There are thousands of exoplanets but are any of them like earth? Surely any life-supporting planet must have a sun like ours. Yet while I was writing *The Soul's Brain*, seven planets were found orbiting a small red dwarf star, TRAPPIST-1.

That sun is cooler than ours, so even planets with close orbits may have life. Put this information together with the growing number of exoplanets they're finding and you can sense the importance of an open mind.

So how many assumptions do you and I need? I'm not sure Occam would be impressed by anyone saying we're the only sentient species in the galaxy!

Resistance to new ideas and intuition come from the same place. If we're to avoid thinking in epicycles, we need to embrace the new, along with all of its possible benefits. Your left brain wants to hang onto known details, while your right brain likes leaping to expansive conclusions. Your intuition will take you to new places, but you can't forget your left brain, because it'll show you the benefits of that place once you get there.

Like any other skill, conscious intuition requires a bit of knowledge and lots of practice. This skill turns into solid bank accounts, thriving relationships and inspiring creativity. Remember that everything in society started as someone's intuition, from Michael Faraday's flashes about electricity and the Wright brothers' visions of taking flight, to the insightful way Napoleon fought his battles to help shape the face of modern Europe. Then there's Katharine Briggs and Isabel Myers creating a measure for your intuition in your personality, the way Steve Jobs worked with technology to create Apple. All these people used expert intuition to change their lives and the world. You can too. But in order to learn something new, to learn conscious intuition, you may need to put aside what you already know.

. . . .

GET SET

. . . .

If all you have is a hammer, everything's a nail
Life, coma and death

Imagine you woke one morning to find the person you love more than anything in severe pain. Light and sound sent them into agony. They were too debilitated to move, so of course you told them to stay in bed. Then they got worse. Soon they couldn't move at all and were speaking erratically. Really worried now, you rang an ambulance. When you got to the hospital the doctors said, 'There's nothing we can do. Prepare yourself.'

No one wants that. Sally certainly didn't. Panicked, she called me for help. When I got to the hospital, she told me her husband had viral meningitis. The doctors had said there was nothing their mainstream medicine could do. When I examined Sally's husband, my left brain saw he was barely aware of me. He answered my questions slowly in a 'word salad' type of nonsense. Mostly he described his symptoms as 'yellow'. Light was painful to him. The swelling in his brain was obvious, from the tightness of his cranial bones and the fluid distension at the base of his skull.

Clearly, his nervous system was in deep trouble. My left brain agreed he had viral meningitis and there was nothing the doctors could do. So much for left-brained facts. Fortunately, my right brain had a different perspective. My intuition tracked the pattern of his illness. It perceived the congestion in his brain as a thick brown sludge, yet underneath that the pattern of his nervous system was intact. The quicksilver-blue (how my intuition perceives a healthy brain) was there. It was just clogged up and under pressure from all that fluid. From a right-brain perspective, there were things that could be done.

You know the pattern of congestion. You've experienced it or know people who have. It's what happens when you get a virus: a cold or flu. You leak everywhere. Sure it's gross but that fluid does an important job. It flushes out the virus. Harry's body was fighting the virus and winning. That's why his brain still showed as healthy in my intuitive vision. But his body was creating so much fluid in its efforts to flush out the virus, it was squashing his brain. That's why you can get a massive sinus headache when you get a cold or flu. It's the fluid build-up causing too much pressure.

I told Sally, 'I need to get the fluid inside his skull to drain. The pressure is squashing his brain.' That meant working on his skull or cranial bones, physically and energetically. I set to work, focusing on the pattern of his healthy cerebrospinal fluid. The base of his skull was the key point. Getting the bones moving there, as well as working with his energy, got the fluid flowing. Then I left. The next day Harry could cope with a little light. He could even talk. Yet it was clear he was still in pain. Again I worked on his cerebrospinal fluid. The next day Harry was sitting up watching television.

Thanks to my intuition, his story had a new and different ending. A happy Sally reported, 'You could see the difference in Harry every time you came. The doctors and nurses were astonished but not one of them asked me what you did.' Their left brains were sticking with their known facts. They didn't want new ones. When the left brain knows hammers, it sticks with nails. It doesn't go looking for screws.

Sadly, not everyone is open to the new. That means no new endings. Mary's story was like that. She came to see me for chronic fatigue. She was married to a very wealthy, controlling man. After I had re-energized her exhausted adrenals, we talked about her co-dependency with her husband, the source of her exhaustion. But a hammer is a hammer. She explained at length why she couldn't change her situation. Despite my best efforts, she wasn't willing to change her relationship pattern, even knowing its cost. When she left, my intuition said: 'She'll be back in two years with breast cancer.' I said a lot of unprintable things to myself, because there was nothing else I could do.

Sadly. my intuition had spoken the truth. 'Can you help?' Mary asked, when she came back two years later.

'It's the same problem. Are you willing to work on your relationship now?' I asked. Once again, she explained why she couldn't. Tragically she's no longer with us.

Change can bring pain because it stretches us. Even positive change can be uncomfortable. That's why they call it 'growing pains'. Understanding the patterns of growth allows us to tell good pain (a sign of growth and expansion) from bad pain (a warning of something negative). If you can't discern the difference between those two, you're at risk of choosing the wrong path, one that doesn't serve you. You may go the wrong way trying to avoid good pain, the pain of the new that comes with growth. That's what I did in my twenties.

I was very ill when I studied veterinary science. I was all ribs and stomach with cystic skin and a swollen belly. I was exhausted every day. The world receded behind a grey wall of fog, as my nervous system threatened to shut down. I was suffering the long-term effects of shutting down my intuition as a child. Closing down so much of myself had shut down my immune system. That, along with an inflamed gut from still-undiagnosed gluten intolerance, had given me severe systemic candidiasis.

Candida is the same organism that's responsible for thrush. However, when it takes over the gut it turns from a yeast into a mould. Yes, just like the mould growing on your bathroom wall. (Yeah, yuck, I agree.) It sends tendrils down between the cells of your gut lining, giving you intense, leaky gut. Bits of food that haven't been fully digested get into your bloodstream, creating further inflammation, congestion and toxicity. If your gut gets as damaged as mine was, you can't absorb proper nutrition. That leaves you further depleted.

I'd stopped myself from feeling the metaphysical or anything more than the obvious and tangible. By so doing, I also lost my ability to feel the physical. I'd shut down my ability to see myself and my unique pattern. Then all I could do was avoid pain, including the positive pain of change. That took me down an unhealthy path. As I wasn't listening to my intuition, it couldn't show me my path. My organs were shut down by the systemic effects of the candidiasis, yet I still held to the left-brained view I knew. Specialists and doctors assured me each successive drug would work, but I continued my slow, messy slide into illness.

I was stuck in my left brain, with lots of details I could be right about. I persisted in trying to force myself into a pattern not my own. Stubbornness is right there in my name after all. 'Wilkins' means related (kin) to will. Okay, it actually means being kin to Bill but the point stands. I was using my ancestors as an in-built excuse for being stuck and in pain.

Your ancestors aren't mine, but you may be using them the same way without realizing. Resisting all pain, even positive pain, is built into your genes and your neurology. You have to choose as I did. What's more important: to be Who You Truly Are or avoid all pain, even positive pain? Because that's what worked for your ancestors?

. . . .

Brain glue
The one-valley world

. . . .

If we go back to when the entire world was the small valley where our tribe lived, we could know everything we needed to know. We'd know where plants grew best, where the first fruits and flowers appeared, where to build or not. In those days, traveling more than five miles was a huge adventure, full of danger and derring-do. This was similar to the world of your grandparents and great-grandparents, in that things didn't change much. That meant it was possible to teach people **what** to think (what worked, or was 'right') and what didn't work (what was 'wrong'). There was no need to teach them **how** to think.

Rules are great when things don't change but not so great when they do. Things in each new valley work differently. Moving around is like figuring out how screws work compared to nails. Of course today there are some of us still living in one-valley worlds. The current focus on fundamentalism or traditionalism assumes the world's problems can be solved by going back to doing things the way they were done a hundred or two hundred years ago. The irony of all that is that many people in those one-valley worlds are using the internet, like Facebook or Twitter, to rail about all the evils of the modern world. The internet didn't exist in the time they want to return to.

Each of us have had our 'one-valley' moments. My mum always did a great roast, her lamb was especially good. Her paella is still one of my favorite dishes today. On the other hand, like many back then, she did overcook the vegetables. The worst was asparagus. She used to get canned asparagus and boil it for about ten minutes. When it landed on my plate it was hot, slimy sticks of sludge. I found it so horrible that I refused to eat asparagus for years afterwards. Even when friends cooked it completely differently. In my one-valley, asparagus was revolting.

One evening after excessive urging, a friend finally managed to get me to taste the asparagus they'd cooked. It was fresh, lightly steamed with just a little lemon juice. What a revelation! Instead of slimy, it was crunchy. Instead of a cloying sludge, it had a crisp flavor. It's now one of my favorite vegetables.

There's a price to everything. The price of becoming Who We Truly Are is giving up who we're not. The price of experiencing a wider world and creating a more abundant life for ourselves is stepping outside our one-valley. Take the stuff with you that still works. Paella is still a favorite of mine and I roast a leg of lamb the same way my mum used to. Yes, it's that good. But I now know how good fresh asparagus is as well.

The problem with the new in a one-valley world is it tends to bring uncertainty, if not danger. I didn't want to risk tasting the slimy sludge I remembered one more time. Yet if I hadn't been willing to change, I would never have found out about fresh asparagus. When circumstances change, what worked before may no longer work. The old rules may no longer apply.

When you focus on **what** to think rather than **how**, you get stuck in a one-valley world. The fight-flight part of your brain acts as if the old rules always apply. But if you want to open up to the amazing opportunities that lie beyond where you are today, you'll have to access the rest-regeneration part of your brain. It holds the key to knowing which new things to embrace, to create your most abundant future.

Imagine you grabbed the superglue without thinking it through. You might end up sticking things together in a way you didn't intend. That's what your old fight-flight reflexes are trying to protect you from. However,

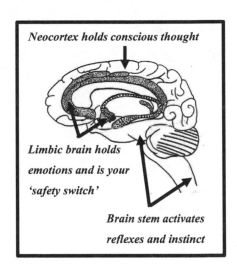

Neocortex holds conscious thought

Limbic brain holds emotions and is your 'safety switch'

Brain stem activates reflexes and instinct

the rest-regeneration part of your brain knows you can get a different outcome if you just focus on **how** you want to align things **before** you start. In other words, holding the focus on the positive keeps your fight-flight reflexes in check. The 'glue' between the oldest (brain stem or instinct) and newest (neocortex or higher reasoning) parts of your brain is the limbic system.

Your limbic brain keeps you stuck in your old patterns when it cuts off your higher reasoning. It triggers your fight-flight instinct. By holding onto your positive focus, you can keep it from doing that. The limbic system responds as quickly as if it were the brain's safety switch. When your brain perceives a potential threat, it cuts in to keep you safe, just like when you stick a knife in the toaster. When you touch a toaster wire with a knife your arm spasms, your chest squeezes. Then the safety switch cuts in. Phew! You can breathe again. Everything's okay, apart from burnt toast and having to reset the fuse box!

In an emergency we don't have time to think, so our limbic system takes over. It gets us out of trouble. Afterwards, it uses our emotions to help us process what just happened. This is a good process but can be problematic, if it treats new experiences as if they were as great a threat as a cave bear. We can miss out on amazing opportunities if that happens.

Our limbic system is master of emergencies. When I was in high school, one morning after swim training I witnessed a girl slip as she got off the train. Kelly fell between the train and the platform. All I could see were her head and shoulders as she screamed, 'Pull me up!'

Kelly was a big girl but weighed less than a bunny rabbit when I pulled her up. She landed on the platform and burst into tears. Her limbic system was helping her process her brush with death. Her elder sister materialized and the emergency was over. Only then could I think again. I wondered what had happened to my schoolbag. I found it halfway up the platform. My limbic system had taken emergency control. It hadn't wasted time forming memories. I still don't know what happened between the time Kelly fell and when I pulled her up.

Your brain's 'safety switch' is brilliant for handling emergencies but it's the worst thing for conscious awareness or intuition. It literally stops you from thinking or being conscious. This is why so many spiritual traditions are focused on letting go of fear, living instead in a state of openness and love.

When we're scared, our limbic system is in control. Brooke was living in that reality. She'd had a difficult divorce. Her children were still young enough for her ex to use his relationship with them as a means of scaring her. He was constantly threatening to take her back to custody court, not bringing the kids back to her place at the agreed time, or telling her they had to change the day he had them over. Her fear over what he would do next kept her in a constant state of anxiety.

Fear of what the constant changes and uncertainty were doing to her kids kept her limbic system in firm control. She couldn't think how she was going to get out of that situation. Yet Brooke was a highly-intelligent woman with a successful professional career. Stressed out of her mind over what she was going to do, she asked me for help. It didn't take much. I helped her understand the one-valley her ex was living in. I gave her some simple strategies she could use to create certainty for herself and her children, despite what was happening in his valley.

That provided enough clarity for her usual confidence to reassert itself and the emotional stress to settle. With just a couple of strategies, her limbic system switched off. She could think again. She realized the situation wasn't one emergency after another, though it was still a difficult situation that needed managing. Realizing she now knew how to create more certainty for herself and her children, everyone was soon calmer and happier. It's easy to understand how that happens with difficult situations, but how about fabulous ones?

When I first worked with Tyler, he had a lot of expertise but very little confidence aside from his work. That changed as he learned to appreciate more of Who He Truly Was. As a result, he was promoted into a management position. Initially, having a team under his authority was terrifying for him. His initial reaction was to get angry whenever there was a problem. That was the 'fight' part of his limbic system trying to attack the problem.

I helped him understand the difference between the valleys. We called one valley or category 'doing your work' and the other one 'managing others'. They both required different strategies, as the trees and houses in one valley aren't in the same place in a different valley. You have to walk the appropriate route for each. When he'd been a team member, he hadn't needed any negotiation strategies. Yet they're the primary skill of a team manager. Once he learned some strategies for achieving optimal alignment in his team, his limbic system calmed down. He no longer saw the problems as a threat to his new position. Everyone in his team became happier. Importantly, he was soon enjoying the satisfaction of seeing everyone work better.

Edward de Bono, the father of lateral thinking, developed a system of six thinking hats to facilitate our ability to think from different perspectives. That's what each different valley is: a different part of our life that requires a different perspective. While our complicated lives these days may span more than six valleys, de Bono's concept is still useful. Each valley has its own obstacles and freedoms. Each different part of our lives enables us to do different things but also carries different obstacles with it. The houses and trees in each valley are the obstacles. The paths and grassy areas in each valley are where we have some freedom. By consciously acknowledging which valley and which terrain we're operating in, we increase our chances of moving forward effectively.

In business, some of our different valleys might be labeled 'negotiating staff differences' or 'handling different clients' or 'liaising with tricky suppliers'. At home, some of our different valleys could be called 'choreographing everyone's movements' or 'keeping the hallway clear' or 'food that tastes good and is good for you'. For our own personal or spiritual growth, we might have such valleys as 'finding me time' or 'creative development' or 'conscious goal or intention work'. Each different valley requires a different perspective. When we acknowledge that, we allow ourselves to align more effectively with the optimal (the easy and graceful) path.

A major key to conscious intuition is keeping your limbic system in a chilled state. Think back to that time you lost your cool. Say

when you exploded during that family gathering or took an inno-
cent joke the wrong way or your paranoia ran rampant when you
weren't in control. All of those not-chilled moments were a result
of your limbic system firing off. In those moments, your intuition
doesn't have a look in. Whenever you connect with anything new
or get emotional, your 'safety switch' will trigger. It just does. Then
you lose conscious awareness and control, at least to some degree.

Being taught **what** to do may have made sense for our grandparents. Things didn't change much back then. Today, however, things
change all the time. What worked yesterday may not work today.
Yet we're at risk of responding to new things the way our ancestors
did. We need to learn to think differently. To think in a way that
enables us to grow and connect with the new, without our limbic
system going off.

Tyler grew so much from his promotion experience he came to
understand that every new situation would present new challenges
and problems. He now knows that's just the new terrain he has to
walk through. The terrain of a new valley. He knows every expansion means that he won't understand where the best path is for a
little while. So now he gives himself time to find it. With that
focus, he's soon walking the new path with as much confidence as
the old. That means he can face the new without going into fear.
As a consequence, he's finally able to take an audacious step and
achieve a dream he's had for a long time: creating his own business.

That's what your conscious intuition is for. It's a system for perceiving the pattern of the unknown, so it's easier for it to become
known. Once we get our fear and limbic system out of the way, we
can expand into the new with confidence. Then we don't have to
tell ourselves stories, in order to justify holding onto the old.

. . . .

Spontaneous remission and other furphies
Freaking fight and flight

· ·

If you ever come across a snake, you want your limbic system to spot it. But if you see a koala, you don't want it reacting, even if someone's been telling you furphies about drop bears, those tall tales designed to entertain and scare you. Or give tourists a hard time. Stories, spin, white lies or furphies are used to 'fight' new ideas. They're a way of pretending that reality hasn't changed or isn't different to what we know. Yet we have to be open to the new, if we're going to get all the abundance that's waiting for us.

In mainstream medicine, when a patient's cancer shrinks and disappears through holistic means (so it's healed without surgery, chemo or radiation therapy) it's called 'spontaneous remission'. However, these patients heal because they've changed their lifestyles and eating habits, taken up meditation and restructured their belief systems, fasted, detoxed and re-aligned their lives on all levels. Doesn't sound that spontaneous, does it?

Your brain's safety switch or limbic system reacts to new ideas as if drop bears were real. It reacts to perceived mental threats by pushing them out of your mental space. Your limbic system drives away new ideas, which is an unfortunate form of self-sabotage.

We need a new habit, a new neurological habit that's more open and comfortable with novelty. When we're in our teen years, we're encouraged to seek novelty, adventure and all things beyond what we grew up with. We're supported to take gap years, do internships and work experience before we settle on a career. We're encouraged to have a wide circle of friends before we choose a life partner, to see a little of the world before we settle down.

This all helps strengthen our neurology, creating more cross-connections within the brain. It's fodder for the awareness we take into adulthood. Being open and comfortable with novelty is a guarantee of ongoing growth. Many years ago, one of my teachers said to me: 'We're either green and growing, or we're ripe and rotten.' There are studies that show those who challenge themselves with new experiences end up more optimistic and fulfilled. This is the natural consequence of the growing confidence that comes with experience. Learning how to handle things you didn't know you could grows your self-belief.

My experience with asparagus taught me that if I at least have a taste of things, I may discover new favorites. The more I'm open to the new, the more variety I have in my life. Thus my life is richer and my understanding grows deeper. So far my openness to novelty has taken me from veterinary school to being trained as a rebirther, to biofeedback counselling, art school and chiropractic school. Each new direction widened my experience and awareness. Each gave me something that enabled me to develop Fractology and the principles of intuition. You're receiving the benefits of my openness to the new in every page of *The Soul's Brain*.

You've probably heard it takes three weeks to change a habit, but it takes twice as long for a neurological habit. Your limbic system needs to take a 'chill pill' for a whole six weeks, if it's to stop throwing a spanner in the works. Or a hammer. If you feel uncomfortable or uneasy whenever you consider doing something new, you may want to do the following 'real life experiment':

. . . .

OPENING TO THE NEW

- Pick a six-week window in your calendar in which you'll have a bit of regular time to devote to your new neurological habit.

- Write the date and how you're feeling today in your journal or on a piece of paper. Keep this somewhere you'll be able to find easily later.

- Commit to spending a little time every day doing something new. This is easier if you write a list of novel things you can experience before you start. There are 42 days in a six-week window. (There's that 'answer to life, the universe and everything' again!)

- It's okay to start with small things. Here are some suggestions:
  - o visit a new cafe
  - o try some strange kind of fruit, like dragonfruit or custard apples
  - o take a different route through your village, town or city
  - o visit a museum or art gallery you haven't been to already
  - o read a book in a genre you wouldn't normally (a small book is okay)
  - o have a go at creating your own Sudoku
  - o do finger painting
  - o try a sport you've never experienced, like archery or white-water rafting
  - o cook that complicated recipe, or cook creatively without a recipe at all!
  - o say hello to a complete stranger
  - o strike up a conversation with the person next to you in line or on a train or bus
  - o make up a game and see how your friends like it

- It's natural to feel a little nervous at first. Be kind to yourself but keep going.

- At the end of your six weeks, write down how you feel.

- Then get out the journal or paper on which you recorded how you felt before you started. How do the two compare? Are you feeling stronger, happier, more confident?

- I'd love to hear about your experience with the new. Please let me know at https://www.facebook.com/drcatherinewilkins/

. . . .

Chiropractors know this 'neurological window' well. Any nerve injury is much easier to sort out if it's attended to before that six-week window closes. After that it can take two or three times as many visits and work, because your nervous system gets an 'injury habit'. Using your breath is one of the best ways to give your limbic system a 'chill pill', so you can use your six-week window effectively. It gives you access to a calmer state, one that supports your intuition. In flight-fight mode you breathe hard and fast. Breathing calmly and deeply will get you into rest-regeneration mode.

Without going into all the ins and outs of it (yes, that's a breathing joke!), the slower your outbreath the more relaxed you'll be. The slower your outbreath, the less your limbic system will take control, so the more you'll be in a rest-regenerative state.

Do the following simple experiment and you'll feel what I mean. This breath helps if you ever get a bit nervous while stepping into the new. Breathing techniques are some of the oldest for creating different states of awareness, including conscious intuition. Ask Mr. Google. You'll get more information than you'll know what to do with. Breathing has a powerful effect on your mind-body connection and your nervous system. Even its oldest part, which is older than your limbic system or mammalian brain. It's even older than your brain stem or reptilian brain.

. . . .

MIND-BODY BREATH

- Notice how relaxed or tense you are.

- Now breathe fast—pant like a dog who's played fetch for an hour. Breathe out hard and fast, gulping in air as if running flat out. Do this for at least ten breaths. Now how do you feel? Has your tension or relaxation changed?

- Now switch. Breathe slowly, deeply and gently. Pay particular attention to your outbreath. Slow it down as much as you can.

Do this for at least ten breaths. Again, how do you feel? Has your tension or relaxation changed?

• Which type of breath is more relaxing?

. . . .

Keep calm and open to the new. It'll give you a life where you'll never be bored. A life where every day will feel like a vacation. When you're on holiday, what do you do? You let yourself learn more, laugh more and gain a fresh perspective. That's what being comfortable with novelty does. Every day there's a new perspective to explore, with surprises and learning that enrich the life you already have. As we open to the new, we open to expansion.

. . . .

Turning the gut brain towards expansion
Your worm brain

Until we get comfortable with novelty, we often prefer to stay stuck in our familiar rut, in the security of what we've always known. We have to be prodded out of our stasis, to start our journey towards expansion and get ready for the new. As much as it's uncomfortable if not unpleasant, this is one of the gifts of fear and pain. Those unpleasant states give us the motivation to move out of our old one-valley world. 'I'm sick of being sick' is something I hear a lot, when clients first come to see me. In order to gain wellness, they need to open to something new. To transform their lives in some way. It's something I understand from my own experience.

When I was a kid, I was constantly nauseous and fatigued. The thought of eating made me want to throw up. I ate only because I had to, but it wasn't fun. Our family doctor did lots of tests including giving me barium meal, which is no kind of meal even if you're not sick. None of it did any good. He couldn't find anything wrong. His diagnosis was therefore simple: I was a hypochondriac. That's the seventies for you. Food intolerances weren't considered then, not in my valley.

Years later, I learned it was all down to gluten. But the doctor was still right, just not in the way he thought. The term 'hypochondria' comes from Ancient Greece. 'Hypo' means 'below' and 'chondria' means ribs. The Ancient Greeks knew that many issues came from the bowel, the area below the ribs. They knew they could free many people from anxiety by correcting their digestive complaints. We now know there's a nerve plexus in our bowels. It produces most of our serotonin, the neurotransmitter or chemical messenger of good mood. That plexus is our gut brain or 'worm brain'. After all, that's what worms are. A mobile gut.

True hypochondria isn't mental anxiety but your worm brain shouting at you: 'Something's not right!' Your gut brain shouts at your head brain through the vagus nerve. The head brain yells back through your spine. The vagus nerve is the tenth longest cranial nerve. It's attached to your head brain, not your spinal cord. It has branches to your heart, lungs, kidneys, adrenals and most of your intestines and 80 percent of it sends information **to** the head brain, rather than receiving it **from** there. We can use that. We can use our worm brain to turn off our safety switch or limbic system and so strengthen our intuition.

Consider irritable bowel syndrome, when your guts are sensitive and cranky enough to cause you pain, poor digestion, bloating, cramping and other not-too-attractive symptoms. We could say that irritable bowel is when your worm brain is **really** unhappy. That was Ned's problem. His irritable bowel was a constant drag. He followed his doctor's protocol. He was strict with his diet, but his irritable bowel continued to be a major issue. When he came to see me, he had lots of facts and figures about the problem. He'd done so much research on his condition his head knew more about it than many specialists. Yet all his information wasn't helping. He knew a lot, but wasn't listening to his worm brain.

I got Ned to work with all of his senses, as in the exercise below. By focusing on how food smelled and tasted rather than the diet sheets, he fine-tuned his relationship with his worm brain. He soon learned that when food smelled good to him, his worm brain was happy. But when it didn't, his worm brain didn't want it and the results would be unfortunate.

As Ned continued working with his worm brain, he learned to control his irritable bowel much better. Then his intuition opened up in other areas of his life. As a highly-practical person, he was surprised at first. But he soon learned that his intuition made everything easier, not just his diet.

The stronger your vagus nerve and digestion are, the stronger all the peaceful functions of your body will be. That's why calming our breathing helps. Yet we can do more.

Turning the worm

'Use it or lose it' really applies to the body. If a nerve isn't stimulated it deactivates, as if it goes to sleep when bored. To strengthen our worm brain and keep our limbic system quiet we need to feed it. Only then can our intuition grow.

· ·

FEEDING YOUR WORM BRAIN

- Think of something you want to manifest or create.
- Visualize it. How will it look?
- Listen to what it has to say or tell yourself about it. How does that sound?
- Feel it. How will you feel once you've created it?

How strong is your connection to your desire? Does it feel comfortable in your space? Get clear on how it feels to hold your desire in your space, then complete the steps below.

- Smell it. What's that like?
- Taste it. What's that like?

Now you're using all five senses, has your connection to your desire changed? Is it easier to feel or hold in your space? Using all your senses integrates your system for a stronger and more complete alignment to your chosen manifestation.

· ·

Most of us think of intuition in terms of clairvoyance, telepathy or empathy. The first is visual, the second auditory and the third kinesthetic. Whenever we use our intuition to perceive a more expansive reality or help us manifest something, we use those three senses. We visualize, think thoughts and practice feeling positive. But sight, sound and feeling are not our only senses.

You have two more senses—smell and taste. Not using them is like deciding that your intuition has to stick to using nails only. Consciously working with **all** your senses is important, especially to start with. Your worm brain processes data through taste and smell. Think about digestion. That's where 'gut feelings' come from. Focusing on **all** your senses strengthens your vagus nerve. It also helps keep your limbic system calm, so you can connect to your intuition more powerfully. As one of my students put it: 'If you want to be connected, you have to **be** connected.' Using all five senses, especially taste and smell, is the empowerment of the true 'hypochondriac'.

Exploring new valleys

With all five senses involved, it's easier to connect to the world around you, including those parts of the world you haven't connected to previously. Connecting to new valleys or realities can feel a big scary deal, as if you're gambling with your beliefs. This is mostly because we feel pushed to accept or reject new realities immediately. It's like having to decide if you want to eat crocodile every week for the rest of your life, before you've even tasted it. It's a gamble and the unknown is scary. Without tasting crocodile first, without giving yourself time for that meat to become known, the chances of making a choice that's wrong for you are high. If we do that, we'll never learn that sometimes screws work better than nails.

So we need time to get to know the new. To taste crocodile meat. In a 'real life experiment', you get to experience any new reality before deciding whether it works for you. Give yourself a set amount of time for this. Decide you're going to believe the new ideas, but only for a while. By limiting the time you try out new ideas, you limit the risk. This lets new realities into your life in a controlled way. The only risk is a little bit of crazy time, not the rest of your life. This keeps your limbic system calm. This kind of real-life experiment is what Malcolm did.

Malcolm was referred by another chiropractor when his mid-back pain wasn't getting any better, despite appropriate treatment.

'The pain's coming from your liver not your back,' I told him. As an accountant, Malcolm lived in his left brain. He found my intuition hard to accept.

'I've had all the blood tests. There's nothing wrong with my liver,' he protested.

For the sake of his left brain, I explained how blood tests use a 'normal healthy range' which isn't necessarily 'healthy' for everyone. It'd be different if he'd been tested when he was healthy, because then we'd see any difference more clearly. I suggested he approach my treatment as an experiment. 'You don't have to believe me. Just help your liver out for a month and see how it goes.' He believed the blood test, not me, but was willing to experiment. Needless to say, his pain went away after he detoxed his liver.

If new beliefs or understandings don't align to the truth of the universe, they won't work. New realities only help us grow if we're stepping into a wider understanding of what is, not because we trick ourselves. You can hypnotize yourself all you like but you still can't walk on air, because gravity is still real. Like gravity, your intuition works because of physics and neurology. They're the natural order of things. You don't have to believe. You have to know how it works, just as you know to not let go of something if it's going to drop on your foot.

As an intuitive healing practitioner, I've lost count of the times people have said to me: 'It's all placebo.' That's another tall tale like 'spontaneous remission'. It suggests intuition is a matter of belief. That it's not really real. But energy and intuition work on animals. I've yet to see anyone brainwash a cat. Besides, placebo is at least 25 percent of the effectiveness of every drug. Sometimes it's as much as 100 percent. If I can reliably produce placebo, I've got the strongest drug on the market!

So whatever your current reality, give yourself time to test the workings of your intuition before you decide whether or not conscious intuition is for you. There's no need to force yourself to decide. Just find out. Read this book at your own pace and do all the exercises. If you like, you can formally acknowledge your 'real life experiment' below:

I hereby grant myself permission to be, do and have whatever is appropriate to align to my new belief that intuition is real and part of the healthy functioning of my neurology, regardless of any consideration for my old beliefs. I will act according to this new principle, live by it and do my best to practice this every day for a period of _____ which will end on

_____.

At the end of this real-life experiment, if the belief has been of benefit, I'm free to adopt it permanently. If not, I'm free to release it.

Signed: _____

Date: _____

· ·

FIRST TRIANGLE

· · · · · · · · · · · · · · · ·

Stability

You know the importance of good posture. Anytime you go to the gym, chiropractor or physio you're told to activate your core. By engaging your central muscles, you create a stable center for your whole system to work from. This decreases the risk of potential injuries. It also increases the effectiveness of your physical effort. Working energetically and psychologically from a stable place is just as important, if not more so. Without it you're at increasing risk, as your energy, awareness and sensitivity grows. Without stability, you'll become more affected by the energies all around you as your ability grows.

If you're unstable, you'll be reduced to constantly going up and down emotionally, depending on the mood of those around you. Your wellbeing and physical energy will become more erratic, as your energy fluctuates with your environment or diet. Your capacity to focus, or even think at all, will be dragged around by everything you overhear or pick up from others. If you're unstable, you'll become ungrounded, disassociated or even sick. The more energy you have coursing through your system, the more important it is for your 'energetic core' to be stable.

Sofie was a beautiful young woman with a profound spiritual commitment. She'd spent many years following different spiritual paths. She'd learned an impressive array of different techniques. Each one she'd learned had opened up her energetic field more. Her intuition had become so refined that even the smallest shift in her environment left her feeling disorientated. Being exposed to any kind of electromagnetic device felt like a physical assault. It was getting so bad she felt she needed to give up her work, as going near the computer left her with a headache.

Jim was a yoga instructor who'd started to work with energetic techniques. This made him sensitive to the energies of others which started to become a problem both in his work and family. Strong emotions began to impact him so heavily he'd have to leave the room or he'd get angry and start an argument. Needless to say that couldn't continue. Fortunately they both came to see me. As well as working on their systems to strengthen them I taught them how to get stable.

Using the techniques of the first triangle, the first three steps in mastering intuition, it wasn't long before their systems grew strong again. Sofie was able to handle modern life once again. She got all those beautiful spiritual benefits without having to give up the advantages of technology. Jim's clients and family were able to resume their usual open and supportive relationship with him.

To achieve your full potential in life and with your intuition, you need a center as stable as Rhonda's. She's an artist who'd used her medium to explore her relationship with herself and the world. Being so creative, she was open to the spiritual and intuitive but had never explored it consciously. Yet she was clearly in a profound state of self-connection and peace. It was astonishing to watch how quickly her intuition opened up and what she was able to do with it. She'd created a stable center for herself which turned into a strong foundation for her intuition once she decided to explore that.

Becoming energetically stable is a gift to yourself. When you're stable, you'll be free to garner the benefits of your increased awareness. You'll grow into and with increasing happiness. The exercise of your growing abilities will bring you pleasure on many levels, both spiritual and physical.

With a strong energetic core, you'll reduce the risk of becoming overwhelmed energetically and neurologically. This means you 'won't sweat the small stuff', creating more opportunities for connecting with the positive at work, with your family and in your relationships. A strong core helps all of us shrug off the small annoyances of the day to day. It keeps us moving towards the expansive future we want to create for ourselves and those we love.

As the saying goes: *Even the longest journeys start with one step.* And the first step in our journey towards conscious intuition is the completion corner of our stability triangle.

. . . .

Step One

The first step in any process often has a much greater effect on the eventual outcome than we realize. In the Lorenz attractor mentioned earlier, even the slightest difference at the start can change the pattern of the attractor entirely. Think of any of your important relationships, whether they're work or social ones. Remember how they started. What would they be like today if the first time you met had gone differently? What if the first time your boss had asked you to do something outside your job description you'd said you would do it only if he paid you a bonus? Would you now be feeling overworked and underappreciated?

When your friend asked you to lend them money, what if you'd replied you weren't in a position to do that? Would your credit card now be straining at its limit? Or what if when you'd seen that gorgeous stranger, you'd found the courage to meet their gaze and say hello? Would you now be in the relationship you've always dreamed about? Sometimes a first step can change the course of our lives.

The first step is also important for your intuition. It can determine whether it becomes a reliable skill or remains nothing more than the odd mysterious coincidence in your life.

Your first step is to create a solid foundation for yourself. A solid foundation for your intuition means knowing how to create a reliable energetic core, as well as knowing your own energy. It's like having your own home. If you don't have that, it's hard to work on anything out there in the world. Without solid ground beneath your feet, you have to waste a lot of energy dealing with it whenever it shifts. Once you have your own energetic core, your progress becomes assured. When you have energetic stability, it's easier to focus your intuition and get clear answers.

If you've ever tried to walk along an unstable surface, whether it's a broken pavement, a log or a pile of rocks, you'll know you're too busy watching where you put your feet to look very far in front of you. It's only once you get to solid ground that you look up. That's why energetic stability is so important. It enables us to use our intuition to handle whatever's coming into our space at that moment. We can also look ahead and create an expansive future path for ourselves.

But before we get to the future, we have to start where we are. And where most of us are is knowing it's all energy.

· ·

It's all energy
The eyes have it

Every morning you wake up and rely on your house being stable. You expect to find your room as it was when you fell asleep the previous night. If that wasn't the case, your morning routine wouldn't be the familiar thing it is. My brain sleeps in past the time when my body gets up, but then I don't need my brain to start with. That's one-valley I know so well I do it automatically: brush teeth, make cup of tea, get dressed. When you dropped off the edge of your bed this morning was your brain working? Did you need it to stumble to the bathroom or pull on your pants? Do you, like most people, do the same things every morning in the same sequence?

That's the seduction of a good system. It works so well you don't need to think. Like starting your car. Today some don't even need a key. Certainly you don't have to check cylinders and pump petrol before cranking a handle for the starter engine. Early model cars didn't have a good system. You had to work hard to get them to work. Just as cars had to develop a better system, you had to develop your morning routine. You knew you had a good one when it made your mornings easier.

'Systems work so you don't have to.' Robert Kiyosaki (author of *Rich Dad, Poor Dad*) told me that years ago. Working with energy becomes a lot easier when you've got a good system to do just that. The systems approach works so well you use it on many levels, sometimes without even realizing. Once your brain starts working, you can see your coffee cup. That means you've activated another system. It's a physical system which gives us a clue as to how our energy system works.

Your body's systems (like sight) work so well you've never once had to get out and push. You're probably not even aware of how they work, because you don't have to do anything consciously. Yet, just like your morning routine, these systems influence how you do things in a big way. It's especially true of your sight because that's your primary sense. A puppy relies on smell and sound more than sight. Humans use sight first and foremost.

When light comes into your eyes, your retinas react. They send a signal into your visual cortex, the picture-processing area at the back of your brain. You get two slightly different images, because your eyes are in different places in your head. Most adult eyes are about six and a half centimeters (about two and a half inches) apart, so when you look at something with one eye and then the other it seems to move a little.

It's that small positional difference that lets your brain calculate how far away an object is. It's why you have two eyes, even though your sight works by having a single point of focus. You learn early on that this single-point focus is important to your survival and doing well in the world. You learned to focus so automatically you don't even notice yourself doing it, though you've got into the habit of looking for small details or focus points to know what to do. Like when you turn round fast—you do it better when you turn your head first and 'spot' a focus point before the rest of your body follows. Same thing when you're driving. You'll corner more smoothly if you're focused on the end of the turn as you move through it.

You move from focus point to focus point. You feel comfortable moving forward only when you've got a clear focus. You know you've completed one move when you start looking for the next focus. This habitual method of progression has a big impact on your thinking, which follows the same pattern. There you also move from focal point to focal point. Focus is so important to the way we operate. This is true of our intuition as well.

The finer the detail you perceive, the better your focus is generally. It creates greater precision. In fact, there's a theory that the Western world developed science because it didn't invent porcelain. China and porcelain were invented in the East. Hence the name. So they didn't need glass to keep things in. But that also meant they didn't have glass to grind into lenses. Lenses for glasses allow people to focus better and work effectively for longer. Many major breakthroughs in science are made later in life, even if they get started early on.

The focused way your eyes work encourages your detail and fact-obsessed left brain. Yet the way your visual system works within your neurology has something to say about your right brain as well. The better we focus, the clearer our intuition will be, though that focus needs to cope with the expansion that comes as our intuition grows.

At least we agree it's all energy

It appears that physics and spirituality inhabit completely separate valleys. Yet they definitely agree on one thing: it's all energy.

We live in interesting times, created by the convergence between physics and metaphysics. Our left brains enjoy the details of fundamental forces, subatomic particles and photons, while our right brains revel in the awareness that energy is in all things. Every day we use technology created by science to access spiritual information that a short while ago would've only been available after years spent in a monastery.

All around us, spiritual truths are becoming more real—like money being energy. Only a few centuries ago, it was gold, silver and copper. Then it became paper. Now it's mostly data held by a bank somewhere in the energy of electronic information.

As our planet becomes more interconnected, the things that divided us are slowly being resolved. In energy we're all one and through energy we move with the creative flow of a conscious universe. It's time to develop conscious intuition, so we can connect with and focus on that flow.

In science, one of the most prevalent forms of energy is electromagnetism. It's all around us in radio waves, microwaves X-rays and sunlight. Electromagnetism is one of the fundamental forces of our universe. It keeps your atoms together, runs your computer and lets you use a magnet to pull iron filings about. It's a balanced relationship, as electrical flows create magnets or magnetic fields, while magnets can pull electrons about to create electricity.

You're constantly dealing with electromagnetic (EM) energy, from every time you check your phone to whenever you get sunburnt.

Whether you heat your food on a stove or in a microwave, you're using EM energy. The complete range of EM energy includes a lot of what you hear, see and feel. It powers your television and radio. You see with cells at the back of your eyes in your retina because of special chemicals, which react to the energy of visible light. That's a tiny slice out of the entire range of EM energy—400THz to 800THz. You hear because your eardrums react to another slice—10Hz to 20000Hz. Your other senses increase this perception range a little, but not much. Below the visible spectrum is infrared, which you feel as heat. But above the visible spectrum is ultraviolet, which you don't feel. If you could feel it, you'd know when you'd had enough sun and wouldn't get sunburnt.

Reptiles can see infrared, which makes sense if you need to warm yourself up in the morning before you get going. It helps to know which rock is hottest. It also helps with catching dinner. Insects can see in the ultraviolet range. Flowers might look pretty to you and me but to an insect they're a landing strip, complete with arrows pointing to the pollen. Even cooler than that is that birds can literally see the magnetic field of the planet. That's how they navigate so effortlessly.

From the perspective of your left brain, the birds and bees are communicating at frequencies where we need technology to join in the conversation. From the perspective of your right brain, the universe is vast and full of wonder. Yet we sense only the tiniest part of the entire EM spectrum through our physical senses. If we could perceive more of the total EM spectrum of our universe, our connection to our world and all things would expand. Increasing our EM perception is a major key to expanding our lives. Yet without a physical sense to detect the energy which gives us our intuition information, how are we to focus on that energy?

One technique for developing conscious intuition is a 'soft focus'. That's where you relax your focus to be consciously aware of what's in your peripheral vision. This helps shift your vision from the detail of your left brain to the whole-image connection of your right brain. It also activates cells in your retinas that react to different frequencies. This is an attempt to get your physical eyes to perceive at least some of the energy outside the normal visible spectrum, so you can get something of a focus. You could use that as a first step.

Mastering your intuition widens your awareness of how EM affects you. You know your nervous system generates EM. I could stick electrodes on your body and get an electrical readout, like an electro-encephalograph of your brain or an electrocardiograph of your heart. Your nerves generate bioelectrical energy and create a biomagnetic field. That field's often called an aura. Auras are usually spoken of in terms of colors rather than gauss (a measure of magnetic flux density). The relationship between magnetism and electricity is very close and dependable. Change one and you'll invariably affect the other.

When I was talking about achieving conscious intuition, I mentioned how intuitives used to be called sensitives. With sufficient sensitivity, you can detect EM beyond what your physical sense organs can, through the interaction of your own bioelectrical system, your nervous system and the EM spectrum. Detecting EM energy without a sense organ to focus your awareness on is called ESP (extrasensory perception). That means you're sensing EM outside the physical organ spectrum—not through the known channels of your senses, but directly with the help of your brain. You're perceiving the effect of other EM energy on your own.

This is why you feel 'good vibes' in some places and 'bad vibes' in others. The flow of energy lies behind a lot of feng shui, the system designed to maximize beneficial energy in your house. Energy is also why your cat will have a particular spot he or she prefers. A cat's capacity for detecting good energy is legendary. Ask any feng shui expert. They'll tell you cats invariably choose the spot in the house with the best energy. Perhaps that's not surprising, considering how recent studies have shown a cat's purr produces a vibration at just the right frequency to strengthen and heal tissue. Clearly, they've evolved to sense and use EM energy. Perhaps that's why cats have a reputation for being close to the spiritual world?

Your intuition is also considered to be close to the spiritual world, yet it's an awareness of EM energy for which you don't have a physical sense. And that creates two difficulties.

First, how do you interpret energy? You interpret what you see, hear, feel, taste and smell with such skill you don't notice yourself doing it. You forget it took you five to seven years of sticking things in your mouth and up your nose, bumping into things and falling on top of other things, for you to learn how to accurately interpret the physical world. Sometimes students of intuition expect to immediately interpret their metaphysical perceptions as easily as they do their physical perceptions, but that takes time. It took you time to know that if something looks smaller, it may be further away. It also takes time to learn how to accurately interpret the EM signals you pick up through your magnetic field, rather than through your senses.

The truth is anyone and everyone picks up energy. Everyone is affected by the EM of our universe. It's in accurately and reliably interpreting that energy that the skill lies.

The second difficulty with intuition is how easy it is to become overwhelmed when you're perceiving directly with your brain. Being a sensitive means you're more affected by stray EM energy. You may be aware of what others are feeling, even if they can't put it into words. That's useful, but how much of that can you absorb without feeling it's too much? If you could sense the entire range of EM, how would you avoid overloading your nervous system?

When Sara came to see me she told me she was allergic to the twenty-first century. She certainly had many symptoms of stress: eczema, poor concentration, muscle aches and constipation. Her system was badly inflamed and, despite numerous healings, she'd had little relief. The only thing that helped was avoiding electromagnetic equipment as much as possible. As most modern technology is powered by electricity, that was difficult. It was also confusing her, as she didn't understand how that could happen. So I explained to her the electromagnetic nature of her nervous system.

Just like any electrical cable, your nerves have insulation. That's what your nerve sheaths are. One of the most important building blocks of your nerve sheaths is omega-3 oils. Fats and oils don't transmit EM energy as easily as water does. Inflammation and thinning of the nerve sheaths are common when the system is overloaded energetically.

Sara started a therapeutic course of these essential fatty acids. That helped her system start to settle. I also took her through the exercises of Step One in mastering intuition. She needed those exercises to get herself energetically stable. It helped her nervous system cope with the demands she was putting on it. Slowly, her system grew more stable and less reactive. She finally reached a point where she could use her computer without paying with a headache.

When the EM effect on our brain is disruptive like that, it's a problem. But if we're stable enough to be aware of it and remain unaffected, that effect can power our intuition. The more we appreciate and understand the effect of EM energy on our brains, the more clearly our intuition speaks to us. So let's look at how we do that.

. . . .

Your nervous system and intuitive language are unique
Finding your style

. . . .

You don't have a sense organ for all the EM energy your brain is perceiving. You still understand your world through your physical senses. In time, you'll develop your own resonant vocabulary. Then you'll be able to 'read' energy directly, giving you a constant source of inspiration and insight. Until then, your brain will do its best to give you the information you're picking up from other electromagnetic energy, in a form you can make sense of right now. In neurological terms, you could say intuition is a form of synesthesia.

In central processing, your brain takes all the different inputs from your physical senses and puts them together into a coherent view of the world. After that you can use the information. But sometimes your wires get crossed and that's what synesthesia is. Like when musicians 'hear' sounds as colors or 'see' numbers as musical notes. The relationship between the different sounds and colors and so on are consistent, so synesthesia isn't some kind of hallucination. It's something that can be useful once understood. Synesthesia and intuition are like a private language all of your own.

Many people have synesthesia, especially creative types. Franz Liszt is a famous example. This Hungarian composer saw sounds as colors. He'd tell the orchestra things like, 'Please gentlemen. A little bluer.' Or, 'That's a deep violet. Not so rose.' At first they thought he was being funny, but they soon realized he meant it. This kind of central processing happens in intuition. Energies outside the physical sense bands are often 'displayed' in your mind, as if they're coming through one of your senses. This is particularly true when you first begin to work with your intuition. It's your brain's way of helping you interpret the information.

When I first worked with my intuition as a conscious skill, I mostly just saw black blobs. Making them go away relieved a client's symptoms, so I came to understand that the blobs appeared where a client's field or nervous system was blocked, such as over the head of someone with headaches.

They say the reward of a job well done is a bigger job. That certainly applies to intuition. As soon as I'd learned to clear my clients' blobs, the blobs I'd see evolved into what looked like X-ray film. This wasn't Supergirl's X-ray vision. I knew how to read X-rays because of my training, so my brain used that to structure intuitive information.

As my ability to interpret the non-physical-sense-organ-EM grew, my intuition underwent several shifts. I now have a 'resonant vocabulary'. That means I can 'read' each energetic signature or resonance as you're reading the words on this page. It's a skill that you can develop too. It's a great skill to have. It grew out of me initially finding **one** way I could work reliably with my intuition. Once you have a way you can dependably interpret what the energy means, you can begin to use it in your life as easily as you use your vision or hearing now.

Alison is a retired counsellor, well versed in the psychological techniques that helped her clients. She originally came to me for healing. She was drawn to the way I worked and the idea that she could develop her intuition to be a strong skill. She was particularly fascinated because she didn't think she was at all intuitive, apart from the rare flash of insight or awareness that many people get. She signed up to be a Fractology student.

One of the first things we worked on was helping her understand her own intuitive language. She realized her intuition was highly visual, when she began to pay attention to the colors she saw around people. She'd seen them before but hadn't understood their significance. As she acknowledged what she saw, she started to decipher the code of the various colors. Then her intuition opened wider.

However, don't think that intuition is always visual. It's not. Indeed, the first person I ever trained hasn't seen a thing to this day, yet his intuition is strong, clear and reliable. Jon ran workshops focusing on self-esteem issues in young men. He was great at what he did and was intrigued about the possibilities of intuition. He'd hoped to see amazing things, because the visual sense is so important in our society. Yet he never did. He felt energy instead. Rather than seeing patterns like I do, or auras like Alison does, he could feel what was in someone's space. He described it to me as being similar to putting his hand into a bag of different blocks. He could sense the different shapes and what matched what. He could even feel if something didn't belong there, like a nail instead of a block. This awareness took his workshops to another level through his own intuitive language.

Your neurology is as unique to you as mine is to me. That gives each of us an intuitive language that's also unique. This can be a stumbling block, but it simply means that intuition requires self-awareness. Your brain formats your intuition through multisensory integration. It puts all the EM data together, to give you a coherent experience. Intuitive information comes through as sight, sound, feeling, taste or smell. The trick is to understand what it means. Take the time to figure out how your intuition communicates most reliably. Getting to know yourself takes time.

Learning how you operate is more than knowing you prefer caramel to chocolate or the other way around. Taking sufficient time is important. You'll achieve more in your life when you understand how you do things best.

Even more significant is demonstrating to yourself how important you are in your own life. Learning how your intuition talks to you has tremendous benefits in many areas, not least in having a stronger connection with Who You Truly Are. Like any other relationship, your relationship with yourself requires quality time.

The next exercise is one I often do with my beginner students, to help them understand their own central processing. It's more about observing how your intuition presents information than about getting it right. Resist the temptation to guess or jump to a conclusion. That way, you can find out where your intuitive strength lies.

. . . .

BOX PROCESS

- Find five or six empty matchboxes. Put a small object in each one. With your eyes shut, stir the boxes around, so you don't know which object is in which box.

- Set your intention to use your intuition to discover which object is where. With your senses open, focus on each box in turn. Write down all the information each of your senses gives you before you attempt to decide where each object is. Use the information from each sense to help you decide.

- Acknowledge what you got correct and, importantly, which of your senses helped you to any correct conclusions.

. . . .

Some years ago, I did this exercise with a group of students and some objects in a shoebox. I got them to record what their different senses told them. Lucy was a successful therapist who wanted to take her work to the next level. Among all her notes was this image she'd 'seen' of a long, straight pointed object. She then wrote her interpretation next to it. She thought it was a 'pen'. She was extremely disappointed when I took the lid off the box. 'I didn't get anything right,' she said.

'What about this?' I asked. I reached into the box and pulled out a six-inch nail. Her intuition had seen it clearly, but she'd interpreted it incorrectly.

When you first start to work with your intuition, it really helps to do what your mathematics teacher kept asking you to do. Show your working out. Find your style, or which of your senses gives you the most accurate intuitive information, and your ability to accurately interpret all EM energy will increase. You'll then have dealt with the first difficulty with intuition.

So let's now look at how to deal with the second one, with the possibility of you being overwhelmed by the energy of the universe.

The universe is a donut
You can't practice detachment
. . . .

How did you feel the last time you sat in a crowded coffee shop? I mean, **really** crowded, where there was so much noise that each person had to shout over the top of every other person and you couldn't move without invading someone's space. Was it difficult to concentrate? To think through whatever you wanted to say? That's what happens when your nervous system's got too much information to deal with. It's overwhelmed.

That's how it feels when you're wide open to the entire EM spectrum. As your intuition activates, you'll be aware of an increasing range of energy. It'll expand more and more, until you're open to everything around you. It can be overwhelming but you can learn to make sense of it. When you do, it'll enrich your life in unimaginable ways.

To make sense of it, you have to focus on one stream of energy at a time. One conversation in the coffee shop of life. With so much noise it's easy to be distracted. But then you'd miss what your friends and family are saying. If the noise gets to you, you'll end up more and more annoyed. Force yourself to be okay with it and the annoyance just goes inwards. It's a bit like fingernails down the blackboard. No matter how much you tell yourself it doesn't bother you, it still sets your teeth on edge.

So how do you manage to hear in the coffee shop? You acknowledge and accept the noise. Paradoxically, that's when you can let go of it. Focus on the feeling of accepting that something **is** the way it is. Then intend for that acceptance to flow to whatever's bothering you and an interesting shift occurs. If you flow acceptance to the background noise, it helps you focus in on the one conversation you do want to hear.

This is also how you clean up the background noise from the universe—the static from all those EM flows. Paradoxically, flowing acceptance to all that energy helps you focus on the one 'phone call' the universe is making to you. That's how you open up your intuition yet not be overwhelmed.

It's said that detachment is a sign of enlightenment and spiritual achievement. Unfortunately, you can't force yourself to be detached any more than you can force yourself to not be annoyed by noise. Flowing acceptance, however, helps you get to that state. And it's something you can practice. It's a cycle. Energy comes into your field and affects your nervous system until you flow acceptance back to it. Then more energy can flow in, which also increases your intuition. Many of nature's processes flow through cycles in this way.

Some cycles are smallish, like sunrise to sunset. Some are medium-sized, like the seasons. And some are larger, like the thousands of years between ice ages. There are cycles within the soil, in the atmosphere and in animals. Rain and ocean water form one cycle. The worms you have to treat your family for, the human as well as the furry ones, live their lives through cycles also. Cycles are all around you. They're part of your life. You breathe in cycles. Your blood sugar and blood pressure work in cycles like a thermostat. All your different systems have a 'default setting' or point of equilibrium. When things get too far above or below the thermostat or default setting, different processes kick in to bring it back to the set point.

EM energy also moves in cycles. In physics, we're told energy is both a wave and a particle. Just as with all magic tricks, it's simple once you get it. Watch a wave moving across a lake and you'd swear the water's moving. Which it is and isn't. Throw out a few ping-pong balls. Then you'll see the real picture. The balls move up and down as each wave passes, but don't really go anywhere. Take a closer look. You'll see how they trace round a circle as they go up and down with each wave.

So energy travels in waves but operates in cycles. That helps to shape our universe. Scientists study this most fundamental of shapes from different angles, which gives rise to various disciplines like cosmology, physics, topology and mathematics.

My father says mathematics is the language of the universe. Mind you, his favorite quote from *The Goons* is:

What are you like at mathematics?
I speak it like a native.

One reason for the supremacy of mathematics is the difficulty of knowing what a building looks like when you're inside it. Taking measurements of what you can see and doing the relevant equations helps. Part of what we can see of our universe is the cosmic background microwave radiation. The afterglow of the big bang. Put it all together and it seems our universe might be shaped like a donut, which is just another cycle shape. So you have a cosmic excuse every time you want Krispy Kreme!

In science, a donut is called a toroid. But ask a scientist what a toroid is and you'll get a fancy description of a donut. Fancy or not, what's the use of a donut universe? Cosmic indigestion? Actually, yes. Kind of.

A donut has the shape of a cycle. Just like a wheel, when it goes round once that's one cycle. If the flow of our donut universe gets stuck, the cycle will stay incomplete. That feels a bit like cosmic indigestion. Any incompletion creates stuckness or a type of indigestion.

Incompletions are what create the time loops in your life. Like when you're looking for your ideal relationship but with each new prospective partner you end up with the same old issues, no matter how promising the relationship seemed at the start. Or when you get a financial windfall, but all too soon you're back counting the pennies. Or you take up a new diet or exercise plan. At first the results are encouraging, but then you reach a plateau and your weight or fitness won't budge any further. Merry-go-round experiences like that are the day-to-day manifestation of incompletions in our lives.

An incompletion happens if the ping-pong ball can't return to where it started. If that occurs, energy keeps going round and round. It's like when you get a thought in your head that just won't shut up. Your head is full of mental chatter and internal arguments. Without completion your energy gets drained, which makes using your intuition a whole lot harder. That doesn't just happen in your head. It happens in your body too. Take insulin resistance. That occurs when your body can't return to its 'default' blood sugar point of about 6mmol/L. Your actual reading can be anything from 3 to 7.8.

When it's too high insulin gets released, telling the cells to absorb the glucose from the blood. If the cells can't or don't 'read' the insulin message to complete the cycle, your nervous system keeps yelling at your cells. Release more and more insulin! That drives your pancreas (which makes the insulin) so nuts it eventually gives up. In other words, incompletion of your sugar cycle can give you diabetes.

When you complete your cycles, you'll build confidence in your intuition as well as increase your energy. Completion is fundamental to our wellbeing. Without completion, it's impossible for us to maintain our energy and we'll remain unstable. With completion, our energy becomes increasingly stable and strong. So it's time we learned how to create completion.

. . . .

Acknowledgments release charge
The point is completion

. . . .

Completion is a foundational skill of intuition, although it's more like a discipline or doing the dishes. It may seem easier to leave the dishes drying in the dishwasher rather than put them away, but not completing that cycle actually creates more work. When the dishwasher still has clean dishes in it, you can't put dirty ones in there. So they either pile up in the sink, which will then require scrubbing, or they get put in with the clean ones making them dirty too. An incomplete cleaning cycle creates more dirtiness one way or another. Having the discipline to complete the cycle and put the dishes away properly is actually less work in the long run.

Loral Langemeier is a bestselling author on personal finance. She's been called 'the millionaire maker'. One of her sayings is: *Money doesn't come to chaos.* The more orderly and organized we are, the easier it is to create a consistent and expanding cash flow. Being orderly and organized is a natural consequence of completing each action as we go. In business, this is particularly true. In order to generate that cash flow, we need to return each phone call, answer each email and respond to each text. We need to do what we say we're going to do for our clients, when we say we'll do it. We need to ensure our paperwork goes into its designated spot and that each service we complete is charged appropriately. Each of these actions needs to be completed. If it isn't, things get out of hand pretty quickly.

The same thing goes for all the other areas of your life. It's true of your morning routine. If you don't make your bed and put away your breakfast dishes, the house soon becomes disorganized. It's true of your relationships. How many arguments are caused by someone not completing what they said they would do? When you complete each action as you go, you keep your 'to do list' to a manageable number. When each action is left incomplete however it stays on your list. Then the lineup gets longer and longer until you feel overwhelmed.

The opposite is also true. If you have a long to-do list, pick the things that are easiest to complete. Do them. Then you can tick them off. Then pick the next easiest and complete those. With each completion your list gets shorter, and you'll soon feel back in control of your life. Then you'll have more energy to tackle those bigger tasks.

In the same way, it can seem easier to ignore the cycles of energy you experience, but the small amount of effort required to complete those cycles pays big dividends in the long run. Your intuition is the cycle of energy flowing in and out of your system. Or if you prefer, it's the infinite universe communicating directly with you through different parts of the EM spectrum.

Communication has a cycle too. Have you ever had someone tell you something? Then tell you again and again and again? That's an incomplete cycle. That person hasn't 'got' that you've heard them, so they keep going until they do. If you don't know what that's like, try speaking to a six-year-old. Acknowledging what people say completes our communication cycles. An acknowledgment tells someone you accept where they're at. We don't really need agreement but we do need acceptance.

You could say, 'I've heard what you've had to say and thank you for telling me,' but that's a bit much. You'd be better to sum the acknowledgment up with a kind of 'verbal punctuation'. Some of the words that do that are: *good, great, well done, okay, alright, thanks, brilliant* and even (my personal favorite) *yay!* Curiously, 'yes' is not an acknowledgment. Remember the point is not to agree or disagree, as that will continue the conversation rather than complete it.

You can think of flowing acceptance as an emotional acknowledgment or the energetic equivalent of an acknowledgment. Remember, an acknowledgment says: *I accept that that's where you're at right now.*

· ·

GETTING COMPLETE

1. Check in with yourself.

   • How are you feeling right now?

   • Especially, how is your energy? Are you feeling positive? Or negative?

2. Acknowledge whatever energy you're aware of. Spend a few minutes doing this.

   • Flow acceptance to whatever you're feeling.

   • Say 'thanks' to any thoughts.

3. When you're more complete, you'll feel lighter, clearer and more centered.

Doing this night and morning is excellent practice, as well as good energetic maintenance.

· ·

You can create increased ease in your space by completing your cycles. Once you get used to that feeling, it soon becomes natural to do it all the time. Much the same thing happens when you learn to activate your core muscles. It takes effort to get them to turn on to begin with. It takes discipline to keep remembering to do it. Then your system figures out it's better to exercise that way and you do it all the time without having to think about it. That happens with acknowledgments. All you need is a little discipline to start with.

But just like putting away the dishes, it helps to understand the benefits. Think of all the benefits you could gain through personal growth or increasing your energy. That's what completion can create for you. So let's take a closer look.

· ·

Acknowledgments trigger expansion
Negative release or positive integration

. . . .

Your energy and life move in circles. I'm sure you've had times when you've felt like you're caught in a 'soap cycle'. That's my term for the cycle of drama you see in TV soaps. It's the same thing over and over. You might feel like you're caught in the same drama; even after doing a lot of work to change things you're back in the same place. Some details may have changed, but your life is more or less the same. Frustrating, isn't it?

All you and I need to do is complete that old cycle. When it's truly complete and not before, things will change. 'The reward of a job well done is a bigger job' because when you complete a cycle, you get more energy. Then you can do more. If you don't do the job well or don't complete it, you just stay with the job you've got currently.

In the movie Groundhog Day, Bill Murray's character Phil is a weatherman, assigned to cover the annual emergence of the groundhog from its hole in the tiny township of Punxsutawney. He gets caught in a time loop and can't leave. He indulges his fantasies and starts to go a little mad, trying suicide several times. Yet each time he's back in the loop. It's only once he learns to accept himself, his situation and everyone else, that he completes the cycle. Then he gets unstuck.

We all get stuck in cycles from time to time. The **way** we get unstuck determines how big our next job is.

There are three different ways we can get complete, though perhaps it's more accurate to say there are three different depths to your completion.

The first approach is actually incompletion—to just leave the cycle hanging. Paradoxically, I have to include it to give you a complete list of options. Whenever your drama–prone limbic system takes over or freaks out over any potential change, you're likely to want to avoid the situation. But that only increases the risk of staying incomplete.

It's like pushing the ping-pong ball under the water so you can't see it. It'll pop back up again as soon as you take your hand away.

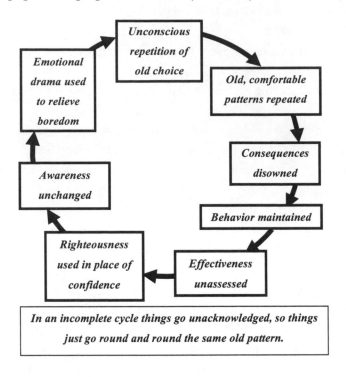

In an incomplete cycle things go unacknowledged, so things just go round and round the same old pattern.

Incomplete cycles get you bogged down. Your tyres spin faster and faster, but you don't go anywhere. You feel drained. Expending more and more energy to stay in the same place is exhausting. Every incomplete cycle is one more bit of background noise you have to deal with, one more piece of static in the EM signal you're listening to. This makes it very hard to hear what's in the present moment.

My dad likes nonsense poetry, along with dad jokes. His take on the poem *Antigonish* by Hughes Mearns is:

The other day upon the stair, I met a man who wasn't there.
He wasn't there again today. Gee, I wish he'd go away.

Apart from Dad being silly, this made no sense to me as a kid. From the viewpoint of incompletions, however, it makes complete sense (pun!). With enough incompletions, people are 'not there'. The 'lights are on but nobody is home'. When your magnetic field is weakened enough from all the static of incompletions, you can't find your own signal. This makes it hard to make proper present-time decisions. So instead of new choices, you just run off old ones. You keep repeating old cycles. In other words, if you're not complete and present, your old incompletions and issues are running the show. Over and over again. Incompletions keep you stuck in repetitive cycles.

However, the better you are at completions, the more opportunity you'll have to move into expansive growth cycles. Just how expansive they get depends on which type of completion you use.

Do you leave your cycles incomplete? Or complete them in such a way that you enlarge your comfort zone? Or complete them so you expand your reality? Instead of staying incomplete, you can get completion by getting rid of something you don't want (completing a negative) or by taking in something you do want (completing a positive).

The most common kind of completion is a negative one. That's what acknowledgments do. When you say 'thanks' to something or flow acceptance to it, you let go of it more easily. It may seem like a paradox, but the easiest way to let go of something uncomfortable and enlarge your comfort zone is to acknowledge it.

When you complete a negative, you let go. You lighten your load. The more you acknowledge everything, the easier it is to move through each step of the completion cycle.

The completion cycle, as shown on the following page, starts and finishes with a conscious choice. What kind of experiences do you want? Do you want to expand the ease and grace in your life?

If you want more than a comfortable life, you need to do more. If you want a bigger life full of expansion and satisfaction, there's a bit more to do. This isn't something your fight/flight limbic system likes, of course.

Do you remember the last time you did a goal-setting workshop? What was it you were told a goal had to be? SMART, right? Which stands for specific, measurable, actionable, realistic and time-based (or something similar). What's that really saying? All goals need to be within your reality.

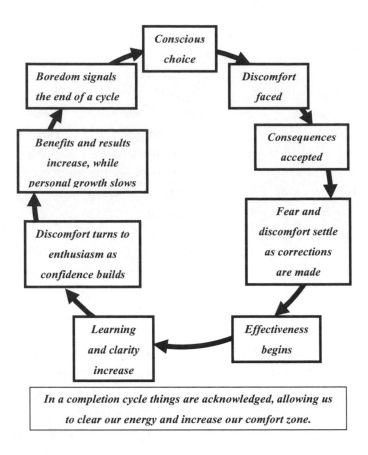

In a completion cycle things are acknowledged, allowing us
to clear our energy and increase our comfort zone.

If your desires are outside your reality, how can they be realistic? And how can you know what steps are needed to create them? Goals are within your reality, even if they require work to get there. But dreams aren't. They're beyond your current reality. They hold the greatest potential for expansion or innovation. But how are you going to get there, if you don't know where 'there' is? A bigger life or expanded reality increases your options, but requires a step into the unknown. For me, it's a lot like walking in the fog. I do that remarkably often, as I live in the mountains.

When I walk in the fog, I can't see very far. Anything at a distance is 'out of my reality'. If I just stand there waiting for the fog to lift, I'll be waiting a while. In the same way, if you don't do anything until you know everything you'll be waiting a long time too. When I walk in the fog, things become slowly clearer as I move towards them. That's what it's like when I step beyond my current reality. Details emerge slowly, as they move from the unknown to the known. In order to expand my reality, I don't need to know what lies beyond it. I just need enough of an idea to know the general direction to take.

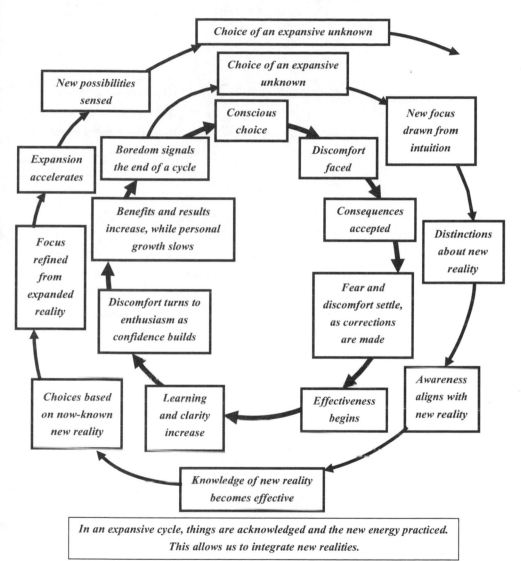

Choice of an expansive unknown

Choice of an expansive unknown

New possibilities sensed

Conscious choice

New focus drawn from intuition

Expansion accelerates

Boredom signals the end of a cycle

Discomfort faced

Benefits and results increase, while personal growth slows

Consequences accepted

Focus refined from expanded reality

Distinctions about new reality

Discomfort turns to enthusiasm as confidence builds

Fear and discomfort settle, as corrections are made

Choices based on now-known new reality

Learning and clarity increase

Effectiveness begins

Awareness aligns with new reality

Knowledge of new reality becomes effective

In an expansive cycle, things are acknowledged and the new energy practiced. This allows us to integrate new realities.

That direction is supplied by your intuition. Truly expansive cycles, like a completion cycle, start with a choice. But because this choice is for an unknown, you start with a feeling. If you use your intuition to tune into how you'll feel once you've achieved your dream or expanded reality, you've got enough of a direction to begin moving in the fog. The feeling that matches your new, expansive state is the start of positive completion. You'll know when you've completed the positive, because that new energy will then feel natural instead of strange.

Positive completion is like getting energetically fit in many ways. A negative completion might be to stop eating chips and ice cream. A positive completion gets you up off the couch and out for a run. Whether it's energetic or physical exercise, it integrates energy into your system. By consciously practicing the energy or feeling of your expanded state, you also decrease the likelihood of self-sabotage.

That's what Julie learned. She'd been divorced for some years and wanted a new relationship. Confusingly, she found that whenever she met a lovely guy she'd become hostile. She told herself it was because she didn't feel safe. It was really because she didn't know what to do with all that positive energy. She wasn't used to it. Once Julie practiced having more positive energy in her space she relaxed. She let her new, wonderful relationship thrive.

Practicing your expanded state turns your unknown new reality into something that at least feels familiar. Each time you step into the unknown, you open your system to a different EM band from what you've received before. It's as if you're used to tuning into a particular radio or TV station and so get a particular view of the world. When you tune yourself differently, you'll get a different station and information. That may change your world view. It'll certainly give you more options and a broader experience. The wider your EM receptivity, the more expansive your life will be.

You don't have a sense organ for ultraviolet (UV) energy, but you need UV to make vitamin D. In the same way, you may not yet have much awareness of abundance in your life. You may not know what it feels like or how to create it. Yet you need that for a truly expansive life and to attain your full potential. Abundance is a positive capacity that builds from expansive completions. You may not yet have the capacity for true abundance, but you can 'exercise' your energy to build towards it. Just like any fitness program, it's important to exercise regularly if you want to get energetically 'ripped'.

A good practice is to do the next exercise first and last thing, like cleaning your teeth. I call this 'bookending the day'. Doing the exercise first thing, just after you've hit the snooze button, sets a good energy for the day. Then doing it again last thing at night, as you snuggle down under the blankets, helps release any stresses from the day. Doing the exercise also shows your subconscious what state you want to live in from now on.

In this exercise, you use universal love and support to increase your capacity for the positive. That makes your right brain happy. But if your left brain prefers, you can do the same exercise with the cosmic microwave background radiation: the afterglow of the big bang or energy left over from the start of the universe. Either one is a source of creative expansive energy.

. . . .

LOVE AND SUPPORT FROM THE UNIVERSE

- Focus on the love and support flowing to you from the universe in this and every moment.

- Allow it in. You don't have to do anything to get this energy, you just have to stop blocking it out. Just relax and let it flow in.

- Do this first thing in the morning to give you energy for the day, and last thing at night to release any stresses from the day. It will also give you more positive dreams.

. . . .

Step Two

Now you've taken your first step towards having conscious intuition. Being able to complete each of your energetic cycles and understand your own intuitive process means you've started a tremendous journey. As you continue this journey, three things will happen:

1. Your ability to stay complete from moment to moment will strengthen.
2. Your self-understanding will grow.
3. Your energy will increase.

The increase in your energy will happen with each and every completion you make. This is why being present, being complete, is such a powerful state.

You next need to learn how to manage all that energy. Keeping yourself balanced is the key to handling an increasing level of energy. That is what Step Two is all about.

. . . .

Your energy is stronger when balanced
Spinning in place

. . . .

Did you ever stand among flowers on sun-warmed grass, then open your arms wide and spin? Turned, turned and kept turning until you lost control and collapsed laughing with dizziness? If you haven't, I'd recommend it. It's fun and will teach you something about your energy. The first few turns are easy. You're going slowly as you spin on the spot. Then you build momentum. That's when you lose your balance. You stagger about and collapse soon after. A spinning top does the same. If it's centered it stays in place; but if it's not, it'll whiz all over the place.

Both you and the top are feeling the effects of angular momentum. As my high school physics teacher said, 'It's hard to get angular momentum really straight.' Fortunately, you don't have to worry about equations. Just remember the last time you drove fast round a corner—it felt as though you were being pushed outwards. If the engine hadn't driven the wheels inwards, the car would've drifted outwards. Smooth driving requires that you balance your angular momentum with acceleration.

When spinning round in the sunshine, your engine is your legs. Just like a top, you need to balance the angular momentum on one side with that on the other. Like the car, you have to go faster to stay where you want to be. Until it all gets out of hand and you fall over! Simply put, the more balanced you are the longer you can spin.

If your system is overwhelmed with incomplete cycles, you can feel light-headed and dizzy. It's much easier to be overwhelmed when you're unbalanced. The more balanced you are, the more energy you can handle. Your EM energy operates in cycles, so as well as completing them, it's important to keep them balanced. If I had to sum up health in one word it would be 'balance'. That's true for the health of your neurology as well.

In your nervous system, there are signals going to your brain (afferent nerves) and away from your brain (efferent nerves). Efferent signals tell your body what to do, while afferent ones tell your brain how well the message worked. These two communication arms create your neurological cycle. This cycle has the same three basic elements of any system:

1. an end result or focus
2. a way to move in that direction
3. a way to know if you're on track or not

The next cycle then corrects any misalignment in the previous cycle, if you're to stay balanced.

You witness this cycle when you spin round, and with any other movement. Your efferent nerves send a signal from your motor cortex to your muscles, which then act on the signal. The afferent nerves then send a signal back to the brain about where the muscles ended, so your brain can figure out if your posture needs tweaking. You need signals both **to** and **from** your brain in order for this system to work. This system works best when both signals are balanced. Too much efferent and you're disassociated. You're living in your head. Too much afferent and your physical sensations demand all your attention. It's hard to focus.

Balance is such an important pattern. It's a large part of making a cycle effective, so it's not surprising to find it everywhere in nature. The evaporation of water and rainfall need to be balanced or we get drought or floods. Herbivores in an environment need to be balanced by predators or the land gets overgrazed, which was powerfully demonstrated when they reintroduced wolves into Yellowstone Park after seventy-five years. The increase in biodiversity the wolves created wasn't a surprise but the halt in the erosion of the river bank was. The wolves changed the herbivores' behavior, causing them to stop spending all their time on the river banks, resulting in a decrease in erosion.

Trees are masters of the balance pattern. Every day they balance the energy of sunlight with water and minerals from the soil. If you've got more of a brown thumb than a green thumb, you need to pay more attention to this balance. You need to help maintain it. Balance was there right from the beginning. It's still there on a sub-atomic level. Every particle of matter has its antimatter partner. The electrons that create electricity, including the bioelectrical energy of your nervous system, are paired with positrons. This balance is about as perfect as it gets.

According to the big bang theory, there's one little lonely extra matter particle for every billion matter-antimatter pairs. This asymmetry is so weird to physicists they're scouring the universe looking for evidence that the 'missing' antimatter bit is out there somewhere. We all like a happy ending.

You participate in the matter-antimatter story much more than you realize. A tiny amount of antimatter falls constantly on the earth from space. You've also eaten it. Think about that next time you eat a banana. They release positrons roughly once every seventy-five minutes from a natural form of potassium called potassium-40. Your body contains some of it too, even if you haven't been eating bananas, but it's not enough for you to fuel the starship *Enterprise*. It's not even enough to boil water for a cup of tea, but it's the right amount to maintain the particle balance of your body.

All things need to be balanced: particles, trees and spinning children (or adults). Your nervous system needs balance too. But before I can show you how to do that, I need you to do something. I need you to raise your hand.

Raise your hand

Go on. Raise your hand. Now how did you do that? You didn't think about which nerves were involved, nor about which muscles had to contract or relax. Nor did you think about how you balanced the shift in your weight, so you weren't pulled onto your side. Your body did all of that while you were probably thinking of other things, like why was I asking you to do this. So just how did you raise your hand?

You **focused** on where you wanted your arm to be. You **intended** for it to be there. **Focus** and **intention**. That's it. Simple. Focus and intention are all you need for your mind to direct your nervous system.

Think of your mind as software to your brain's hardware. You can program your software however you like. It isn't just your nerves that need balance. Their support system needs it too. Many ancient traditions speak of the flow of life force up and down the spine. In Sanskrit, it's called *kundalini*. Descriptions of this energy don't fit the afferent-efferent nerve flow, but correlate well to something else flowing in your spine.

The kundalini is actually described as three flows. There are a balanced pair on the outside which spiral around each other to create a central space for a third flow. This image can be seen in the caduceus, an ancient healing symbol still used by medical practitioners today. This 'diagram' resembles a vital flow that moves through your spine. This flow isn't from your nerves, but the liquid support system for your brain. It's called the cerebrospinal fluid. You might remember it from what happened to Harry.

Caduceus, also called the Staff of Asclepius, the Greek god of medicine.

The cerebrospinal fluid is produced in the middle of your brain by special capillaries. They're special because they're so leaky they let a lot of the liquid part of your blood move into the spaces round your brain. This 'leakage' becomes the cerebrospinal fluid. The cerebrospinal fluid flows through spaces in your brain called ventricles, down through the middle of your spinal cord. At the base of your spine, it flows out of the middle to reach the outside between the spinal cord and the bony vertebra. Then it flows back up towards your skull. The outside of your brain has special veins called sinuses. These resorb the cerebrospinal fluid and allow it to rejoin the bloodstream.

The cerebrospinal fluid is basically a kind of blood plasma. It gives your brain and spinal cord extra nutrition, which the nerves need as they're so active. This fluid also helps remove all the waste such busy little cells produce. The cerebrospinal fluid is so essential for the health of your nerves, as they start screaming if it's not flowing properly. Keeping your cerebrospinal fluid balanced is a great way to keep stress out of your spine and nervous system. It also has other advantages.

There's a strong correlation between the health of your cerebrospinal fluid and the health of your brain. Keeping that flow balanced increases your sense of wellbeing. It helps you think more clearly, sleep better and feel better. It is a great support to a positive and optimistic outlook. This means it also supports you to be more open to the expansive opportunities which will be coming your way, as you open up your intuition. Put another way, the stronger and more balanced your cerebrospinal fluid, the greater your wellbeing.

When you go to university, you learn all sorts of odd things. One of the oddest from chiropractic school is that there's very poor correlation between X-ray findings and back pain. It's odd because most chiropractors and doctors use X-rays to look for problems in your spine. X-rays are good for checking for general problems, like fractures or arthritis. But X-rays aren't much help in getting you pain free. On the other hand, there's good correlation between back pain and blockages of your cerebrospinal fluid flow. Unfortunately, a reliable technical test for this flow has yet to be developed, so X-rays are still used.

I say no **technical** test because with any such blockage your nervous system will obviously be stressed. That affects your EM field. With a little bit of training, it's possible for your intuition to perceive that effect.

Andrew is one of my chiropractors. Yes, chiropractors see other chiropractors because it's a bit difficult to adjust yourself. He was one of my tutors and, over the years, we've had many discussions about the link between energy and neurology. His style of chiropractic involves something called a nervoscope: a device for measuring the EM field along the spine.

Like many experienced chiropractors, years of observing the EM system of the body has honed Andrew's intuition. He's an excellent chiropractor. He always gets a shift in the EM of a body he adjusts. After one of our discussions he said to me, 'You've made me realize I'm much more aware of energy than I thought.' I find that's true of many experienced practitioners who've worked for years with the health of the spine.

As they come into balance, you may notice your body's relief. Just as good physical posture is easier on your muscles, good EM posture is easier on your nerves.

The more balanced your energy is, the more balanced your cerebrospinal fluid will be. Then it's easier to notice other EM energies. One of the most effective ways of doing this is to balance your energy first thing and last thing. Bookend the day with balance through this next exercise. It's even more effective if you build on what you've already learned. Allow in the love and support of the universe before you do the balance. Then you'll have more energy to work with when you do balance your spine.

. . . .

ENERGY BALANCE

- Focus on the upflow and downflow in your spine. You can focus on your energy or nervous system flow, whichever works better for you. The effects are the same.

- Intend for both flows to perfectly balance each other.

. . . .

Balancing your energy requires getting your energy to move the way you want it to. That's a little bit of work or exercise for your energy. The more clearly you can focus on what you're doing, the more effectively you can do it. That's what I'm going to show you how to do next.

. . . .

What goes out must come in
The other side of chaos

. . . .

Have you ever been to a chiropractor? Did they talk to you about your posture? When you stand, sit, walk and sleep with good posture, your weight is balanced by your center of gravity. Good posture significantly reduces any possible musculoskeletal problem. Balance helps your muscles work effectively and with less strain.

When your body is out of balance, you pay a heavy price. Especially when your lifestyle or work makes it hard to maintain good posture. Your body needs physical activity to maintain balanced processes.

Sedentary lifestyles are now among the top ten causes of death and disability worldwide. Not moving your body doubles your chances of heart attack, diabetes and anxiety. It also increases the chance of putting on weight, which in turn brings a whole host of other problems. Being overweight is simply another symptom of imbalance in the body. When you take more calories in than you use in a day, your diet is out of balance. But adipose tissue (or fat cells) don't only store excess calories. Fat also stores toxins. If your body is out of balance, it's not eliminating all the toxins you're consuming or your metabolism is producing.

Your body doesn't like toxins wandering around causing issues, so it builds storerooms. That's those same fat cells. Your body puts the toxins inside your fat cells, to keep them out of the way. If you've ever been on a calorie-controlled diet or watched a friend go through it you've experienced this. After about three weeks, the weight loss has taken down enough storerooms for you to start to feel like crap. Mostly because the crap or toxins have lost their room and board. They start to circulate again. A cleansing or balancing diet, together with lifestyle changes to support a healthy balance, can be more effective in the long run. Even if you don't lose weight so fast initially.

Balance is essential, including the balance between sleep and waking. Scientists have identified the health risks of insufficient sleep.

Getting good sleep is as important to your health as nutrition and exercise. But as you know, sleep is one of the first things to go when your life gets out of balance.

Our planet also needs to be balanced. When there's more pollution going into the environment than what natural processes can break down, the planet has a problem. A recent report suggests there'll be more plastic than fish in the sea by 2050. I guess you could say that, in a toxic sense, our planet has a weight problem!

Balance is especially important energetically, though this often requires undoing old habits. There are many who've learned to flow energy out when working with others or working on manifesting what they want, but they've never learned how to draw energy in. The long-term effects of this imbalance can be draining. Think of it like your budget. If you spend $5 more than you earn every week, you won't notice it for a while. But if you keep doing that year after year, you'll end up in trouble.

Patricia was like that. She was a beautiful woman with a thriving spiritual practice, who'd become so drained she could no longer work. She was energetically exhausted. When she did the following exercise, she quickly realized her energy went only one way—out. Once she learned to keep her inflow and outflow balanced, she quickly recovered. Then she was able to return to her work.

The first time you do this exercise you may find, as Patricia did, it's easier to flow energy out than it is to bring energy in. Many people start that way, because energy always responds to our focus and intention, whether we're conscious of it or not. We generally talk about flowing our energy out to the world so, unconsciously, that's how it goes.

. . . .

ENERGY BALL

- Place your two hands together, palms touching each other.
- Focus on both your palms.

- Intend for your energy to flow out from both of them. If it helps, think of this as extending your magnetic field.

- When you feel the energy (or magnetic field) between your palms, cup the outside of the growing field of energy, as if you're holding a ball. Allow your palms to move apart as the energy ball gets bigger. When your energy ball is big enough, take the next step.

· ·

- Focus on both your palms again.

- This time, intend for your energy to flow back into them, as if your palms were energy vacuum cleaners. As the energy between your hands reduces, and the energy ball begins to shrink, allow your palms to come back together.

Do this several times. Flow energy out, then in, then out, then in. Do it until you can draw energy in as easily as you can flow it out and vice versa.

· ·

As with Patricia, it's important you have a balanced relationship with energy. Doing the above exercise strengthens your intention. It clarifies your focus and teaches you to keep your system energetically balanced. It's also helpful if you're not yet confident of perceiving energy. This exercise activates your subtle awareness. Keep practicing until the outflow and inflow are as easy as each other. Keep practicing until you can feel both.

That's what Dan had to do. He'd had a very interesting time through the sixties, taking all sorts of substances that did weird things to his brain. As a consequence, his health was poor. His energy was very low when he first came to see me. After many detoxes, he began to feel a whole lot better. Yet his energy still wasn't as strong as it had been when he was young. He would swing from feeling lightheaded to dragging himself around. A classic case of energetic imbalance. He'd cleared his system but still needed to rebuild its capacity to stay balanced.

Dan soon understood that both feelings were the result of his energy being at one extreme or the other. Once he learned to keep himself balanced, he found his strength returning. He realized that keeping his system balanced was a much easier, more peaceful way of operating. It gave him the space and energy to deal more calmly with his life. Then he found he no longer missed all those interesting substances.

The importance of balance is known in many spiritual traditions. It's even encapsulated in the yin-yang symbol which you probably know, and the flower of life which you may not. The yin-yang symbol comes to us from Chinese Taoism. It encapsulates their understanding of balance as the constant flow between the feminine (all things dark and mysterious, receptive and empty) and the masculine (all things bright and assertive, radiative and full). The flower of life has come down to us from Ancient Egypt. It has perfect form, proportion and harmony. That was their understanding of balance. For them, it was the true balance of creation held throughout space and time.

Yin-yang symbol

Flower of life

In Ancient Egypt where Plato and other ancient Greeks went to study, there wasn't good or bad, but order and chaos. Chaos happened when things got out of balance, when the kind of harmony seen in the flower of life was lost. The regular flooding of the Nile brought renewed fertility and abundant harvests every year. The Egyptian civilization was built on that. When the flood was out of balance—either too low causing a poor harvest or too high bringing damage and destruction—chaos ensued, threatening their civilization.

The ancient Egyptians learned to predict and manage the different flood levels. The Nile influenced everything, including the Egyptians'

understanding of themselves. Understanding gave them better man
agement of the balance of the flood. The Egyptians stored grain or
built extra canals and walls. It also let them view their internal balance
differently to the way most of us view ours today.

Our internal balance is a result of our relationship with ourselves.
If our view of ourselves is in harmony and proportion, then all of
our aspects work together to create a beautiful and balanced life.
Unfortunately, the way many of us view ourselves creates imbalances
in our lives and intuition.

. . . .

The key to self-trust
What color is your shadow?

. . . .

When your destructive aspects peek out and disrupt your relationships or stop you from achieving your dreams, it's tempting to blame your shadow. What's the shadow? It's the part of you with the worst reputation. At least that's how it's generally perceived. It's like that moment at the Christmas party when you met your boss for the first time, and were so desperate to impress that you made a fool of yourself. Or that other time you had great plans to get fit and signed up to join a Saturday morning running club. Then every Friday night you drank so much you slept through the run.

Doing things that get in our own way is self-sabotage. Our shadow gets the blame, yet that's not all the shadow is. Rather that's what an **unhealthy** shadow is.

It's a bit like what you eat. When you don't understand about nutrition, you might eat all sorts of things that taste great but are terrible for you. That's your shadow. Once you know a bit more, you understand your shadow. Then things get healthier. The shadow is a bit like the yin part of the yin-yang symbol. It's a dark, mysterious part of us. It's the part we don't know. The part we don't yet fully understand. Yet yin energy has an incredible amount of power. Integrating it fully into our lives opens the door to our true mastery.

As we grow, we invariably run into these parts of ourselves. Read the lives of the great masters and you'll notice this pattern. The moment of their awareness, enlightenment, holiness or realization is fraught with significance. It's at that moment their shadow appears to be integrated. That happened for Christ as he came out of the desert and for Buddha as he meditated under his Bodhi tree. I've seen it happen to many of my clients and students. I call this moment being offered 'the devil's contract'.

When you're getting really close to having everything you want, when your chosen desire is almost about to manifest, your energy is really strong. Yet your alignment to your integrity may not be complete just yet. What turns up looks like your desire, but isn't aligned to Who You Truly Are. When you're close to true success, it can seem like you can get everything you want, if you only give up a little of yourself or your integrity to have it. The problem is that'll never work.

In relationships, a devil's contract may appear as the love of your life, only they're already involved elsewhere, so your connection would start as an affair. In business, a devil's contract may be a lucrative contract with your dream client, only they're insisting you circumvent some regulation. In life, a devil's contract may be an invitation to join the cool crowd, the beautiful people; but when you do, you realize the group is dominated by a bully. In each situation, it may appear as if you're going to get what you want and the only cost is giving up a tiny piece of you.

No matter how amazing, how bright and shiny your desire is, nothing will ever compensate you for giving up even the smallest piece of yourself. If you take up the devil's contract, your desire will fall to ashes as it won't give you the joy you were seeking. You'll end up echoing what Maxwell Smart in *Get Smart* used to say: *Missed it by **that** much*. That happens so frequently I've come to expect it in my own life, as well as the lives of my friends and clients. I've also come to expect the true desire to turn up, shortly after the devil's contract has been refused.

It may appear as if the devil's contract is the work of your shadow. That would certainly follow the general psychological model where your shadow is that part of you which houses your 'inner murderer' and all the other dark, horrible bits you can't trust. But it's actually a paradox. It's the lack of integration of all of our aspects which creates the misalignment with Who We Truly Are that enables the devil's contract to appear.

By separating ourselves from our shadow, by attempting to keep it caged up in our subconscious to keep everyone safe, we open the door to the devil's contract. It's another by-product of our one-valley view. One-valley rules of good/bad will make the shadow wrong. The problem is that when you think of your shadow that way, you'll never entirely trust yourself. And you definitely won't trust any strange or weird impulse you get. How do you know if it's coming from your 'evil self'?

Thinking of your shadow as a repository of evil makes it hard to develop reliable intuition because your intuition, especially to start with, often occurs as strange or weird impulses. Believing your shadow is evil, bad or generally up to no good makes any impulse suspicious, including intuitive ones. If you can't trust those impulses, you'll block them. You'll also block the development of your intuition.

If you think your shadow will lead you from your path, you'll want to suppress it and stick to what's familiar. You'll assess every stray thought or feeling for wrongness. That throws you back into your fight/flight limbic system, or to your left brain with all its yes/no or right/wrong detail.

As in the yin-yang symbol, there is light in the darkness of your shadow. Your shadow houses your greatest gifts. Your shadow is where your genius is waiting to be discovered. Your shadow is also where your intuition remains, until you bring it into full conscious awareness. If you stop to assess every intuitive impulse because you don't trust yourself, you'll delay the development of your intuition. Acting immediately on any impulse helps your intuition to grow much faster.

Now that's not a smart thing to do, if you can't trust your shadow. But what if your shadow wasn't evil, but simply the parts of yourself you didn't know? We all have aspects of ourselves we don't fully understand. That's what's in our shadow. All those different aspects serve a purpose. They're essential for you to become more of Who You Truly Are. At first your shadow may not appear to be helpful, but it is.

There's a part of me that's quite ruthless. No, it's not a comfortable aspect, but it's there. For a long time, I tried to squash it into my shadow but it demanded to be acknowledged. It would appear inappropriately. As one of my friends said, 'Catherine, you always say the right thing at the wrong time.' The more I tried to suppress my ruthlessness, the more it expressed itself in unfortunate ways. Then I began to work in the healing arena and realized I needed this aspect.

Healing often requires we face things we'd rather avoid. Having to push clients to face deep hurts and terrible pain is never nice, always uncomfortable and often necessary. Being able to call on my ruthless side gets this essential but painful job done.

Happily employed now, that aspect of me is no longer really part of my shadow, the dark unknown and unacknowledged part of me. It's become an asset. Indeed, one of my former students, now a Fractology colleague, said to me, 'You're a ruthless teacher. You know we can do it, despite all the reasons we give you as to why we can't. You never let go of the knowledge that we can do it until we do.'

Unshakable faith in people is a form of ruthlessness. As you rehabilitate your shadow, you too will discover unexpected gifts. Many of my clients are clever decent people who've been thoroughly conditioned or trained to be nice. All their assertiveness has ended up in their shadow, so they say 'yes' to things that don't serve them.

That was Luke all over. One of the most decent men you could ever hope to meet, he was at the desperate end of stress. He was exhausted but couldn't rest or sleep. His head was too full of worries. He was constantly thinking of the things he was being pressured to do. He wanted to make everyone happy but had a problem—he was so nice he couldn't get angry.

Anger helps us maintain our boundaries. It lets other people know when they've gone too far. Think about other people's reactions when you want to persuade them to do something. If they say they'd rather not, you'd probably persist; but if they got angry, annoyed or irritated you'd stop. That's what anger is for. To let people know when they've crossed the line.

But what if your anger, like Luke's, is in your shadow? And you're not letting it out? You'd probably end up agreeing to all sorts of things that don't work for you. That's the curse of being too nice. It's a huge source of emotional and physical exhaustion. Once Luke allowed his shadow out, he could acknowledge what worked for him. He was clearer on what he wanted and that it was okay to say 'no'. His stress and exhaustion faded. He didn't turn into an angry man. Far from it. But his anger could do its job. It could protect him and his boundaries.

Just like Luke, you need your shadow. It holds necessary keys and insights into your true genius and authenticity.

Many people find it hard to realize their purpose until they rehabilitate their shadow. That was Tess. She was desperate to find her true path in life, but was at a loss to know how. She did a lot of admin work to get by but wanted more. It wasn't until she integrated her shadow and the passion that was hiding there, that she realized she really wanted to be an artist.

I think about it this way: the creative source (whatever that is for you) is surely at the very least a decent engineer. Engineers are masters at making things 'fit for purpose'. When you want a widget you make it so the most efficient (read easy and graceful) thing for it to do is whatever you want it to do. You don't stick a cogwheel where you need a flywheel, then yell at it for getting stuck. Or start thinking it's conspiring against you.

Nature exhibits this same level of beautiful efficiency. Whatever it produces is fit for purpose. Physicists see this in the functioning of our universe, as Stephen Hawking explained:

> The laws of science, as we know them at present, contain many fundamental numbers [to do with particles and forces]. The remarkable fact is that the values of these numbers seem to have been very finely adjusted to make possible the development of life.

You too are finely adjusted, to make possible the development of your own life. By not owning your shadow, you end up throwing off the balance of that adjustment. By invalidating or not trusting yourself, you keep yourself out of alignment and off balance. You need **all** the bits currently residing in your shadow to fulfill your function in the universe. If you continue believing your shadow is bad, you won't ever find out how those aspects help you on your path. But if you get to know those aspects with the intention of figuring out how they're part of the true design of your life, you'll find you're stronger and more capable than you ever thought possible.

Your shadow is part of the order of your life, rather than its chaos. And not just any order. It's an ordered pattern that expresses your essence to its full potential. The ancient Egyptians understood that their shadows strengthened them against chaos. Here is an excerpt from Normandi Ellis' *Awakening Osiris*, an inspiring translation of the Egyptian Book of the Dead:

I have walked that road between mountains, longer than night, whiter than salt, where the hearts of men are made fragrant as hyacinth nodding. To the fields I've traveled and back. I am the same man made new. My hands carry the power of love, I hold my hard, ancient life like crystal. My shadow binds itself to me. My soul whirls, rushing overhead, grazing my hair with the flurry of its wings. Gods sail in the dawn with a cargo of souls waiting to be born. I am the first to walk this road, bringing the reckoning of years. With the eye of sun I see the continuous motion of days, words only silence could have brought to my ears, and light in the eye of the world to come. My soul, shadow and I are walking.

There are those who know nothing of walking in light, who dwell in caves or creep from the rocks, who doubt that the songs of sparrows are real, who live by the club and the knife. They would seize a man's dreams and speak them with fetid tongues. They'd tear out his heart and scatter his bones. Their road is dark, but just as well traveled as mine, though their shadows and souls refuse to walk with them.

From Chapter 31: *His Soul and His Shadow*

When we understand that imbalance or incompletion is the cause of our problems (and not wickedness or any other form of being wrong), we're much better equipped to create the lives we desire. It's so much easier to complete a cycle and balance our system than to cure all the evil in the world. If you make aspects of yourself or your shadow wrong, you'll avoid calling on them when they're the best part of you for the job. Playing right-wrong with yourself keeps you a little one-dimensional. When you integrate your shadow, you have a vast array of parts that'll increase the width of your soul and energy. It's then so much easier to deal with everything life has to throw at you.

When you and your shadow are one, you have a whole smorgasbord of different aspects to call on for any given situation. Need to deal with a difficult family member? Your patient side can do it. How about a difficult client? Your assertive aspect works better. Have a party to plan? Let your fun side do it. Need to complete that assignment or project? That's what discipline is for. Want to be innovative? Out comes your creative side.

You were born with a tool set, but you've only got access to the complete set once you've integrated your shadow. Keeping your energy balanced helps with this integration. It'll help you appreciate that it's the balance between your different aspects which enables you to create good in your life, not focusing on particular aspects and suppressing others. That's also true for your intuition. The more balanced your energy, the easier it is for you to balance all parts of your life, including your analytical and intuitive parts. So let's get your energetic balance even stronger.

. . . .

What goes up must come down, especially in your own system
Clean and jerk

· ·

Whent your system is neurologically and energetically balanced, you become more effective. You experience this all the time physically. Now you have to take it one step further for your intuition.

When you are carrying heavy bags, does it feel easier if they're on just one side? Or if you split the load into two so the weight is even on both sides? Of course, it's easier to carry weight that's balanced. But it's more than that, isn't it? When the weight is balanced, you can carry **more** weight.

Your muscles work rather like a pulley system. This means they use one load to offset another, if it's a balanced load. Your body works best when your weight is distributed evenly around your center of gravity. That's why good posture works. When you're holding something against gravity, it has kinetic or stored energy. Kinetic energy is potential energy. It could be a reaction waiting to happen, like in a bomb or a battery. Or the energy of an object accelerating after you drop it.

With an equal amount of kinetic energy on either side of your body, it's easier to stay upright and centered. In the same way, making sure your kundalini energy is balanced in both directions in your body keeps you metaphysically upright and centered. If you keep the upflow and downflow of energy in your body balanced, you'll stay grounded and present. Then you'll be able to work with increasingly intense and powerful energies.

As you continue to practice the energy balance and energy ball exercises, two important things happen. Firstly, your ability to stay neurologically and energetically balanced grows stronger. Secondly, your awareness of your EM energy grows clearer. That's an important part of the development of your intuition.

One of the most common questions I'm asked is: *How can you teach intuition?* That's a good question because when you learn something physical, like how to make a chair, your physical senses tell you how well you're doing. If the legs of your chair are different lengths, you'll know it when you see it or sit on it. The experience of your chair gives you what you need in order to learn. Feedback. Afferent nerves carry feedback to your brain and complete the cycle of learning. That feedback enables you to correct and improve. It's how you build lesson upon lesson until you've mastered each new skill. This applies to making chairs as well as any other skill, including mastering intuition.

You can start the cycle of feedback by simply focusing on what you want to do. There's an old part of your brain called the reticular activating system (RAS for short). It's a bit like having your own personal secretary reminding you what's important to watch out for.

When I was in my twenties, one of my flatmates bought an MG. My family's not into cars, so I'd never seen one before. I thought MGs must be really rare, but within a couple of weeks I was seeing them everywhere. It wasn't that those cars had suddenly flooded onto the streets of my city, but the attention system in my brain had decided I needed to look out for those cars, in case my flatmate was in one of them.

This is what you need to get your brain to do with your electromagnetic energy, if you want to develop conscious intuition. Just like it was for me and cars. It's not that your brain isn't aware of intuitive information. It is, but you need your 'secretary' to watch out for it. Practicing the energy balance and energy ball exercises will make that happen. That's the trick to teaching intuition.

The truth is, I don't really teach intuition. I just show my students how to be aware and make use of what their brain is already doing. Once you're aware of your electromagnetic energy, you'll get clear feedback. That makes it simpler to keep your energy more complete and balanced. Once your EM energy is more complete and balanced, your energy becomes more stable and has a foundation you can continue to build on. Importantly, you'll also build confidence and certainty in your own awareness. Once you get your EM energy on your 'secretary's' list of what to watch out for it becomes part of your peripheral awareness. These are the things you notice when you need to, without having to obsess over them. You don't obsess over your big toe, do you?

Your big toe has a huge impact on the way you walk and stand, but you're not generally conscious of it as it's in your peripheral awareness. If you want to you can focus on it anytime and get an 'update' on how it's going. Furthermore, if you stub your toe or walk barefoot on a gorgeous carpet, your big toe grabs your attention immediately. That's also part of your attention system, bringing focus to where it's most beneficial. It's how energetic awareness and your intuition work most effectively. Once you've started to work with your intuition, it becomes a conscious part of your attention system.

This type of peripheral energetic awareness is the first real step towards intuitive mastery. It enables you to apply your awareness in effective beneficial ways for your life. It starts with putting conscious attention on your energy through the energy balance and energy ball exercises. It soon grows to the point where you're aware of the energy running up and down your spine. When you can tell the upflow from the downflow in your spine, you can use your awareness to refine your energetic balance further.

Awareness of both separate flows means you're starting to have some conscious control over your neurological cycle. You can now also safely begin to increase the amount of energy in your system, because you can keep the load balanced. That's like increasing how much you can carry once you've got your load balanced.

Here's a quick quiz. If one of your flows is stronger than the other, will you:

- decrease the stronger flow?
- increase the weaker flow?
- do both, so they meet in the middle?

You can experiment with each option. Feel which one suits you best. I bet I can guess which one it'll be. If you think about balanced and unbalanced flows, you'll be able to guess too.

None of us like to be suppressed. Just ask your shadow. Indeed, the whole point of learning the logic of your intuition is to grow and expand with grace and ease. A good principle is to never shut down your energy. If you always choose to strengthen the weaker flow, you'll enjoy this process much more. Then you'll be more willing to keep your energies balanced.

Consistency is key in life and with your body. This is why 'book-ending' your day with your energetic maintenance is so useful. In time it'll retrain your system to maintain a balanced and complete state.

Bookending the day with a balanced energy requires you do the following exercise night and morning. This combines the completion you learned earlier with keeping your system balanced. Only do this when you've done the previous exercises enough to feel the upflow and downflow.

. . . .

DAILY BOOKEND FOR BALANCED KUNDALINI

- Flow acceptance to anything negative in your space and/or acknowledge anything that feels incomplete.
- Focus on the upflow and downflow in your spine.
- Feel for whichever is the stronger or weaker flow.
- Focus on the weaker flow.
- Intend for the weaker flow to increase in strength, until it perfectly balances the stronger.

. . . .

As you continue to bookend your day in this way, your energy will grow clearer. Any static or background noise from incompletions will drop away. Your space will be clearer. Connecting to Who You Truly Are will be easier.

Realizing the true benefits of your intuition will be your new normal, just as it became for Meg. She was already highly intuitive when I met her. That wasn't what she needed help with. Her difficulty was how hard she found it to distinguish between what she perceived energetically with what was there physically. This hampered her from using what she saw to her benefit, especially when she was tired.

I remember one evening after dinner she was driving me home. Suddenly she braked heavily, throwing me against the seat belt. With the tires squealing, she brought the car to a rapid stop. Fortunately there was no one behind or they'd probably have rear-ended us. I looked at Meg and said, 'That was an invisible person. You're allowed to drive through those.' She'd seen a spirit on the roadway and confused the spirit with a human person. She'd braked desperately to avoid hitting the person in spirit, though that's not an issue for spirits.

Meg's inability to distinguish between the spiritual and physical made it hard for her to operate effectively on either level. She was able to navigate between both only when she learned to keep her energies balanced. Soon she was able to use her intuition in her business. Then her business helped her expand even more. Both she and her intuition continue to thrive.

Such experiences will teach you a lot about energy. They'll also teach you about Who You Truly Are. Ultimately, that's where your stability comes from. When you gain a depth of clarity around your own essence, about your own soul, you'll attain a level of certainty and stability that'll see you through whatever life may throw at you.

With clear self-awareness, the windscreen of your perception is clean of any mud. You can see clearly in life and with your intuition. It's a self-reinforcing cycle. The more you know Who You Truly Are, the clearer your intuition becomes; and the clearer your intuition is, the more you'll learn about Who You Truly Are. That's the source of so much of the expansion that intuition generates.

So let's get you started.

· ·

Step Three

Now you're completing your cycles through using acknowledgments, understanding your own intuitive process and keeping yourself balanced, you're on the verge of stepping into a wider reality. You're on the brink of a more expansive life than you've ever known. However, there is one more step required before you can step up with complete confidence.

The development of intuition is often equated with spiritual development for one simple reason: they both require you grow your self-awareness. The self-awareness you need to grow your intuition is, like intuition itself, an energetic awareness. This is what Step Three is all about. In this step, you'll learn how to be fully conscious of your own resonance, your own unique EM signature. This will give you an entirely new way to understand your life, the universe and Who You Truly Are.

. . . .

Where am I?
Point of reference

· ·

Have you ever woken up and for a moment didn't know where you were? Maybe you slept in a new place so for a second nothing made sense? Confusing impressions tumbled through your addled brain, mixing disorientation with turmoil as you struggled with shades of panic. Just like in the movies your first question was, 'Where am I?' A moment later with a wave of relief you found the answer. You remembered where you were. Bewilderment faded and everything made sense again.

Knowing where we are gives us a stable anchor. Without that it's difficult, if not impossible, to understand the world around us. Nothing has meaning in itself—all meaning comes from the relationship of one thing to another. My father used to joke, 'Everything is relative, and you're my relative.' Apart from the groan factor, this is true.

Right now, you're reading this page. But how do you understand what the different squiggles mean? Someone taught you that a particular collection of letters relates to a certain meaning. Probably when you were first learning to read someone wrote C-A-T and drew a stick figure of one such creature next to it. Even then, you knew that C-A-T didn't mean the stick figure. It didn't give meaning because of the way it was drawn. The drawing was a reference point. It enabled you to grasp the idea that putting those three shapes together in that order referred to that warm, furry, purry creature.

By themselves, letters don't mean anything. Even words mean nothing. Look at them. They're just squiggles on paper. We give them meaning. It's what we agree they refer to and the relationships they hold that have meaning.

As we collect more and more references, we build them into an increasingly complex system of connected significance. That's how our ability to understand and derive meaning grows. Once our original reference gets us to the meaning, we often forget about it.

Just as we don't generally remember the stick figure when we read 'cat'. We use points of reference all the time. We know the table is hard when we refer to a cushion, or our coffee is hot when we refer to the water from the cooler. These references enable us to understand our world and when things are working or not. Carpet should be dry relative to water. If it isn't, then someone has some explaining to do.

Among all the references we use, there's a constant we all share. It's so important to our survival it has influenced the shapes of our bodies and the functioning of our nervous systems. Can you guess what it is? Remember that once our reference creates a **meaningful** relationship we tend to forget it. The constant is the three dimensions of our world: up/down, left/right and forward/backward.

Look around the room. You'll see your three-dimensional references in the walls, floor and ceiling. The three dimensions define the limits of our world. They also give us a framework to understand everything in our everyday lives. If you lose sight of them, you'll instinctively scramble to get your references back. Like when you don't know where you are when you wake up or if you get tumbled about in the surf.

Your physical body uses reference points. A large part of your nervous system is dedicated to keeping track of where you are in those three dimensions. Your body is obsessed with keeping your eyes parallel to the horizon. If your pelvis gets out of alignment, your spine twists about, sometimes severely, to keep your eyes level. Your eyes have a powerful connection to your brain. So much so that the way they move can indicate any possible problem. Level eyes automatically orient you to your three reference dimensions.

Your eyes give you another set of three reference points: your left eye, your right eye and the focal point where each eyeline meets. You're so naturally attuned to this three-point reference system, it influences your thinking and your memory. The belief that things happen in threes is a longstanding one. Your eyes and their focus together make up three reference points. You also access your memories as another set of three: your memory along with its time and place.

Think of that summer when it was so warm the ice cream dripped down your arm, or the year you left school or had your first job. Now, how did you find that memory? If we have the place, like the shop where we bought the ice cream, we find the time by asking ourselves: *When was I there?* Or if we know the time, like the year we graduated or got that job, we get the place by asking: *Where was that?* Once we've got both, our brain focuses on where they connect. Then we pull up the 'file' of that particular memory.

We do this with any memory, even ones that are hard to recall. Once we have those references of where and when, the details start to come. Ask yourself: *When was I there?* and *Where was I?* Go with whatever answer you get. Focus on that time and place. Accept whatever details come to you. They might be a little fuzzy at first but if you practice with those reference points your ability to remember will improve.

Reference points allow you to remember. Or navigate in the physical world. One look and you know if you're inside or outside. If you're in the country or the city. You get details such as sidewalks and cars that fit inside your reference points. Details give you further meaning, like where it's safe to walk. They also tell you about other things in your space. Like right now the cat is getting in my way because I can't see the computer screen, which explains why I've had to type this several times!

We automatically refer to the dimensions of our physical existence. Our neurology developed this way. We're so used to it that we don't even notice. But what happens when our set of three references are not there? When we're out in the metaphysical? When our intuition has opened up and it's all energy? Or we're somewhere with a different number of dimensions? What are we going to use as our reference when we're beyond the physical and don't have the horizon to tell us where we are?

This lack of a reliable reference explains why it's often so hard to understand the meaning of our intuitive flashes. Our intuition tells us we are One with all things. That's what we experience when we're working through our EM awareness. EM energy is everywhere throughout time and space. Reality and the universe are so vast. If we're going to make sense of it all, we need a way to think about all of that with the same kind of clarity our physical references give us.

. . . .

There's more than three dimensions
Everywhere and nowhere

. . . .

Jonathan Livingston Seagull understood: *[If we] overcome space and all we have left is Here. Overcome time, and all we have left is Now.*

When we're working with our right brains on energy or in the spiritual dimensions, we don't have the three physical dimensions of our world. We lose our normal references that tell us where we are. What can our eyes and brain align to when we're nowhere? Or everywhere? We feel horribly disoriented when we wake not knowing where we are.

When we're doing metaphysical stuff, our systems can't use the three dimensions of physical space as references. Yet our brains are designed for doing just that. Our brains and bodies are connected to the third dimension. They're three-dimensional like the house. That's what our brains and minds are used to working with. It's confusing when we need to process information from (say) seven dimensions. And what about eleven dimensions? Having more dimensions is not just a spiritual idea. Einstein's relativity gave us a fourth dimension by combining time and our three dimensions. String theory gives us even more with ten dimensions. And when the different forms of string theory are combined into M-theory, we have eleven dimensions.

String theory aims to get gravity to make sense in quantum mechanics. Instead of particles, we have vibrating strings. Just as a fan looks solid when spinning fast, a string looks like a particle when it vibrates at a high enough frequency. Different string vibrations create different particles. One vibrating string even creates the graviton, which theoretically carries gravitational force. Relativity and string theory seem like a foreign language to most of us. String theory is still awaiting the development of technology for it to become part of our lives. For the present, just think of it as the fun guy at the physics party, who's always telling outrageous stories. String theory gives us a mathematical understanding of parallel universes. It also has a model for a particle that creates gravity.

The trick with string theory is that it can't be tested with current technology. Einstein had the same problem. He was a bit different from other physicists—not just because he was brilliant, but in how he accessed his brilliance. He liked to visualize—to experience the concepts he was playing with, instead of simply working them out with numbers. By doing so, he worked out many things technology couldn't test in his time. Like what happens as we get closer to the speed of light. When we connect with energy or spiritual planes we're doing what Einstein did—doing 'thought experiments' and experiencing other dimensions.

Einstein used mathematics to turn his thought experiments into something he could share with others. Most of us need a more user-friendly method, if we want to share our 'thought experiments' or intuitive visions. If we want to share what our intuition reveals with everyone, we need a method everyone can get. Fortunately such a method exists. It's in-built. It comes with your internal tool kit. We've already talked about it. It's fractals. That pattern that's repeated over and over to build up a more complex pattern.

If you walk in nature, you'll see fractals in every tree and fern, mountain range or ocean wave. If you go to the museum, you'll see them in the formation of nautilus shells and crystals. If you go to the markets, fractals are there in vegetables and overhead in the clouds. You're surrounded by patterns that repeat over and over again creating more complex patterns. These are fractals.

Your mind knows how to recognize a fractal. Without any effort, you can tell the difference between a plastic flower and a real one even from across the room. Your in-built 'fractal finder' seeks out the pattern within all things. It can tell you which flowers are fake and which are real. It can show you how to align your visions for others so the vision becomes real for them too. Fractals can also help us understand some of the heady stuff in string theory.

The fractal nature of our world is that patterns are repeated on every level. The more closely we examine our world, the more world there appears to be. Think of a coastline. If we measure it from space we get one length. If we come into a low orbit and measure it again it's longer. If we do a flyover in a plane it's longer again. This happens because the closer we get, the more details we measure, like the crinkles in the coastline. If we measure around every bay rather than straight across the bay it's going to be longer. We know instinctively that walking across a bridge from one side to the other is shorter than walking around the bay.

Each time we include more crinkles the measurement gets longer. That's how dimensions get 'folded up' inside others. Fractals and their workings help our left brains discern many things that our right brains intuit through immediate connection. It all depends on how we're looking at the fractals, or what references we're using.

How many dimensions are there? According to physicists, as many as they need. This proves two things: physicists make worse jokes than dads do and physicists use mathematics as their reference. The number of dimensions depends on which theory they're using. Superstring theory uses ten. Supergravity eleven. And the original theory (now called bosonic string theory) has as many as twenty-six different dimensions.

Think of our coastline again—its length depends on whether we're measuring it as we walk, fly or orbit about the earth. Physicists study physical phenomena to develop their theories but the number of dimensions depends on what reference they're using. However most of us don't refer to higher mathematics every day. We're quite happy with the three dimensions of space-time to which our neurology is perfectly suited. If we get disoriented, we simply check them for things to fall into place. But when we're in the spiritual realm or thinking about extra dimensions like Einstein, what do we do then?

Without a stable reference point, things keep shifting about. It's like a graph with a whole lot of data plotted but a zero point that keeps moving. It's a bit like that scene in *The Hitchhiker's Guide to the Galaxy* after Ford Prefect and Arthur Dent are picked up by a space-ship with an improbability drive. As they're outside the shielding, they initially experience the improbable. They see an ocean where the shoreline is washing up and back rather than the waves. Without a stable reference point, we can't rely on anything staying put.

Yet we expect the metaphysical to operate the same way as the physical. We expect to see intuitively in the same way as we do physically. Don't worry, as this is where we all start. The thing is, we're all aware of energy. Even those who claim to be unaware of, or don't believe in, spiritual energy will react when the energy changes in a room. Clearly, picking up energy takes no great skill. We do it all the time.

The skill lies in **interpreting** the energy. Look around the three dimensions of your room. You'll automatically interpret what your senses tell you. You know that shape is a chair and that's a window. You can tell by the look of an object how hard or soft it probably is or how near or far it is. You could even guess how much it's likely to weigh. You do all of this without much conscious effort, if any.

The problem is that we expect to interpret energy as easily and simply as we do our physical world. We forget we spent the first several years of our lives getting more food on our face than in our mouths, missing the potty more often than we'd like. We were constantly surprised and astonished before we learned to interpret our world. Those around us who'd already learned about the physical world didn't expect us to do it immediately. They knew we'd get there in the end and we did.

If we're going to develop any skill in interpreting the metaphysical, we need to give ourselves a similar grace period. Without that, our results will be hit-and-miss at best. We also need a reliable reference point. Unfortunately, not everything in our world is something we benefit from. Do you want your references to be negative or positive? That's a simpler choice than you might believe.

. . . .

Resonance is catching
The trouble with tribes

No matter what we're doing in the physical or metaphysical, we like to know we're doing well. We want to know our efforts will be rewarded. That what we're doing is of value. That it's going to benefit others as well as ourselves. We need to assess how effective and productive we're being. Once again, we need a reference. Something against which to measure what we're doing. Only then will we know if we're on track or not. If we're on track, all we need do is keep going. But if we're off track, we need to correct.

By constant correction we can go a long way. They say the first moon landing was only on target about 3 percent of the time—for the rest of it they were correcting their flight path. Even the biggest, hairiest goals can be accomplished if we correct enough. References tell us when we need to correct, as well as how to do it. They add ease and grace to our paths.

I spoke earlier about our tribal neurology. The way our brains tend to work because of what our ancestors got up to, creating a right/wrong orientation in our thinking, instead of leaving us open to correction along the way. Unfortunately, staying on track is much more difficult without correction. It's then way too easy to think of ourselves as wrong when things don't work out. The internal conflicts it generates is also a huge drain on our energies. Internal conflict is inevitable if we use a right/wrong reference, because these references always come from **outside** ourselves.

Who gets to decide what is right? Who decides what's wrong? Whoever it is, it's generally someone else. Someone outside your own system. Like your parents or boss. If you're using a right/wrong reference, you're using someone else's rules created around something other than Who You Truly Are. Furthermore, rules assume things never change. They might work for a while but when things shift about they stop working, yet you might keep following them anyway.

Understanding why rules don't work depends on the cycles. Rules keep you trapped in the same old cycles and make it hard to expand into new expansive realities.

Whatever your opinion about following rules, the fact that they're created externally is a problem for your intuition. You have no control over the energy outside of yourself and, sadly, it's often not the kind you'd want to refer to anyway. Energy has a resonant effect similar to entrainment. Your brain has a tendency to fall into line with the frequency it's exposed to. Like a musical beat. That's called 'brainwave entrainment'.

Have you ever noticed how meditation or working with energy is stronger when you do it in a group? That's one of the effects of entrainment. It helped our ancestral tribes work closely together. Today, entrainment can assist when we're working in a team.

We all have a tendency to fall into sync with the strongest signal. Put on loud music when you're doing your chores. How long before you're doing them to the beat? We tend to adopt any strong signal as a reference, even if temporarily. This effect is increased if we let right/wrong thinking get us focused on what's external.

Here's a quick question: *Is there more positive or negative energy in the world?* Turn on your news feed. You'll see how much attention humanity gives to negative states. It's another unfortunate side effect of our neural inheritance from our ancestors. Keeping us focused on the scary stuff ensures we're aware of all possible threats. While this had survival value at one time, it no longer serves us. There are too many people in the world feeling anxious, angry or depressed. So do we really want to refer to their energy?

Let's test this right now. Focus on your heart space and open it wide. Now open it wider. Wider again. What happened? Open your heart space wide enough and chances are you'll feel wobbly or uncomfortable. You may even begin to feel a little anxious or depressed. If so, your heart space has fallen into line with the dominant emotional energy that's out there; you're in sync with all that negative emotion. If you've had a lot of experience with grief, anxiety or anger you're even more at risk of this. If your system refers to those states inside and out, you'll have a 'negative emotion habit'. With all of that going on, how are you ever going to transform your life into one of peace, love and abundance?

You do it by changing the reference your heart space is using. When you open your heart space like you just did, you unconsciously select the strongest emotional signal as a reference. By consciously choosing a referential energy that puts positive 'training wheels' on your heart space, you recondition yourself to work with more supportive energies and states.

Deirdre's poor little heart space needed that desperately. She'd endured a neglectful upbringing from narcissistic parents, which led her into a mentally and emotionally abusive marriage. With the support of friends, she'd found the strength to get a divorce. But her life didn't get any happier because her heart didn't know how. Her heart had used fear and depression as its references for way too long. Her heart didn't know what else to do.

Deirdre had done some work to release her anxiety and depression. That helped a little, but happiness still eluded her so she came to see me. I explained that different emotions were different resonant states and that her heart had a depression habit. Just like breaking any habit, the best approach was to develop a new one. 'But how do I do that?' she pleaded. 'I can't remember ever being happy.'

Her tough life had left Deirdre believing in very little, but she did believe in angels. So that's what we focused on. I encouraged her to bring the heart of the angels through her heart space, as you can do in the exercise below. Much to her astonishment, Deirdre felt an immediate shift. With that support her heart space shifted, entraining to a different state. Just like taking on any new habit or breaking any old habit, she had good days and bad days for a while. But that first experience gave her enough hope to keep practicing. In time, her anxiety and depression lifted. Her heart space opened to safety and happiness.

The exercise below shows you how to do this. It's quite simple, because you want your heart space to use your new reference all the time. While you could argue this is still using an external reference, it's one you're consciously choosing. You can pick a reference that works for you, no matter where you are spiritually. One that makes your path in life easier.

. . . .

THE HEART OF GOD

- Focus on your source of creation (God, universe, angels, your higher self).

- Intend for you to connect to this source. Be open to whatever comes.

- When you feel a connection, ask (or intend) for your source to open its heart space through the center of your heart space. Remember to allow it through.

- Once you feel the heart of your source flowing through your heart space, it's safe to open your heart space. Notice any difference in how that feels, especially how much wider you can open it, once you have that strong reference point in its center.

No matter how many people there are on the planet, your source (God, universe, angels or higher self) will always have a stronger resonance. With that at your center, your heart space will entrain to it, rather than to whatever negativity there is in the world.

. . . .

The most effective way to use this exercise is to bookend the day. Do it first and last thing. You can add it onto your other exercises.

The heart of God (or universe) is an excellent reference for our heart space. If we're to get our left brain and our right brain to understand each other, we need a reference for our intuition that's just as good. We need intuitive 'training wheels' that support us. We need to make it easier for us to progress in our spiritual mastery.

As it turns out, we've always had what we need. You may have heard it said that all the answers lie within. That's true—and it's a whole lot easier if you know where to look. Let me show you where that is.

. . . .

It's not what you know, but who— and the most important who is you
It's all about us

. . . .

Spiritual reality is vast, so our intuitive reference has to be just as vast. Or at least it needs to be always with us, no matter where our consciousness is focused. There's one thing that's always with us. No matter the dimension. No matter the time. No matter the universe. No matter the life. No matter the energy or reality. Our intuitive reference is always there. It's always present within our physical and spiritual experiences.

That reference is you. That reference is me. Our intuitive reference is our own consciousness. This is the only thing that's always with us. We can use our own authenticity or integrity as a reference, rather than a right/wrong framework. Instead of asking: *Is this right?* we need to ask: *Is this me?*

However if we're going to do this, we need a bit of a rethink. In physics, we learn that the act of observing alters things a bit. A lot of that has to do with how we measure stuff. Like hitting an electron with a photon of light. That'll tell you where the electron was, but it'll also change where the electron actually is.

You've undoubtedly experienced the observer effect in your own life. You know you behave differently when your parents are watching than if you're out with your friends goofing off. You also know you behave differently when that hot guy or girl is nearby, just in case they **might** be watching. Remember the saying: *When the cat's away, the mice will play?* This is another statement of the observer effect, as the mice behave differently when observed by the cat.

So we have a dilemma. We recognize the act of observation by its effect, which means we're still using external references like our three dimensions. How do we change this? How do we stop using external references? How do we learn to refer to ourselves and stop having observers affect us?

How many times have you heard: *The answers lie within?* It's true. Our whole system is designed to be a self-referencing system. We just need to know where to look. It's most clearly demonstrated in our immune system.

Your immune system says, 'This is part of me, so I'd better look after it' and 'This isn't part of me, so I'd better get rid of it.' Your immune system is a physiological self-referencing system. Each of us has a point in our body located over our thymus, which is an important part of our immune system. Barbara Ann Brennan, in her seminal book *Hands of Light*, calls it the 'soul seat'. Judith Currivan has written a book about it entitled *The 8th Chakra*. (Chakra is a Sanskrit word meaning 'wheel' and is commonly used for the primary energy points in our body. Like many electromagnetic energy systems they rotate.) As this point is located just above the heart, it's also called the 'high heart'.

I like the term 'soul seat'. For me it's the best fit. Just as we're connected to how we feel all over, our feelings are centered in our heart space. We're connected to Who We Really Are all over, but the center of our connection is the seat of our soul. Our soul seat. You find your soul seat by starting at your sternal notch, the small hollow at the base of your throat between your two collar bones. Come down your breastbone to the level of your second rib—usually the width of three or four fingers. You'll find a ridge there. Our breastbone is actually two bones, the manubrium and the sternum. The ridge you're feeling is where they join. Your soul seat is right at the top edge of it.

The thymus lies under your soul seat. It's a kind of high school for white blood cells. After your bone marrow makes white blood cells, they're sent to learn what things to look out for. The thymus is one of their schools. Ever heard of T cells? They're one kind of white blood cell. The T stands for thymus. It's a potent self-referencing point in your body for your physical health and wellbeing and is also your spiritual center.

Once you're consciously aware of how to work with your soul seat, you never need get lost again. You're going to learn the first step in how that works right now.

Soul seat awareness

While it's true all the answers lie within, it helps to know where to look. Our soul seat is our strongest, most powerful guide through life. Once consciously activated it acts like a compass, guiding us on our truest path. This awareness enables us to let go of right/wrong thinking. We can replace that with authentic or integrity-based thinking. It's one of the best places to look.

Make sure you can locate your soul seat. Then do the exercise below:

. . . .

SOUL SEAT AWARENESS

- Focus on your soul seat. Notice how it's feeling right now.

- Is it light or heavy? Constricted or relaxed? Glowing or dark?

- Now tell yourself a lie. Tell yourself a lie as if you're trying to convince yourself it's true. You could tell yourself you're wearing a swimsuit or your hair is pink with green spots. While you're lying to yourself, how does your soul seat feel?

- Now let go of the lie and tell yourself the truth about your clothing or hairstyle.

- How does your soul seat feel now?

This soul seat awareness exercise is available in meditation format as a free download for readers of *The Soul's Brain*. Please go to www.fractology.info and put in the code HAYHOUSESSA.

. . . .

When we do something that takes us away from our True Selves, we put our soul seats under stress. We can do that even with a silly thing like a small lie. Whenever we reconnect to Who We Truly Are, our soul seat relaxes and opens up. That's what happens when we tell ourselves the truth.

Did you feel that? However your soul seat feels right now is okay. The more you exercise it, the better and lighter it'll feel. If you find it difficult to tell how it's feeling, that just means it hasn't activated yet. Like a muscle, it won't work very well if it's not switched on. If your nerve pathways don't turn on for some reason, you end up with inactive stabilizing muscles giving you back or shoulder problems. You can turn them on by focusing on them and telling them to. In the same way, if your soul seat hasn't activated yet you need to work on it until it does.

. . . .

SOUL SEAT ACTIVATION

- Activate your soul seat by breathing into it for ten minutes. Breathe calmly and deeply, while visualizing your breath passing in and out of your soul seat.
- Do this each day until you feel your soul seat, then do the soul seat awareness exercise again.

. . . .

The more your soul seat becomes part of your normal awareness, the more you can use it like a life compass. Using your soul seat awareness with food is especially helpful, as your body's needs change constantly. Your soul seat guides you to what serves you best every moment. Want a piece of fruit? Focus on eating a banana and notice how it feels in your soul seat. Then focus on an apple, orange or mango in turn. Notice how each one feels in your soul seat. Eat what feels best.

Like any muscle, our soul seat awareness gets stronger as we practice. We want it to be strong enough to be always there. Like a constant compass pointing to what truly serves us. Think again of your big toe. It's part of you, yet most of the time you don't think about it. You only focus on it when something negative happens like stubbing it, or something positive like a foot rub. That's how your soul seat works best.

. . . .

SOUL SEAT COMPASS

- Strengthen your soul seat by focusing on five things each day. Focus on the yes/no, warmer/colder or positive/negative feedback it gives you.
- This works best if you focus on one thing at a time.

. . . .

A strong soul seat strengthens your immune system. It can also show you your path in life. With that strength, your physical self is more able to support what truly belongs to you and release everything else. The same goes for your spiritual self. The more you connect to Who You Truly Are, the more open, expansive, energized and vibrant your soul seat will be, until it shines with a clear golden glow.

Just as you can strengthen your soul seat, you can also damage it. Any time you invalidate yourself or don't support yourself, you risk doing that. Each step you take away from Who You Truly Are darkens it a little. A person with a damaged, clouded or missing soul seat is a 'lost soul'. They've lost all connection to Who They Truly Are. They can't remember their connection to their Source. It's through your connection to your Source that the greatest, most expansive vision of your life is realized. So it's not surprising that depression, hopelessness or despair often accompany a damaged soul seat.

Another symptom of a damaged soul seat is immune dysfunction. This is what Casey had when she came to see me with Crohn's disease. Crohn's is a particularly nasty autoimmune disease. (There aren't many nice ones.) With Crohn's, the immune system attacks the bowel. It's painful and unpleasant. It can have severe negative effects on the patient's social life and career, because of the restrictions to eating and movement it brings.

When I first saw Casey, she couldn't feel her soul seat at all. It was completely numb. At the time she was so ill and depressed she couldn't work, despite heavy medication. Her diet was severely limited and her bowels felt like a war zone. After two months of breathing into it every day. she could feel her soul seat a little when she concentrated hard. Yet even that much awareness accelerated her progress. Soon she could feel her soul seat strongly enough to use it as a guide. She naturally focused on her food and supplement choices to strengthen her bowels. Gradually her ability to tune into what she needed improved, as did her soul seat.

The first thing she noticed was she wasn't feeling so depressed. After that came improvements in her general energy. As she continued to use her soul seat compass to guide her choices, she was able to avoid re-inflaming her system. Her soul seat awareness kept her system, including her immune system, more balanced.

Casey still has occasional flare-ups but manages them better. She recovers faster and feels her bowels are slowly getting stronger. This is wonderful news. Yet the most important difference is that her soul seat guidance has enabled her to stop making choices based on other people's wants and expectations. Casey is now choosing what serves her. She's no longer controlled by her illness or other people's concerns. She's returned to regular work and is planning family holidays without fear of another attack. She has her life back.

This is what happens when we put ourselves at the center of our own lives. Our energy is at its most stable when everything we do is a natural expression of Who We Truly Are. That happens naturally when we become self-referencing. In other words, leading such a centered existence is natural when we are the reference we use for every perception, every energy we encounter and every choice we make.

Self-referencing is the key to living a truly authentic life and fulfilling our purpose, but for many of us that goes against our childhood conditioning. This is a big subject that could be a whole book in itself, but the next section will get you started.

. . . .

All the answers really do lie within
Sacred selfishness

O ur only stable reference in the metaphysical is ourselves. The clearer our soul seats are, the stronger our abilities for self–referencing become. But sometimes there's a stumbling block. How many times has someone asked you to 'be reasonable'? I know I've heard that a lot! When people ask us to 'be reasonable', they're asking us to follow their reasoning or expectations. Put another way, they're asking us to act according to **their** reality. This is a problem we come across time and again when we're growing and expanding.

Each time we take a step up, we step out of our old reality. We're no longer conforming to how we did things before. We're no longer following the reasoning that created that reality. We're being 'unreasonable'. Another one is, 'don't be selfish'. This means: *Don't do what you want to do; do what **I** want you to do*. It goes against what we were taught when we were little, but there's a world of difference between being selfish for our spirit and being selfish for our ego.

You have a purpose. Whether it's to create a work of art or heal the distress of the world, invent a new technology or reinvigorate an old one. Your purpose requires your unique gifts, experiences, energy and viewpoint. If you don't complete your purpose it'll remain undone, for no one else can do it. So it's important you do it. Yet you need resources, time, acceptance and support for that. It's selfish to demand these things. But if you don't demand what you need to fulfill your mission in this lifetime, it won't get done. And the future of our planet will be altered.

If someone tells you that following Who You Truly Are or your soul seat compass is selfish, it means what you're doing doesn't suit that person. Admittedly we can be selfish to justify our limitations or protect our vulnerabilities. That's being selfish for our egos, which does create problems. Mind you, being 'selfless' can be a good way to avoid our true purpose. The relationships I had when I was younger were like that. My partners and boyfriends were decent, kind and sexy but mostly an excuse for me not to get on with what I came here to do. They were a wonderful distraction, but a distraction nevertheless.

The best relationships make it easier for us to be more of Who We Truly Are, not less. And this includes our relationships with ourselves. Both you and the world will be better when you accomplish your purpose for this lifetime. Holding an unwavering focus on that is having Sacred Selfishness.

Fractals are self-referencing

The need for Sacred Selfishness is inherent within the hologram itself. In order to connect fully to the hologram, you have to stay focused on your **own** pattern or resonance and live from that space. Remember we learned earlier that our holographic reality has a fractal structure? That means patterns are repeated again and again and each pattern is made up of a smaller version of the same pattern. Fractals teach us about pattern logic and balance. They also show us the importance of self-referencing. Every part of a fractal is made up of smaller versions of the same pattern. So if one part is lost or damaged, we can check in another part of it to 'reboot' the pattern and get back on track.

That's what Diane had to do. She was a lovely woman who, to all appearances, had a successful life. She lived in a beautiful home, had a career and was still married to the father of her children. The problem was she was exhausted. She'd spent her whole life focusing on others: first her parents, then her husband and now her children. Her empathy and sensitivity meant she was acutely aware of what other people needed or wanted. She'd always focus on that. Over time, Diane had lost her ability to self-reference, to check in with what she wanted.

When she came to see me to find out what she could do, I showed her how to use her empathy and sensitivity from a place of Sacred Selfishness. I helped her turn those great awareness skills towards herself, her own pattern and energy through her soul seat. She was soon able to find her own energy but was still frustrated and exhausted.

Then I showed her the next step. I explained to her it wasn't just **what** she did but **how** she was doing it that was important. I showed her how she could focus on each thing she did from her soul seat to make sure it wouldn't collapse and, what's more, that it'd expand and grow stronger. In that way, she learned to do the 'Diane things' and soon had her energy back.

By learning to operate in a similar way to a fractal, Diane created more energy for herself. She did what a fractal does and operated from alignment with her own energy and patterns. It took her a while to learn how to do that and still take care of the other people in her life, but she did it in time. That's the paradox of Sacred Selfishness.

By looking after ourselves, we end up more capable of looking after others. This is why inter-dependency, which I'll discuss in the third triangle, is founded on independency.

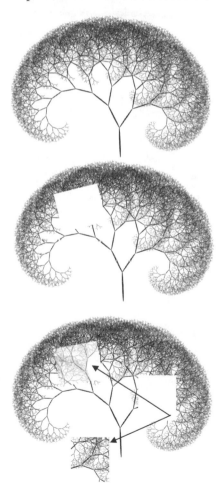

For those who like a picture, here's how fractal self-referencing helps create healing. This is a little more data for your left brain on Sacred Selfishness. On the right is a tree. It's not a natural tree but one created in a computer, using a fractal program. Now imagine part of the tree is broken or that a whole section of it is lost.

Then you'd have something like what you see in the second image of the tree. You'd have a big gap in the middle of the tree. How would you go about healing it? How would you know what to do?

In the third image, you can see what you do. I've taken another piece out of the tree, turned it around and plonked it down again. Of course, in healing you don't cut out the piece. It's more like copying and pasting than cutting and pasting. I've just done it like that so you can see how the pattern in one place is the same as the pattern in another place. That's why self-referencing works. You can use your essence, your pattern or resonance as a template to reboot the parts of you that aren't working as well as you'd like.

This is self-referencing. Each bit matches every other bit. If a fractal is broken or confused, it just needs to look at where it's clear and strong to regain its certainty. This is what creates the deepest healing.

When we lose our connection to ourselves we become unwell, on one level or another. Until we regain our ability to refer to ourselves we'll remain unwell, as our system won't know how to operate optimally. Our system will follow some other pattern. Just as a fractal reboots to repair itself, so can we.

Through completing our cycles, keeping our balance and activating our soul seats we achieve a powerful foundation for ourselves, creating greater wellbeing on all levels. This stable foundation means you're now ready to move to the next stage in developing your intuition. It's time to move onto the second triangle and develop real intuitive strength.

. . . .

SECOND TRIANGLE

· · · · · · · · · · · · · ·

Strength

Now that you've worked on your foundation, your energetic core and have some energetic stability, you're ready to get energetically fit. It's time to get strong. Clients often ask me if my work drains me, especially as there are days when I see eight or even nine clients back-to-back for hour-long sessions. My answer is always 'No!' If you're not fit, doing even gentle exercise is exhausting; but once you are fit, strenuous workouts are invigorating.

If you're the energetic equivalent of a couch potato, you'll be drained when you use your intuition or operate through your energy. But if you're energetically buff (because you've practiced the principles of *The Soul's Brain*, so you know intuition is a skill and you're now experienced enough to know you can rely on it), you can use that intuitive edge to give yourself extra insight in business or perform healing and be energized by it. Over the years, I've met many wonderful healers and intuitive managers who've yearned to make it their full-time career or use their skills more consistently—but they didn't have the strength.

Intuition is never going to be more than a hobby if you're exhausted after seeing one or two clients, or after one meeting. Without energetic fitness, you'll stay on your 'intuitive couch'. You'll only ever use your intuition in quiet calm spaces with beautiful, harmonious energies. Such spaces are wonderful to work in but unless you can work in more demanding environments, which unfortunately is much of our modern world, your ability to work with your intuition is going to be limited. If you have to wait for the world to hold its breath for your intuition to work, it'll never truly serve you. Your ability to live as Who You Truly Are will be hampered.

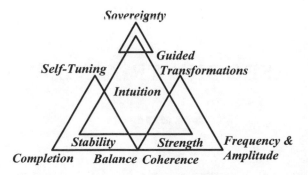

But if you build up energetic strength and intuitive flexibility, you can use your right-brained awareness wherever and whenever you choose, without any need for special circumstances. It's that kind of strength that the second intuitive triangle, the triangle of strength, can show you how to achieve. Once you've got that, your ability to create what you want in life will increase significantly.

Step Four

By now you can complete your cycles, understand your own intuitive process, keep yourself balanced and know your own resonance. That's a solid foundation you've created for yourself, a stable platform on which you can build a powerful intuitive structure.

Step Four is the first step in the second triangle, which is all about gaining intuitive strength. You'll need that, if you want your intuition to have the reach and consistency of an intuitive master. With intuitive strength, your energetic signal will become so clear and strong you'll produce amazing results. At times it may seem like magic. Only it isn't.

If you took a packet of matches with you as you time traveled back to Ancient Rome, you'd probably be greeted as a powerful magician. So many of the things we do could appear as magic, if you didn't understand the technology. Whether it's being able to speak and see someone halfway across the world; seeing inside someone's body without cutting them open; capturing an image in a display box; creating light without candles, heat without fire or music with no visible instruments. Modern-day magic is all around us. All of those things are modern marvels, yet we know none of them are magic.

We know they're the result of technology built upon scientific principles. Similarly, you can produce marvels with your intuition, but it won't be magic. It'll be the result of your skill and awareness built upon sound principles. Or perhaps I should say **light** principles. As I discussed earlier, it's all energy. The more you understand about light and energy and how they work, the better able you'll be to work your own light and energy.

. . . .

You want to be a laser, not torchlight
Driving at night

. . . .

When I was learning to drive, we lived in the country. This gave me room to practice but often meant I was driving at night. Like mushrooms, I didn't like it at first but have grown to love it since. Nowadays I live in beautiful mountains a couple of hours outside the city. Driving along tree-lined roads after dark, watching the headlights bring trunk after branch into sharp relief, reveals a whole different perspective to places I know well. Yet as powerful as they are, car headlights don't go far into the night even on high beam. Like torchlight, they're dazzling if you stare into them but they illuminate only a small area.

A torch can be powered by a huge amount of energy, yet all it does is throw a little light around. Their energy only goes a short way. Compare that to what a laser can do. A laser can level land or travel to the moon and back in mere minutes. It can cut and weld metal, or heat treat it to reduce wear on parts. It can measure great distances or see the tiniest details with incredible accuracy.

Lasers perform essential functions in business by reading scanned barcodes, and in military defense by neutralizing mines and unexploded ordinance. Lasers are used in surgery, most notably eye surgery where incredible accuracy is essential. They're used in games and surveying. They align components and perform photochemistry. In physics, they're used to trap atoms into Bose-Einstein condensates. In sci-fi, they're envisaged as futuristic weaponry but they've already developed into anti-aircraft and anti-missile weapons.

The power and versatility of lasers is amazing. Importantly for the understanding of our intuition, they also create holograms. They do all these astonishing things because lasers are coherent light. But what does that mean?

Torchlight is made of many different frequencies, all going in different directions at different speeds. With each photon of light banging into every other photon, they waste a lot of energy getting in one another's way. It's as if every photon of light is fighting all the others to get to where it wants to go. More scientifically, you could say torchlight is disorganized. In that sense, coherent light is its opposite: it's superbly organized.

A laser has coherent light. That means it has only one frequency, but its organization goes further. Every little wave of its energy goes up and down at the same time, in the same plane. So every bit of energy builds on and supports every other bit of energy.

You can demonstrate the difference in these two types of light very simply. When you shine a torch on a wall, you'll find the light dispersing or spreading out as the distance between the two increases. As a consequence, it doesn't take very long for the power of its light to be lost. On the other hand, increasing the distance makes little difference to a laser's coherent light. You'd have to put astronomical levels of distance between you and the wall before the laser started to lose its power— even with a simple laser, like the ones used to point at whiteboards.

It's the state of complete **internal** support that gives lasers their power. This is the same kind of power that enables a voice to shatter glass—the power of natural resonance. If a singer's voice is loud enough and at just the right frequency, it's possible to build the natural vibration of a wine glass to the point where it literally shakes itself to pieces.

Everything has a natural resonant frequency or innate speed at which it vibrates. It's what famously happened to the Tacoma Narrows Bridge. Its material, width and length created a bridge with a natural resonance at the exact same frequency generated by the wind that flowed up the chasm. Each push of the wind caused the bridge to vibrate more and more, just like when you push a child on a swing. When you time it right, each push builds momentum and the swing goes higher and higher.

The Tacoma Narrows Bridge vibrated so much it shook itself to bits. You can watch the old black and white videos of it happening on YouTube. That disaster is one reason you may notice a lot of cables on bridges these days; they're there to break the vibratory momentum and ensure such a disaster doesn't happen again.

As with everything in creation, shaking things to bits with resonance can be negative but it can also be positive. Like when it's used to break up kidney stones, which is so much better than having to cut open the kidneys to remove the stones. All of this boils down to the simple fact that one of the most effective ways to increase your energetic strength is to increase your own coherence. For that to happen, you'll need to go a little deeper into your soul seat.

· ·

You are your resonance
Soul seat attunement

Remember your soul seat is the center of your connection to Who You Truly Are. In the section on **soul seat awareness**, I focused on its physiological link to your immune system and how you can use that to consciously support your integrity. If you do that, you won't be distracted from Who You Truly Are.

By taking your soul seat awareness to a deeper level, you can increase the coherence of your energy. Just like anything and everything in creation, you have your own unique resonance. Your soul seat is your own 'radio station', playing your resonance for your whole system to tune into.

Indeed, many dis-eases and frustrations in life come from having an incoherent system. If all your different organs can't hear your unique signal, they start operating out of alignment with each other. Without your signal keeping everything in your body coordinated, you'll get a toxic build-up or have poor digestion or other possible, sometimes serious, problems.

A lack of coherence in your system can create many problems. Have you ever wondered why sometimes when you've been working on manifesting something, it turns up pretty much straightaway? Then at other times nothing happens? Or even more frustrating, you just get a whole lot of chaos? We've all been through that. Like most things, it's easier to manage and correct when you understand that the reason why it happens is the same as why a laser is so much more powerful than a torch. When you're working on a manifestation and it doesn't happen with grace and ease (with laser power), it's because your energy has the alignment of a torch. In other words you've illuminated your intention but haven't the coherence for true power.

Lack of awareness around our self-alignment or coherence can be obvious. Many times I've asked clients to lie on my chiro table, face down, only to find their legs angled off to one side. When I pick up their legs and straighten them to align their spine and legs, they tell me it feels as if I've made them crooked. Their body is used to their self-misalignment; it's operating as if the misalignment needs to be maintained. That also maintains physical problems that come with the misalignment. If a healthy alignment is to be created and maintained, they have to work on it consciously for a while.

In the same way, you may not be aware of any incoherence or self-misalignment in your energy but the internal conflict that comes with incoherence and misalignment is never ideal. Changing any incoherence in your energetic signal to greater coherence has tremendous benefits. It'll help you manifest with increasing ease and grace. It's also hugely beneficial for your health and intuition. You create more coherent energy by working deeper into your soul seat.

In the soul seat awareness, you focused on the surface of your soul seat, which gets disturbed by other signals coming into your space (like the surface of a pond being disturbed by wind). That's the tension you feel when something doesn't serve you—the disturbance created by the intrusion of a foreign signal in your 'radio station'. Like when I'm driving in the mountains and get more than one song coming over the radio. To achieve coherence, you need a good connection to your own signal.

Remember that a laser has all its energy photons lined up, so if you're going to get your energy to be more coherent you're going to have to line it up also. That means you need to know what to line your energy up to. Your soul seat helps with that, when you go deeper into it.

The disturbance to your soul seat that you feel in the **soul seat awareness** exists only on the surface. When wind disturbs the surface of water, there'll always be calm, clear water underneath. Just ask any scuba diver. Admittedly, you may have to go deep to find that calm, clear space. This is again part of the nature of energy and how it travels in waves. The deeper the water, the more likely the wave won't reach the bottom.

So if you focus deep enough into your soul seat, you'll always come to a calm, clear space. That's where you connect most easily to your own resonance or 'radio station'. This is true even when life is at its most stressful—you just have to go deeper, the more your soul seat is disturbed. If you need, turn back to the **soul seat awareness** section and review it now. Once you're sure where your soul seat is you can do the exercise below:

. . . .

SOUL SEAT ATTUNEMENT

- Focus on your soul seat with the intention to connect to its clear, calm space.

- Allow your awareness to move deeper into your soul seat, until you're immersed in that clear, calm space. This depth may change from day to day.

- Once there, focus on the resonance in that space. However you connect to your 'radio station' is fine, as a vibration or just a feeling. The most important thing is that it's as clear and strong a connection as possible right now.

- Once connected to your unique signal, intend for every cell in your body, and all your energy, to tune itself up to that resonance.

This soul seat attunement exercise is available in meditation format as a free download for readers of *The Soul's Brain*. Please go to www.fractology.info and put in the code HAYHOUSESSAT.

. . . .

The more you do this exercise, the more effective it becomes. The more coherence your energy has the stronger it gets, increasing your ability to create even more coherence. Sometimes when you do this exercise, you may feel a part of your body or energy resisting. Often a little extra 'push' or a stronger intention is all it needs. Think of it like a flabby muscle. Sometimes it takes a little extra work to get it to activate.

However, there will be times when even a little extra push is not enough. If you find parts of you resisting being 'on station', it means there's an incompletion there. Whenever you feel that, focus on the resistant bit and flow acceptance to it. Or acknowledge whatever comes up for you. Once it's complete, it won't be stuck in the energy of the incompletion. Then it'll tune up to your signal.

Once your energy is more coherent, you'll gain increased ease. With your energy deeply aligned, any internal conflict of the past will begin to disappear. Your ability to use your energy to manifest and create what you want in life will increase. That's not surprising when you realize the universe itself uses lasers and therefore coherent alignment to create itself. The universe uses lasers because it's a hologram and you need the clarity and precision of coherent light to produce those amazing holographic images. Viewing our reality in this way makes a lot of sense in both psychology and physics. It also tells us why energy is so fundamental and why energy is aligned along fractal lines. That's the truth that underlies most of the world's creation myths.

. . . .

Creation is a hologram
In the beginning was the hologram ...

....

Every culture has its own creation myth. These vary but have some elements in common. Most go something like this:

> *In the beginning everything was One. It was undifferentiated and so nothing really existed. Then the Creative Source split the One into Two. This first act of separation enabled many more things to follow. However some of what was created ended up separated from the Source causing it to become a negative force.*

That's the spiritual point of view. The scientific point of view is our universe is probably a hologram.

You know what a hologram is: a 3D (three-dimensional) image, created from information on a 2D (two-dimensional) surface. There are poor examples on your credit card and tourist postcards. Better ones are projected into a room so you can walk around the hologram. It's just like your room with all its three-dimensional furniture, only in a hologram the furniture is built of light, so you can walk through the chairs and couch as well as around them.

The physical universe operates the same way, except that it's more dense. Think of water as opposed to treacle or molasses. It's easier to walk through water than treacle, because water is less dense. Just as air is less dense than water. The physical hologram we live in here on earth has the same structure as holograms built from light, but the universe's hologram holds so much energy it makes it too dense to walk through

Strong evidence for the holographic nature of reality was scientifically confirmed in January 2017. A multinational study gave researchers observational evidence that our universe is a vast hologram. Scientists studied the pattern of the cosmic microwave background radiation. (The Hubble telescope made it possible to examine this afterglow of the big bang.) They found the holographic structure explains our universe nicely and published their paper in *Physical Review Letters*.

What does all that mean for us? That our three-dimensional lives actually are a projection from a flat two-dimensional field.

Let me put it another way. Imagine your life's a 3D film. As you watch the film of your life, you perceive height, width and depth, which are all recorded on and projected from the flat surface of the film's screen. That's how holograms are projected into space from the holographic film which is also a flat surface. Put simply, holography explains our universe so well it's possible it might even solve one of the biggest conundrums of science: how to get relativity and quantum mechanics to work together. Holography gives us a 'Theory of Everything'—a framework to understand spirituality right alongside all the different sciences.

How does this all fit together? I'll go over how to make a hologram and then you'll understand.

To make a hologram, first get yourself a laser. You have to start with coherent light or **energy that's completely the same**. Coherence is the Oneness that existed before the beginning. Then the myths tell us to split the Oneness into two. That's the second thing you do to make a hologram. The laser is split into two beams. Remember how our eyes work? We need two eyes (two visual references) to create perspective. So naturally, we need two lasers. But we need them to be coherent with each other, which is why it's best to split the original laser beam into two.

A laser doesn't lose its focus. So to start with, our hologram is a tiny dot. We have to use lenses to spread out both beams. We have to increase the space both lasers cover. Each now-wider beam is then redirected to meet each other using mirrors. One beam goes straight onto the holographic plate (the reference beam), while the other is bounced or reflected off the object you want to make into a hologram (the object beam). Both beams of light are then captured on a holographic plate.

The holographic plate can be developed like any photo, though it doesn't look like a normal negative. It has no light or dark areas. It's just a scatter pattern of light. To see the hologram, it's necessary to shine light, preferably the same laser light, back through the holographic negative.

Put the creation myth side-by-side with hologram production and you may notice the following:

Creation Myth	Hologram
Before creation all was One Source.	A laser creates a hologram and is coherent light. It is only one frequency.
Creation splits Unity into a Duality. Examples of dualistic pairs are matter and antimatter, light and dark, or the physical and meta-physical. They're the poles of creation.	The laser is split into an object beam and a reference beam.
Polar pairs aren't 'opposite'; together they're One, not zero.	The object beam and reference are the same coherent light.
One polarity connects to the Source of Creation. The other is disconnected from that Source.	The reference beam is the same as the original laser. The object beam is changed by being reflected off the object.
The One Source is everything and everywhere within creation but isn't immediately apparent.	The holographic plate or film holds a scatter pattern of light, the light of the original laser, but is not a recognizable image.
Connecting to the One Source is required for manifestation.	The image on the holographic plate can only be seen when coherent light is shined on it.

Creation Myth	Hologram
As above, so below.	If you break a hologram, each piece contains the entire original image. So a holographic negative, or scatter pattern, must have a fractal structure.

Understanding the similarities between the spiritual and holographic is a powerful insight into the connections between our left and right hemispheres—especially the principle of 'as above, so below', which you witness when you smash a hologram. This most unique of holographic properties, that each piece will have the same image in it as the original, holds the real key to our intuition.

When we smash a hologram we don't get a jigsaw puzzle, but many copies of the **original** image. On a practical level, that means there's always a version of you that's already who you want to be, is doing what you want to do and has what you want to have. This Ultimate You has the same fractal you do. It's out there in the hologram somewhere.

Working to create your expanded, more abundant life without a clear sense of what it is, looks or feels like can be a long arduous process of trial and error. But as Thomas Edison, inventor of the lightbulb said: *There's a better way to do it—find it.*

The fractal structure of the hologram gives us a much better way. You learned earlier how focus and intention work to flow energy where and when you want it. That also works for tuning into the holographic version of yourself, this ultimate you, that'll get you where you want to go. Understanding this is of great assistance when getting your beliefs into alignment with what you want to manifest. To start you on your expansive path.

It certainly helped Lee change his life. Lee was working in a job he detested and he felt like it was taking his soul a little bit at a time. He was doing the work because his father had done it before him. He was good at his job, but he just wasn't the accountant type. He was more creative. A part of him died a little more with every tax report. Something had to give.

When Lee came to see me, his system was already showing advanced signs of stress. His doctor was talking about a long list of drugs he was going to need, just to keep him going. Fortunately, Lee's wife insisted he come and see me before going down that path.

Initially, I focused on Lee's stress and getting his health back into balance. In Fractology, that always includes assisting the client to find a way to tune into their own system. Not surprisingly, the despair that his creative side was feeling surfaced. Lee needed to put that side of him to work, initially by dreaming up what his ideal life would be. But he was reluctant. 'What's the point of focusing on something that'll never happen?' he asked.

'Because it's already happened somewhere in the hologram,' I told him. 'You just have to navigate towards it.'

Many of us look at our current life and focus on what's reasonable—what we believe has some chance of happening. The problem is our soul's yearning often lies way beyond reasonable or realistic goals, out in the mists where our dreams exist. Yet they exist for a reason. Our souls have no limits. When we give ourselves permission to connect to our dreams, true magic happens. This is a more practical application of the spiritual truth that Who You Truly Are already exists. You are already perfect on one level of your consciousness or another. You don't have to become perfect. You simply have to learn to connect to your perfection. That's what your soul seat and fractal help you do.

In the same way, your ideal life already exists. You just have to connect to it. The more you connect, the closer your life will come to resemble that perfection.

Lee was still dubious, so I suggested he do a real-life experiment. At the very least, it would provide a mental escape from dealing with numbers all day. That was something Lee understood, so he gave himself three months to work on the experiment. Every day he did his best to tune into his ideal, creative life. He did it in the way you learned to do earlier, with all five of his senses. He wasn't sure what that life would be like, but he did what he could to feel the way he would feel, to see what he'd see, to hear, smell and taste the things that'd be around him in his ideal life.

As so often happens, the timing couldn't have been better. His family were moving house and the new place needed renovating. With his focus on his ideal creative life, Lee decided to do more of the work himself than he would have otherwise. Designing what had to be done gave his creative side an outlet. He was soon enjoying that far more than his accountancy. He did a great job; so much so that when he was finished, someone approached him to buy the place. The profit was handsome enough to make it worthwhile to move the family again.

Now Lee is happily flipping houses for a living. He's also making more money than he did before. He still uses his accountancy skills, but only to keep track of his own expenses. He's far happier and his soul is alive. By focusing on his ideal life as best he could, he changed his life in ways he hadn't thought possible.

This is something you can do too. You can navigate through the holographic universe to where your life is what you'd love it to be. If your beliefs get in the way, try this same experiment. Give yourself time to play with this important process. Give yourself permission to dream as big as your soul. You'll be amazed at where it takes you.

. . . .

FRACTAL DREAMING

- Acknowledge to yourself: My ideal life already exists in the Universal fractal. I just have to connect to it to begin to live it.

- Focus on it as clearly as you can. Find the most exciting part of your dream. Don't worry about how it'll happen. That'll come later. For now, all you need do is connect to it.

- Focus on each of your senses in turn. How will it look? Sound? Feel? What will you taste? Smell?

- Practice that experience every day, until your dream begins to get clearer. Then you can take the next steps.

· ·

- As your dream gets clearer, ask yourself: What's the most exciting, inspiring core of this dream for me? That's the part your soul's most powerfully connected to.
- Once you have the exciting core of your dream, focus on its energy, or on your energy when you're connected to that inspiring core.
- Focus on the energy of your dream's core. Intend for your energy to tune up to that. Keep doing it until that energy feels natural. Then wait for the magic!!

· ·

The hope and inspiration of using fractal dreaming is a great support to our psychological, energetic and spiritual wellbeing. But fractals are more than that. They also have a direct link to our physical health. Your body is already using fractals every day for optimal functioning.

· ·

Fractals keep you healthy
Holograms and mathematics

The highly-focused nature of lasers makes them perfect for creating holograms. Without the laser's power and clarity, the level of detailed information necessary for a hologram wouldn't be possible. Without coherent light, the underlying structure of a hologram wouldn't exist.

Mathematics is a useful way of describing information such as the interactions between the object and reference beams in a hologram. It's even possible to use mathematics to program a computer to print a pattern onto a holographic plate. That's how you create holograms of imagined or fantasy objects. This means my father was right … mathematics truly is the universal language!

This fractal, called a Sierpinski triangle, is created by removing the central triangle from an equilateral triangle over and over again. That process can be described in a mathematical equation.

Mathematics equations also describe fractals. Remember, a fractal is a pattern repeated over and over to build up a more complex pattern. It's an iterated function, where the result of one 'run' of the equation is used to start the next one. You can understand how that process creates an image made up of smaller and smaller versions of itself. Remove a part of a Sierpinski triangle and you have a triangle.

Fractal equations are why CGI (computer generated images) look so real, as in *Avatar*. The computer-generated world is amazing, yet somehow too pristine. It looks real because your right brain can find the fractal pattern underlying all that amazingness. Yet it looks a touch unreal because you're unconsciously used to all the fractal patterns in the world being messed up by the tough stuff in life.

Fractals are everywhere in nature—from rivers and clouds, to shells and vegetables. They're also in your own body. Your lungs, circulatory system and brain all have fractal structures. It's this fractal structure that enables your body to work so efficiently. Without fractals, you'd suffocate.

Look at the Sierpinski triangle again. Notice how the length of its edges gets bigger with every iteration. If you measure the length of the outside of the shape when it's a simple triangle, it's one measure. As soon as you take away the middle triangle and measure around that too, the perimeter gets longer. Every time you take away the center, the border gets longer.

Your lungs are like a Sierpinski sponge. The Sierpinski sponge is a 3D fractal, created by removing the middle cube over and over again, in the same way we saw with the Sierpinski triangle. That's how your lungs pack so much surface area into such a small space. If that fractal structure is lost, as happens with emphysema, there isn't enough surface area for oxygen to get through.

When you break a fractal, you get the same image. It's just not as crisp and clear as the original. The small bit of holographic plate you're left with after it's smashed contains fewer photons of light. Whether you view the world through physics glasses or spiritual glasses, you know every photon contains information. Every photon of light gone from the plate, every iteration or repetition of the fractal lost, means there's less information in the image.

Memories are one way your brain stores information. Left-brained science keeps hunting for where memories are stored in the brain, as if your memories are packaged like photographs in a box. But your brain works in fractal-like ways. You need light or energy to activate your resonance and your memory, so that you have a clear, stable focus to achieve coherence. If a part of your brain containing a particular memory is damaged you can still recall it, given time or a relevant stimulus; just never as clearly as before.

Fractal health

You and your body are part of the holographic universe, so it's no surprise that fractals are important for your health. They're critical to the healthy functioning of your body. When I was at university, I learned the heartbeat was a 'regular sinus rhythm' and was taught how to see the regular T wave in an ECG (electrocardiogram). That particular squiggle in an ECG, the most commonly used part of the readout, indicates all kinds of problems if it changes shape.

I don't know if you've ever seen a raw ECG before it's 'cleaned up' with a computer program. It looks like a dog's breakfast, and takes a practiced eye to discern the relevant parts of the wave. This irregularity is crucial, as your heartbeat isn't meant to be regular. It's meant to be 'regularly irregular'. This is its underlying fractal pattern, which in this instance is called 'fractal recursion'. Without fractal recursion, your heart will stop.

The rate of loss of fractal recursion means some heart attacks can now be predicted with astonishing, almost clairvoyant, accuracy. Once the heartbeat becomes too regular, it's as if the heart just stops. Scientifically, the loss of fractal recursion means information is lost. Fractal recursion holds a lot of information. Without it, the heart can't do its job properly.

It's not only your heart that does better with fractals, the same goes for your gait, the rhythm of how you move. There's a fractal recursion to how you move, so any diminution of the fractal component of walking or running is an early sign of a neuromuscular problem or disease.

Just as the hologram of our universe is generated by its fractal, your existence is encoded in the fractal structure of your energy. Your fractal is as unique to you as mine is to me and everyone else's is to them. In a very real sense, it's the pattern of your consciousness. You're a self-referencing system. The more you live in alignment to your fractal, the more you're connected to Who You Truly Are. So the easier and more graceful things become, your path opens up and you create the life you were born to live with increasing enjoyment.

But if you create a misalignment, things can go to a painful place pretty quickly.

You're not meant to be right or wrong. You're meant to be **you**. Who You Truly Are is divine perfection, but that perfection isn't something any philosophy can give you. The only perfect thing you can be is a perfect you. The more powerfully and robustly you can hold your alignment to your fractal—to Who You Truly Are—the more your life is going to reflect that perfection. Right there is the key to much of the power of the spiritual or personal development path. And you already have the means to increase your personal power in this way. Once again, you just need to take what you're doing with your soul seat to another level.

. . . .

Stay 'on station' for an amazing life
Oh, the power!

. . . .

When you operate from right-wrong or good-bad you keep second-guessing yourself, which gets in the way of developing your intuition. You also cause interference in your own signal and run the risk of messing up your fractal. The more you practice tuning yourself up to your own soul seat resonance, the more 'on station' you are and the more you'll notice this. If you practice being 'on station', you'll soon get to dislike any kind of internal conflict generated by thinking of yourself in terms of right-wrong. As you leave such internal conflict behind and focus on remaining coherent, you get to know Who You Truly Are. Maintaining your alignment to your own fractal will give you great certainty and confidence. This moves you from co-dependency to independency.

As discussed earlier, coherence is a great source of power. As you achieve that coherence for yourself, you'll grow in personal power. The more we progress on our path, the more we become Who We Truly Are and the more powerful we become. Then we're more able to manifest those things we want in life.

What do you want? To be a sexual dynamo? To have an expansive amount of money? Are those things good or bad?

The answer to the last question is the same as the answer to every question. It depends. If there's more energy in the sex or money than is contained in your own resonance, it'll pull you 'off station'. You'll end up aligned to something other than your fractal, the pattern of your integrity and authenticity. When there's more energy in the resonant signal of your soul than the sex or money energy being experienced, then the sex and money will align to your integrity, rather than the other way around.

When you're fully connected to Who You Truly Are, you won't be interested or tempted to follow a path that diminishes you. The awareness of what it'll cost you in terms of internal conflict and 'loss of resonance' changes the priorities of your choices.

In other words ...

- When our hearts work properly, they default to love.
- When our minds work properly, they default to truth.
- And when our bodies work properly, they default to bliss.

Love, truth and bliss are a powerful combination. They hold the power of Who We Truly Are. We can't become Who We Truly Are without becoming powerful.

My younger brother likes to play war games. He's especially fond of a game called *Diplomacy*. It's a board game in which you get to practice negotiation, pretending to be one of the old powers of Europe. It's an interesting way to develop the skill of negotiating. One of his comments on the game can, I believe, be applied in a wider context: 'Power itself doesn't have a + or - sign in front of it.'

Power is the ability to do something, to act or cause an effect. It's not inherently good or bad in itself. Hence the lack of + or - sign. However when we're in our one-valley world, it might be easy to think of power as positive or negative. Power can be constructive or destructive, especially to our own integrity. Power is just like control, which is neither good nor bad in itself.

Stopping a child from running out into the traffic is a form of control. That's why I use the words 'appropriate' and 'inappropriate' (rather than 'good' or 'bad') to describe the value of an action. A thing is appropriate or not depending on whether it's aligned to and strengthens your integrity and the integrity of those around you.

This is what catching a cold teaches you. Just as with everything in creation, a virus has its own resonance. It's neither good nor bad in itself. From 5 to 8 percent of your genome originally came from viruses. Some viruses help fight infection, while others help create maternal placentas for pregnancy. Viruses that are behaving appropriately increase your ability to hold your resonance. Inappropriate ones don't. Viruses can introduce a foreign or interfering resonance into your system. If you allow your system to align to that resonance you'll get sick, but you can make a different choice.

The following exercise will only work for you if you've practiced your soul seat attunement **before** you get a cold. If you've strengthened your own resonance enough for it to do a bit of heavy lifting when you need to then this is simple. And you need to when you catch a cold or flu. You can, of course, practice this without the cold. When you turn up the volume of your own resonance, you're effectively forcing whatever is in your system to align to your integrity, resonance or fractal pattern or leave. This is a practical demonstration of the power of your integrity.

. . . .

PUMP UP YOUR SOUL VOLUME

- When you have a cold or flu, focus on your soul seat and the resonances you find there. You may be aware of a foreign resonance or interference in your signal.

- Set your intention to connect to the clear, calm space deeper inside your soul seat. With the disturbance to your resonance caused by the virus, you'll probably need to go a lot deeper than normal to connect to that clear, calm space.

- Focus on your soul seat resonance.

- Intend for every cell in your body, and all your energy, to tune itself up to that resonance.

- You'll find the virus will create resistance, so you'll need to pump up the volume. Use your intention to turn up the volume of your resonance until you're 'shaking the walls'.

- You'll experience two releases. These are subtle shifts in the level of resistance. The first occurs when the virus loses momentum. You'll feel better, but the virus will still be in your system. You may be tempted to stop at this point but if you do, there's a chance your cold or flu may come back.

You need to turn the volume up even more until you get the second release, which is when the virus clears out of your system.

· ·

Without the ability to know our integrity, we're at risk of collapsing into the resonance of other things including viruses. We can collapse into other people's resonances, which complicates our relationships no end. Or into ideas which are trending, which can distract us from what truly serves us on our path. By owning the power of our soul seat, of our integrity, we learn how to be Who We Truly Are **regardless** of what energy is around us. We learn how to stay 'on station' with increasing strength in an increasingly noisy world. This is the unconditional power of an independent being.

By pumping up the volume of your soul seat resonance, you've enabled yourself to access more personal and energetic power. This is the beginning of real personal and spiritual strength. You're beginning to get energetically fit.

But if you want to get really vigorous, you've a bit more to do yet. The next step is to build on what you've already accomplished.

Step Five

You now have a solid intuitive foundation. You can complete your cycles and understand your own intuitive process. You keep yourself balanced and know your own resonance. You've also begun to improve on that foundation, by building intuitive strength through increasing the volume and coherence of your resonance.

The next step in building your intuitive strength is to increase this coherence by improving your ability to focus. The more you understand what enables you to tune into each specific focus, the more you'll be able to do that. This is what Step Five is all about.

. . . .

Observing energy, a different perspective
It's all resonance

. . . .

Shut your eyes for a moment and visualize yourself. What do you see? Is it the same as what you see in the mirror? How about when you dream? Do you look the same as in your physical life? Why? Why not look like Gal Gadot? Or Jennifer Lawrence? Miranda Kerr? Chris Hemsworth? Kit Harington? Zac Efron? Or your own imagined, perfected self?

Who You Truly Are isn't your body. Just like the hologram, what you see about you is a 3D illusion created from photons of light, aligned to a fractal structure. Your true nature is a resonant field of energy. That's why tuning yourself to your soul seat works so well.

So why don't you see yourself as a resonant field of energy when you visualize yourself? If that is what you saw when I asked you to visualize yourself, then well done. Yet whatever it is you visualized is a clear result of the reality valley you're in. Most of us see ourselves as the physical body we're used to seeing every time we pass a mirror. We learned to identify ourselves as that body very early on. Maybe someone showed you a mirror when you were very little and said, 'Look! That's you.' However we came to it, it is now fixed in our awareness so strongly that it's hard to change.

In *The Tibetan Book of Living and Dying*, Sogyal Rinpoche tells how the transitioning spirit first encounters a resonant field of energy. If the spirit's unable to connect with that resonant field, the spirit passes from there to places of different forms, searching for where things feel familiar. The important point is that the resonant field of energy is our true nature—not the physical form which we may visualize when we shut our eyes.

I discussed earlier how your neurology generates an EM field, which some call your aura. If Who You Truly Are is confined to your physical existence, or to what you see in the mirror, then when your body is no longer functioning that's the end of you. On the other hand, if Who You Truly Are **is** a resonant EM field, then you do go on within the hologram—even after your body is no longer functioning. So if you think of yourself as just your body, then when your body dies you'll perceive yourself as ending. But how about if you focus on your 'software', instead of your 'hardware'? If you focus on the EM field, rather than your body?

All physical things, including your body, come to an end. The proteins and other molecules that make up your body will be recycled, one way or another. Eventually they'll become part of some other life form. If you think that all you are is a physical body, then that is your destiny. But your energy has a very different destiny. Physicists tell us that the photons or energy packets that were present at any particular event in the universe's vast multi-billion year history still exist. Your energy will also continue to exist, long after your physical body has gone into other parts of the planet. Your resonant field continues long after your body has gone.

What if your true nature **is** that resonant field? When you understand that it's your true nature and you learn to identify yourself as such, there's no question. The EM field continues, just as photons continue. Therefore, so do you. But how can we be nothing more than a resonant field of energy? Putting aside the fact that **everything** is a resonant field of energy, how can we get about in life and generally operate as a resonant field of energy?

You know how to operate as a body, because you learned to do that early on in your life. Sure, you fell down a few times but you now know how to operate your body. You just haven't had the same training in doing things as a field of energy yet, though you already have some of the tools you need for just that. You've used those tools to balance your energy flows and to tune yourself up to your soul seat resonance. These tools produce tremendous results, whether you're using them physically or energetically.

Ironically, the primary benefit of working energetically in the physical is the exact same thing that often makes it so frustrating. It can be frustrating that your life changes so slowly in the physical world, yet that same creeping pace gives us our best ability to learn. It's practically impossible to appreciate and learn about anything unless we can observe it in a consistent way. When things are slow, they're easy to observe.

So how are we going to observe energy with more consistency, when it's so fast? We do it by using the same tools you've been using to do all the other things you've already learned. These tools are **focus** and **intention**. They make up your most essential intuitive tool kit. They're also the way you get your neurology to do what you want it to do. With these two basic tools, you can do extraordinary things. You just need to know how to apply them so that they are truly effective.

· ·

Stable connections are conscious connections
Getting cozy

. . . .

You can call any connection in your life a relationship. Just like all your relationships, the healthier ones are more stable. The more stable your energetic connections, the healthier your energy will be. That creates the space for more effective learning. The only issue is that energy has a powerful photonic ability to whiz about the place, which your body can't possibly match.

So how can you work with this? Simple. Once you consider where you're at from the other's point of view, a connection becomes clear. In other words, if you want to connect with energy, you need to use its innate properties, its resonance. If you're willing to 'meet' the object's energy at its resonance, you'll connect with it. You already have the tools you need for this next exercise: your ability to focus and set an intention.

. . . .

GETTING TO GRIPS WITH RESONANCE

- With your hand on your chosen object, intend energy to flow from your hand into it.

- Feel the energy the object is sending or reflecting back to you. Are they the same? Of course not! You're made of different things.

- Intend for the energy flowing from your hand to exactly match the energy flowing from the object. The energy in your hand will shift. Hold the intention until the energy of your hand and the object feel the same. Once they do, you've established resonance.

- Test it by attempting to lift your hand off the object. When you're at resonance, it will feel difficult, as if your hand were heavy because you're resonating at one with the object. You may even feel that the object is now part of you. Energetically, you've come to grips with it.

- Changing the resonance in your hand will break that grip and release you.

- When you're finished, always focus on your soul seat resonance and intend for the energy in your hand to tune back to your own resonance.

. . . .

The first few times you do this exercise, choose something made of one material, such as glass, crystal or a piece of metal. Being made of only one material means its resonance will be relatively simple; just one frequency and amplitude is the simplest type of resonance. Your mobile phone is made of so many different materials it has a very complex resonance, made up of several frequencies and amplitudes together.

What you're aiming for is to create and release a resonant grip over and over again. Each time you do this, you'll get that same 'stuck to it' feeling. You may want to practice this exercise until you're familiar with the feeling of holding an 'energetic grip'. One of the powers of a conscious mind is its ability to use focus and intention to shift and change resonances at will (or to change its energetic grip from one resonance to another). Through the mind-body connection, you can guide the subtleties of your nervous or EM system to match the resonance of any object you focus on. That's how you change your grip.

The ability to create a strong resonant grip is a powerful one. Once you have a strong resonant grip, your ability to connect with any energy will increase. So your awareness of the properties of that energy will also vastly increase. That gives you the ability to gain all the information the energy contains. Through your resonant grip, you can do everything you can do in your physical life but from a space of pure energy.

You've just taken your first step towards operating as a pure EM field. This is an exciting and powerful step, because it means your awareness is getting close to becoming so strong that it draws more awareness to you in an ongoing, generative spiral. It's possible for you to reach a point where your awareness can connect you to the resonance of anything in the world you focus on. Then that resonance will give you the information contained within it, so you end up even more aware.

That's something my students often experience. At first, the ideas I teach are new and often strange. But their clarity slowly grows, as they continue to work on the exercises you're now learning. Then they reach a point where they feel they've shifted mental gears. Intuitive information begins to flow into their awareness without any conscious effort on their part. This is how they know they've passed the point of critical mass in their growing awareness.

In order to master any skill, we pass a similar point of critical mass in our awareness. It's the point at which you shift from having to concentrate consciously on what you're doing, to being able to do it without thinking about it.

You went through that point when you learned how to drive a car. Initially, you had to concentrate on matching your direction and speed, as well as traffic and all the other elements involved in driving. Then you reached a point where you no longer needed to focus on it consciously. It all just appeared to happen, because your driving skill had fully integrated into your system. Your driving awareness had reached critical mass. The same thing happens when your awareness reaches critical mass.

Being able to shift into resonance with other things is an essential step towards achieving critical mass in your intuitive awareness. However that won't be much use if you don't know how to apply your resonant awareness. Applying resonant awareness requires principles, not rules. Just as it's easier to grow our intuition when we shift from right-wrong thinking to integrity-based or pattern-based thinking, it's easier to do things energetically when we shift from following rules to following holographic principles. Let's see how this works.

. . . .

Rules are made to be broken—
principles are made holographic
Five fits all

. . . .

When you were growing up, your parents probably told you to do things you didn't want to do. When you protested or asked why you had to, their response was no doubt something like: *Because I say so*; or *While you're under this roof, you'll live according to my rules*.

Rules work when you're living in a one-valley world. Problems occur as soon as you enter another valley, where there's another set of rules. Like the teenage years. And another and another subsequent valley. What works in one context or reality may not work in another. What's right in one place may be wrong in another.

History is riddled with examples, from giving opium to babies when they were teething to using mercury as a 'cure all' for anything from a grazed knee to syphilis. The problem with rules or right/wrong thinking is they're always based on a fixed reality. Principles are context-based, which means they first consider which valley they're in, so the alignment of their application is appropriate.

We need to learn to think of the context, if we're going to apply our resonant awareness effectively. Unfortunately, we're not taught about contextual thinking much at school.

In the same way principles work in every context, regardless of whether it's a physical, energetic or intuitive context. There are five principles for effective intuition: focus, intention, acknowledgment, completion and integrity. Together they form the Power Pentagon.

Here's a ready reference table for you:

Power Pentagon

Principle	Definition
Focus	Where and when you want a result
Intention	What result you want
Acknowledgment	The means to complete a cycle
Completion	End point of a cycle
Integrity	Alignment to Who You Truly Are, measured by coherence, your resonance or the clarity of your fractal pattern

For many of my clients, what I do appears very complicated. It isn't. Like a fractal itself, it's just lots of simple things going on at once. It's lots of different ways of applying the above five principles.

You've learned some of these principles already. You've learned to use focus and intention to move energy, also to acknowledge any incomplete cycles to create greater sense of completion in your life and increased integrity. Working with the principles is so much easier and more effective when you can figure out your fractal priority.

Each of our lives is simply a different context, requiring a different priority. For Mark, his issue was his focus. He was overwhelmed by everything he wanted to do and how much he wanted to grow. He couldn't do anything, despite his strong desire to 'get on with things'. By getting him to focus on each small step in turn, on where and when he needed to put his energy, he was able to direct his aware-ness where he needed to. He was soon making progress. He realized the fractal truth that we don't need to know everything. We just need to know enough to find the alignment of our own path in life.

Intention rather than focus was what Lea needed to work on. She'd had very controlling parents, so had never developed her will. Growing up, it hadn't been safe to be clear on what she wanted for herself. I got her to exercise her will by setting tiny intentions. She started with such things as: *I'm going to get up from the chair* and *I'm going to walk to the door* and *I'm going to open the door*. As she achieved each tiny intention, she was able to set a slightly bigger one. As her intentions became more robust, she was finally able to take control of her life.

Without acknowledgments, we get incomplete on many levels. Ava had that issue. She was a talented empath, which was causing her a great deal of confusion. She felt so much from other people she couldn't find her own feelings. Lack of acknowledgment had energetically entangled her with many other people. She was almost living their lives more than her own. Learning to use mental acknowledgments, such as 'thanks' and 'brilliant' for thoughts and emotional acknowledgments in the form of flowing acceptance to whatever she was feeling, got her disentangled. Then she discovered her own needs and wants. With increased clarity, she could meet her own needs. That was her key to a far happier life.

If you get so busy you don't have time for yourself, you know how Evan felt. He was constantly on the ragged edge of exhaustion. Yet his accomplishments were few. He had very little to show for all his hard work. By the time he found me, he was severely frustrated as well. We talked about completions. I got him to shift his focus from **doing** stuff to **completing** stuff. It wasn't easy at first. He was keenly aware of all the demands placed on him. But he kept at it. Each day he wrote a short list of only two or three things he'd commit to completing that day. He made sure he completed them before he did anything else. It took a while, but the chaos settled. Completing things one step at a time helped him make more headway. Each completion gave him personal satisfaction and more energy for his next task.

Bradley's a family man with his own business. He's helped a lot of people over the years but he wasn't helping himself, so his health was beginning to suffer. To add to his pain, he was confused. He enjoyed his work or had done before he got sick. Bradley didn't understand where it had all gone wrong. It appeared to be an integrity issue, so I got him to focus on his soul seat. He couldn't feel it to start with. I explained to him that he'd been so busy taking care of the needs of his family and clients, he'd lost track of himself and his own unique pattern in life. He committed to giving himself a couple of months to practice focusing on his soul seat, with the same dedication he gave to his business. Soon we were discussing how to realign his business systems, so they were more 'Bradley systems'. With a more aligned life, he learned to support himself as well as others. He then rediscovered his enthusiasm for his business and got his health back.

My students and I can do what we do because we work with those five principles in each and every situation. We also ensure we have a good grip on every resonance, giving us an exact and specific focus. That's supported by knowing the characteristics of photonic energy in a little more depth.

Many of us are familiar with the idea that different energies have different frequencies, but did you know they also have a different amplitude? If you've worked with energy before but only worked with the frequency of energy, you're using an incomplete tool set.

. . . .

Frequency and amplitude
What's your speed?

The characteristic of energy waves that people are most familiar with is their frequency. We see that every day. Each and every color is a product of a different frequency, from fire-engine red to forest green; also the lower or higher pitch of every sound. If your ears couldn't hear the different pitch of different notes, it's possible you wouldn't be so comfortable with the idea of frequency.

The reason why one color or sound appears different to another is because of the speed at which its energy is vibrating. When more waves of energy go past you in the same amount of time, it's a higher vibration. A faster vibration like the color violet or the note high C is a higher frequency. A slower vibration like red or middle C is a lower frequency. Around your home, if you strike something with a higher frequency (like a crystal glass), you'll produce a higher sound. Striking something with a lower frequency will produce a lower sound (like a cupboard closing).

You may have heard it said that the more spiritual you are, the higher your frequency will be. It's true that the clearer and more coherent your energy becomes, the 'lighter' your energy feels. That's due to the decrease in static and interference with your energy. It's also true that there's more energy in a higher frequency than in a lower one; just as there's more energy in running than in walking.

Yet there's a limit to how much faster an object can vibrate without falling apart or changing into something else. Each material has its innate resonance or 'radio station'. This is true for physical materials, such as glass and wood. It's also true for humans. Angels may have a higher frequency than humans; but while you're still human, you're best to operate within the 'human bandwidth' of frequencies. So if frequency doesn't change that much with personal expansion, what does?

How big is your game?

Energy is often talked about in terms of frequency. Even if you haven't thought of your intuition in terms of tuning into different frequencies before, you'll be familiar with UV light being a different frequency to visible light. The frequency of energy is definitely important. It's the primary characteristic used to decide what type of energy we're dealing with.

Gamma rays have a different frequency to radio waves. The frequency of microwaves is different again. The frequency tells us how fast the energy is traveling. But there's another characteristic that tells us how big the space that energy holds is. That's amplitude.

There are two types of radio waves. The one you use most is the one close to television waves. That's FM. The other one is AM radio. If you want to change an AM station you have to change the amplitude. So what is amplitude?

The fatter the wave, the bigger the amplitude or the more space it's going to take up. Think of woodwind instruments. They produce all those beautiful sounds by creating a standing wave within the vibration chamber of the instrument. A small instrument, like a piccolo, is going to create a wave with a much smaller amplitude than an bigger instrument, like a bassoon. The bigger the chamber or hollow section of the instrument, the bigger the wave's amplitude needs to be to fill the space inside.

The bigger our amplitude, the wider our EM space. That means we can energetically cover more ground. If we're still living in our one-valley world, we need only a relatively small amplitude. The widest amplitude we'd ever possibly need is the width of our valley. However if we get out of our valley and start operating in a number of different valleys, then we're going to need a much bigger amplitude. Each valley is a different context, so we have to operate differently in each. We'll also need a wider amplitude to support our increasing flexibility. We're going to need an amplitude big enough to hold the total width of **all** the valleys we're operating in.

In a very real sense, frequency tells us what kind of game is being played. Whether it's a glass game or porcelain game, a metal game or wooden game. Or even if it's a human or angelic game. On the other hand, amplitude tells us how big the game is. The bigger the game, the more awareness we need to play it.

In spiritual terms, the frequency of a person speaks to how their soul is expressing itself, while the amplitude speaks to how expansive that expression is. For the sake of our own life's game, let's look at both frequency and amplitude a little closer.

. . . .

Resonant realities
Matching speeds

. . . .

My brilliant editor, Jason, is a musician. He's never been my student although he chose to do all the exercises in *The Soul's Brain* as he worked through it. When he got to this point, he realized he'd never thought before about working with energy in terms of frequency and amplitude:

> *It was definitely informed by my experiences as a musician. I experienced the frequency as a tone that wavered at first—like when you're tuning a guitar string and keep going too far in one direction, and then the other. After a few moments, the 'tone' became clear and strong and stopped wavering. The amplitude was a little more abstract. It felt a bit like trying to get my body to match the width of it—like coming to an understanding of how broadly I needed to stretch myself out to encompass it. Sort of like feeling for the width of something in the dark, and stretching your arms out to see how wide it is. Once my 'energetic hands' felt the edges, I had a good grip on it.*

Working with the frequency and amplitude of energy has huge practical benefits, not the least of which is increased clarity. The kind of clarity that enables many famous intuitives to 'translate' energy into the physical or into words. Esther Hicks is one such famous intuitive. She writes bestselling books using the material she channels or translates from an energetic consciousness she calls 'Abraham'. When interviewed by Oprah Winfrey on her program *Talk to Me*, Esther shared her belief that everyone can tune into the vibration of consciousness or intuition and translate that into words. She even believes everyone is already doing it—from a basketball player who's in the zone, to musicians and artists who are expressing energy through their creativity.

The clearer you are on what you're translating, the easier it'll be. Clarity comes from focusing on both frequency and amplitude. As I mentioned, I generally find frequency is easier for most people than amplitude, so let's start there.

First, assemble a few things made of materials with different resonant frequencies from around your house. Glass has a pretty high frequency, while metal is a bit lower. Porcelain or your dinner plate will be lower again, while something made of wood will fit into the bottom end of your 'household frequency resonant range'. Collect two or three objects made from each different type of material. Then you'll be ready to get started.

What you're about to do is simply an extension of the resonant grip exercise you did before. This next exercise will grow your awareness and clarity of how each different frequency feels. You notice different sensations with your hands. You don't even have to think about what's happening consciously, as sensation happens whenever you touch something. The physical world is dense enough for you to discern the difference between hard and soft, rough and smooth. Each sensation has a big impact on your nerves. That's why the feeling of a certain object seems obvious. But feeling more subtle impacts with your EM or neurological system takes a more conscious focus.

. . . .

FEELING THE VIBE

- Get your first resonant grip. I suggest you start with the wooden object, as it has the lowest frequency. Note the feeling of being connected to that frequency.

- Do the same with a contrasting object. I suggest glass for its higher frequency.

- How did the feeling of the resonance differ? Did the higher frequency differ from the lower one?

- Feel another two objects made from the same materials—wood and glass. Does the feeling between the two differ in the same way?

- Once you can feel a big frequency difference, focus on feeling a smaller frequency difference, like between glass and metal, or metal and porcelain.

· ·

One of the objections to intuition is that it's intangible. Yet if I were to poke you with a sharp stick, then hide the stick before you saw it, would you say that the feeling was intangible? No! So why not? As you never saw the stick, how would you know the feeling was real? You'd know because you've **felt** something like it before, so you know what that feeling means. You know how to interpret the feeling. Once you know how to interpret the feeling of a frequency and amplitude with your intuition, it will feel as tangible as if I **did** poke you with that stick.

Once you've practiced with frequency so that you've got a sense of the difference between frequencies, it's time to turn your attention to amplitude. One of the best ways to think about these two essential characteristics of energy is that frequency will tell you what you're dealing with, while amplitude will tell you how expansive it is.

Take Colin, who meditates and does yoga. He works with mindfulness and compassion. Yet he was experiencing more and more pain in his chest. He couldn't understand why his heart space would be in such pain with all the good work he was doing. That's why he came to see me.

Colin was very aware of energy and could tune into an impressive range of frequencies. Oddly enough, that was his problem. Remember how important balance is for keeping our energy stable? Colin's heart could stretch a long way in frequency, but hardly moved around his amplitude. How would your body feel if you kept stretching forwards to touch your toes, but never did backbends. The stiffness you'd get in your spine was the same kind of stiffness Colin was getting in his heart space.

Amplitude was a new idea to Colin, but he understood how it would help his heart hold a space big enough for all those frequencies he wanted to connect with. Once his amplitude range was as robust as his frequency range, his heart pains disappeared. Then he felt stronger than ever.

For most people, frequency is easier than amplitude. That's mostly because amplitude is such a new idea for many people. Some find amplitude easier once they know how to focus on it. Once again, knowing how your own neurology works is a huge help.

Celeste is a professional homeopath. This is her experience:

I feel more uncertain when I'm trying to find the frequency, and find getting a grip on the amplitude first is easier. It's like I sense the size of the signal, feeling it in the space in front of me, as well as in my body. Once I've got that sorted, it feels like I've taken the confusing 'noise' out of the signal and cleared the deck for me to feel its characteristic frequency.

As with all things, allow yourself to work with frequency and amplitude in the way that works best for your system. As long as you end up with a good grip on both, you'll do well.

For this next step, the objects of your 'household resonant range' need to have a different amplitude, but similar frequency. That way you'll be able to discover how your system gives you information about different frequencies, as opposed to different amplitudes. Learning to distinguish between the two is an essential step on your path towards intuitive mastery. Here are some suggestions:

- Glass and quartz crystal have a similar frequency, but quartz has a wider amplitude.
- Steel cutlery and singing bowls both have metal frequencies, but the bowl has wider amplitude.
- Porcelain contains calcium from bones, so it has a similar frequency to calcite or jade, but those crystals have wider amplitude.
- All woods have a similar frequency, but softwoods (like pine or balsa) generally have a lower amplitude than hardwoods (like oak, walnut or mahogany).

Go for a wander round the house. Look for things made from similar materials, so they have the same frequency but different tolerances to vibration. Ping a glass tumbler and you get a dull 'tunk' that stops almost immediately, because it doesn't vibrate much. Ping a crystal glass and you get a high 'ting' which lasts a few seconds. That tells you crystal has a bigger amplitude. In physics, amplitude is measured by the amount of force applied over an area. This tells you that amplitude is directly related to the intensity or power of a sound or wave. The more amplitude a wave has, the more it's moving from one side to the other. That means it carries more force. So when you're looking for objects to fill out your 'household amplitude resonant range', it may help to think of things made with the same frequency or from the same material but with different levels of power.

Most people find shifting amplitudes stranger than shifting frequencies. If you've ever done dowsing or watched a grandfather clock, you probably paid more attention to the **speed** of the pendulum as it swung back and forth. This is the pendulum's frequency. But the **size** of the swing from one side to the other is the amplitude. This is the direct measure of the power of the energy your dowsing pendulum is responding to or of the power stored in the winding mechanism of the grandfather clock.

When you look at a light, you probably notice its color most of all. Once again, the color of a light has to do with its frequency. Yet the light's brightness is another significant quality. The brighter a light is, the more power it has. The brighter a light is, the greater the amplitude of the light wave coming from it. So you can understand how important it is to understand amplitude. It's a major key to understanding your own power. So be patient with yourself. Take the time you need to fully appreciate amplitude along with frequency.

As your appreciation of amplitude grows, your power will grow. The more powerful you become, the more important it is for you to remember your occupational health and safety for the metaphysical. The more powerful you get, the more deeply you can affect your own energy along with the energy of others. Whenever you've moved into resonance with someone or something other than your own soul seat, it's important to come back to your own resonance.

Remember Ava the talented empath? She wasn't doing that. Partly because she was moving into resonance with other people's energies, without being aware she was doing it; partly because she didn't know how to get back to her own energy. That's why she ended up so drained, lost and confused. Energetically, she'd got to a point where there was very little of Ava in Ava's life. By learning to acknowledge what energies she was tuning into and later learning to consciously tune back into herself, she became much healthier energetically. She was then able to make more positive use of her talent.

Tuning back into your own resonance is important for two reasons. It helps you get clearer on the resonance you're tuning into, giving you a constant point of reference you can compare other energy to. It also stops any interference from the other resonances in your system. This works even better once you're working with frequency and amplitude, because it gives your awareness an unprecedented level of precision. The better your resonant grip works, the clearer your soul seat resonance becomes as you release any resonances that are not your own. It's that reduction in the static within your resonance which makes you feel lighter, as you become more self-aware.

Now you're aware of amplitude as well as frequency, you can tune into your own resonance with much greater clarity. This will speed up the expansion of your awareness.

. . . .

Measuring coherence and your own power
Gripping resonance both ways
....

You've got two eyes, so your nervous system is configured to having two reference points to create a stable focus. In the metaphysical, frequency and amplitude are your two reference points. That means you can grip an energy two ways for a much more stable connection. The more you practice working clearly and specifically with both amplitude and frequency, the clearer your focus will be. The clarity of your focus will then create more coherence in your own resonance.

Coherence is the key to your own true power. You can use frequency and amplitude to create coherence in your own resonance through the following exercise. If you find frequency more accessible, do the steps in the given order. However if you find amplitude easier, reverse the order of these steps and do the amplitude first.

....

A COHERENT SOUL

- Focus on the clear, calm space inside your soul seat. Focus on your resonance.

- Now refine your focus; focus on the frequency of your resonance.

- Once you've got a grip on your frequency, focus on the amplitude of your resonance.

- Once you've got a grip on both your frequency and amplitude, intend for every cell in your body, and all your energy, to tune itself to that.

....

Soul seat attunement created through a specific focus on your frequency and amplitude is much clearer and stronger. Notice how tuning up your soul seat felt different for you with this more precise focus. A more coherent signal means there's far less noise or interference in your resonance. If you bookend the day with your own resonance, or tune into your frequency and amplitude on a regular basis, your intuitive clarity and resonant strength will increase rapidly.

It's a good practice to anchor this attunement to set actions you do during your day, to help you remember. As with other 'bookends', it could be first thing in the morning before you get up and last thing at night when you get into bed. It could be when you have a cup of tea or coffee through the day or when you're on your way to work. Take a moment to focus on your specific soul seat frequency and amplitude as you do these everyday things.

Doing a precise soul seat attunement while sitting on the train or bus or in the traffic can be challenging, as there's lots of distractions. But if you persist in doing this practice in those situations you'll get more robust. Then your resonant coherence will remain intact, even in life's distressing moments.

From a purely resonant point of view, rather than a psychological one, the quality of a resonance gives us four clear stages in the development of our signal: from white noise and interference to coherence, then to a signal that is richly harmonic. We're all more advanced in some areas of our lives than others, so we find we're at the beginning of our signal development in some situations yet have a masterful signal in others.

Four EM stages

When we're not paying attention, it's easy for our resonance to get messed about—unless we've practiced holding that kind of robust focus. Our system can fill up with static and white noise, from the resonance of viruses to the energy of anyone we've spoken to or thought about. If this happens enough, it's possible for our resonance to be more static than signal; to be nothing but white noise. With nothing but white noise in our system, we have no choice but to be unconscious of Who We Truly Are.

You could say **unconsciousness** (the first EM stage) looks energetically like a television screen filling up with snow, or the chaotic energy found in an ordinary torch. If someone's soul seat is like that, they can't find their resonance. They need a bit of self-connection to begin to find their true signal. That's why putting a bit of conscious intention into self-connection is essential. Simply breathing into their soul seat for a few minutes each day is a useful first step.

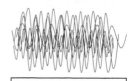

Unconscious resonance is all static or white noise.

The second stage, called **co-dependency,** comes when we've got some ability to perceive our true signal. We still have interference, but we've cleaned up our signal to the point where our true resonance comes through clearly some of the time. Yet we still lose our signal when we're exposed to a strong enough outside resonance. The upside is there's some chance we'll find our clarity again.

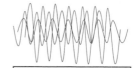

Co-dependent resonance holds a lot of interference with the true signal.

If an unconscious signal is a torch, then a co-dependent signal is an LED light. The truth is we tend to connect with others by either collapsing into their signal, or projecting our resonance strongly enough to bring the other person into resonance with us. Either is messy and co-dependent, as it messes up someone's signal. Either way, someone ends up with interference in their resonance, which results in a loss of self-connection. A better way to connect is through harmonics, which we'll discuss shortly.

Understanding these dynamics helps explain why many people feel as if they're losing themselves through their work or relationships. Exposed to powerful resonances that overwhelm their own, they begin to think the other resonance **is** their own. They end up depending upon the source of that resonance to create their life for them.

This is why falling in love can sometimes feel like a drug, as if something foreign has taken over your system. It can be exhilarating and intoxicating, but co-dependent love is the result of losing your own signal and taking up someone else's signal. It's why we can lose ourselves in those kinds of relationships. The same thing can happen at work, if your boss is very charismatic. You can end up replacing your own career goals with whatever idea your boss has for you. Yet no matter how good the intentions of others, they can never create a life for you that suits you. Their choices won't be exactly your choices. That's why co-dependency doesn't work.

Up until this point we make progress by 'negative gain'. To progress, we need to get rid of the negatives. In resonant terms, we grow by deleting interfering signals. The more we clear frequencies and amplitudes that aren't ours from our resonance, the easier it is for us to perceive our own true resonance of Who We Truly Are. Once we get to this point, we need to switch gears and move into 'positive gain'. Positive gain is the ability to put in what we **do** want, rather than take out what we don't. In the resonant sense, this refers to the ability to find and strengthen our true signal. This level of self-awareness and the ability to tune up our soul seat resonance moves us into the third stage.

As our signal becomes more coherent, it becomes easier for us to move to **independency**—the third EM stage. When we first get to this point we can be hypersensitive to any interference, as our newly-clear signal may still be a little fragile. That's why people in early-stage independency can often appear to be shielded or defensive. They've just found their signal. They don't want to risk anything interfering with it.

Independent resonance is clear and strong with increasing coherence.

With increasing practice of the positive-gain skills we can relax. Once we're familiar enough with our signal and are confident we can get it back, even if we lose it badly, we don't need to guard our signal so heavily. This usually occurs around the time the person's resonance begins to develop true coherence. Now their energy begins to develop laser-like qualities, bringing their life into alignment and creating an even stronger signal. It's the power and strength of that coherence which gives their signal increasing robustness.

Coherence is necessary if we're to move into **interdependency**, the fourth EM stage. One of the things I'm constantly reminding clients and students is: *Interdependency is founded on independency.* In interdependency, we learn a completely different way of connecting to others. This is why interdependency is the master key to co-creation.

At first glance, an interdependent signal can appear similar to a co-dependent one, as there are a number of different resonances together. However, there is an incredible and significant difference. In co-dependency, every signal is of equal value. You could say it's almost like ADHD—there's so much energy it's overwhelming! It's not clear which signal we should pay attention to, as in a relationship where you're confused about where your priorities lie. In interdependent relationships, your priorities are clear.

In co-dependency the energy is incoherent, so every note causes interference with every other note. All the different energies are fighting each other and getting in each other's way. This makes it hard to increase the power of your signal because if you do, you also increase the power of the chaos. Think of a radio where you're getting a lot of static. It's hard to hear the program you're listening to because of all the white noise. You might think that if you turn up the volume it'll be easier to hear. But if you do, it's actually harder because the interference gets stronger. Paradoxically, turning down the volume can often make the program clearer, even if you have to concentrate to hear it. Perhaps that's one reason why meditation is so helpful when we start our journey towards Who We Truly Are.

In interdependency, our coherent independent signal becomes the foundation for a much richer signal. Our original coherent signal is now called the fundamental signal, as all other frequencies and amplitudes will align to our fundamental one. Our signal has gone from a singular laser to being hologram-worthy. In other words, there are many different notes all playing together, but they're not chaotic. An interdependent signal is richly harmonic.

In an interdependent relationship, we understand we need to love ourselves just a tiny bit more than we love our partners, family and friends. We know we have to do this, because if we love the other person more than we love ourselves, we'll inevitably end up giving up on our integrity. When we love another more than ourselves, we put a higher priority on their needs. But when we love ourselves a tiny bit more, it opens the door to the possibility of true negotiation, to finding a way that works for both people without either losing their integrity.

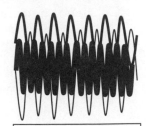

Interdependent resonance is coherent and is enriched with harmonics.

In interdependency, we can open to others' energies and still stay centered on our own signal, because every note is **aligned** with every other note across harmonic scales. This means that when you increase the power, the signal doesn't disperse or become chaotic. Harmony and alignment remain. So increasing the power results in more effectiveness, not chaos. The rich harmonics of an interdependent signal means it's full of awareness or information.

One of the problems with the right/wrong or more co-dependent way of handling energy is that other resonances interfere with our signal, so we instinctively reject them. That means we also reject all they have to offer, including opportunities for learning and growth. Energetic interference gives fear a strong place in our lives, because that drives the rejection response. This changes utterly and profoundly once we achieve interdependency.

When we achieve interdependency, we have a robust capacity to bring any new resonance into alignment with our own. So new resonances aren't to be feared and rejected, but rather welcomed and appreciated. Any new resonance is a new opportunity for learning and fun, for a new level of connection and understanding. This perhaps is what Einstein meant when he said: *I have no special talent. I am only passionately curious.*

Interdependency creates an attitude of open curiosity to life, which makes it much easier for us to be open to all the universe has to offer. We achieve interdependency once our internal and energetic systems can easily and naturally make positive use of anything new. This leads to relationships and lives based on inspiration and wonder, founded on the certainty that our lives will continue to strengthen our awareness of Who We Truly Are, and will grow to reflect that perfection more with every passing day.

You can experience this for yourself. Earlier, I got you to 'pump up the volume' of your soul seat. Now you're focusing more specifically on the frequency and amplitude of your soul seat resonance, so you can create greater coherence in your signal. With that coherence, you can produce a more powerful signal for more ease, grace and alignment.

. . . .

COHERENT POWER

- Focus on the clear, calm space inside your soul seat. Focus on your resonance.

- Get a grip on the frequency of your resonance.

- Now get a grip on the amplitude of your resonance.

- Once you've got a good hold on both frequency and amplitude, intend for every cell in your body and all your energy to tune itself up to that resonance.

- Now pump up the volume. Increase the power of your resonance to its maximum.

. . . .

Notice any difference. How does this compare to pumping up the volume without such a specific and coherence-inducing focus? With increased coherence, it's much easier to increase the strength of your signal. It's clearer and the increased focus makes it even easier.

Importantly, there's no increase in dissonance as you increase your energy. This means more power, more ease—rather than more power, more discomfort.

Regardless of how much power and energy you think you may or may not have, bringing your resonance into a coherent, laser-like state produces greater effectiveness. The internal alignment makes it much easier for you to attain peace and ease in your personal life. It supports you to walk your path in grace. And that grace will continue to expand as you grow towards energetic interdependency.

Becoming interdependent is a significant transformation. I believe it is this transformation that the collective consciousness of humanity is working towards at present, though it may seem otherwise. If we're to make our own transformation with more ease and grace, we need to understand what's happening. Only then can we 'get with the program' and align to what is happening. When we work appropriately with transformation, we experience it as inspiration that is so expansive, there is no room for fear.

Step Six

With a solid intuitive foundation created from completing your cycles, understanding your own intuitive process, keeping yourself balanced, as well as knowing your own resonance, you've started to build a truly impressive intuition. You can now increase the volume and coherence of your resonance to a truly powerful level. With the added awareness of frequency and amplitude, your intuitive range has increased. You're intuition is now becoming reliable and is something you can apply to your life for increasing success in all areas.

You're on the verge of a powerful transformation, which is what Step Six is all about. Being able to navigate each transformation on our life path with increasing ease and grace is a powerful way to support ongoing growth. The more we grow with confidence and certainty, the greater our personal expansion will be.

. . . .

95% of the universe is missing
Luddites, saboteurs and holding back the darkness

It takes strength and robustness to deal with chaos, especially the chaos of transformation. It's never easy to get out of your one-valley and go exploring. New realities are extra scary if they involve potential loss of income or other survival necessities, as many people are experiencing now with increased automation. Fear makes them want to stop and turn the world back from its current transformation.

Facing the necessity to reskill or otherwise adapt to a new reality is stressful, but it's not the first time this has happened. A desire to return to the 'good old days' before technology took away jobs was really big a couple of hundred years ago. The Luddites in England and the saboteurs in France protested against the new weaving machines replacing their textile jobs by smashing those machines. In their one-valley world, the Luddites and saboteurs believed the machines were leading to bad changes. Many were starving. Yet the transformation they were trying to halt was leading towards ultimate abundance, the likes of which hadn't been seen before. The Industrial Revolution changed every aspect of life. The standard of living increased consistently as incomes improved and more goods became available at more affordable prices.

Our world is undergoing such a shift in work and abundance again, because of automation. Jobs and job practices are changing, as the world shifts from petrochemicals to renewables. It's enough to cause anyone to demand a return to the 'good old days'! One way or another, the future is going to be different.

This is one powerful reason why developing conscious intuition is so important. When we step from one reality to a completely new one, the patterns are completely different. The facts haven't changed, but they line up as you've never seen them before. Trying to work with the facts in the same old way no longer gets us good results. We need our intuition to show us the new pattern, so we can align our efforts to that. Then our actions will be effective, with expansive results for ourselves and those around us.

Remember epicycles? Those cycles within cycles within cycles that were used to hold onto the old belief of planets moving in circles around the earth? The planets hadn't started moving in new ways, but the invention of lenses and the telescope meant they were observed more clearly, revealing a new pattern, a new alignment.

Transformation always brings new challenges and opportunities, like having to earn money in a new way—similar to what happened in the Industrial Revolution and is happening now for many people. It can also show us the limitations we've lived with up until now.

Years ago, when I was still working as a country vet, I remember examining a cat and asking the owner, 'And how are you today?'

'Awful,' she replied. 'I've got a terrible disease. I've been diagnosed with idiopathic pyrexia.'

Sounds terrible, right? Every time humanity has peered over the edges of the known into the unknown, our first instinct has been to pretend we know all about what's there, even if what we know is 'there be dragons' or even 'dark dragons'. But no. 'I'm sorry,' I said. 'Idiopathic means of unknown origin, and pyrexia means fever. The doctor has diagnosed you with a fever caused by something he doesn't know.'

Pretending we know what's there makes life seem less scary. But just like epicycles, when we can observe more than ever before, the chances are there's going to be a new pattern for the new context. We won't understand the new stuff until we 'get' the new pattern.

That's the true difference between change and transformation. Change is simply moving from one part of a known pattern to another, but with transformation it's a completely new pattern. When we view transformation this way, we can understand the steps involved.

· ·

The steps of transformation
The science of transformation

. . . .

One of our greatest intuitive powers is our ability to 'get' a new pattern in an instant. The difficulty is in communicating it. Intuitive truth is like emotional truth. It's personal to us and speaks to us in our own personal language.

Scientific or left-brain truth is more like mental truth. It's based on what is, as opposed to emotional truth which is our personal response to what is. Translating our intuitive or emotional truths into mental truths makes them easier to communicate. The first step is to realize what our intuition or emotions are responding to.

In science, the pattern of a new context is eventually captured in a new equation. This is why Einstein's equation for gravity looks so different to Newton's. They were both working with the same left-brained facts, but they lined up differently, as Newton didn't think about light and Einstein used light as his new context. He wanted the relationship between light and gravity to be clear, so there was a new pattern.

If you'd like a simpler example, have another look at the Sierpinski triangle. Think about each different repetition of the rule that creates the fractal, so the whole complete triangle is one context. The triangle with the middle removed is a different context, and so on.

Another way to think of any fractal, including the Sierpinski triangle, is that every iteration is a different context. Each one gives more details, letting us view the triangle in a different way.

Our intuitive vision of the whole lets us see the same pattern repeated over and over. From the context of **one particular iteration**, the bits can seem to be a completely different pattern. Einstein's advances don't make Newton wrong. Engineers have to think about gravity, but they don't have to worry about what happens to it close to the speed of light. Einstein's views were transformative because he took us to a new context, one that took our understanding of our universe to a whole new level.

Shifting to a new level is characteristic of transformation. Most things studied in science are reversible. They go both ways, like gravity. Gravity draws you back to the surface of the planet or, by applying enough force, you can achieve escape velocity and 'break free' of gravity. Reversible or two-way processes are change—not transformation. You can always change back. Water that goes into ice can always go back into water.

Transformation goes in one direction only. Once it's done, it can't go back. Sugar that's become toffee can't become sugar again. You've done some irreversible things in your own life. At some point I'm guessing you've learned some things you couldn't unlearn, whether you wanted to or not. Also you've got older and, I'm sorry to say, that's a process that only goes in one direction. Aging may make you feel out of control around your personal transformations but, thanks to the work of Ilya Prigogine, you can gain mastery in this important area.

Ilya Prigogine also thought Newton had left something out. Born in Moscow a few months before the Russian Revolution, he ended up in Belgium working in physical chemistry. For him, it wasn't the speed of light but the direction of time that he wanted to understand. Irreversible systems have an arrow of time which was incompatible with Newton's stuff and quantum mechanics, as both are reversible theories. Theories of change. Prigogine was fascinated by the mystery of the incompatibility of the reversible foundation of science with the irreversible behavior observed in chemistry, hydrodynamics and biology. He was fascinated by transformation.

Prigogine wanted to know if the arrow of time, of transformation, was a fundamental property of nature or an illusion. He thought the arrow of time must be fundamental—something Newton had missed. In 1977, his fascination with the science of irreversible systems earned him the Nobel Prize for Chemistry, mostly for his theories on dissipative structures. What's a dissipative structure? You, for one thing. Anything that can respond to (and thereby dissipate) stress is a dissipative structure.

In physics terms, the definition of a dissipative structure is a little broader: anything that wastes energy through waste heat, rather than by using it to do work. Your car engine does that. You know things are getting worse when it starts wasting heat and overheats.

Things work fine when everything's in equilibrium or close to it. Systems in equilibrium are what Newton studied, but Prigogine examined systems far from equilibrium. When you can let go of the amount of stress you're under, things remain much the same. Your car works properly when its cooling system keeps it in equilibrium, so the temperature stays the same. However when not in equilibrium, things start to behave differently. When you're under more stress than you can handle, you're also on the verge of a possible transformation. It's at that point Newton's thermodynamics don't work so well.

The first thing that happens when a system is stressed beyond its capacity is it starts to break down. It can break down a little or a lot, depending on how far beyond its capacity it's pushed. You know that feeling. If someone pushes you just a little bit more, you're going to explode. But it's okay, depending on what happens next. There are three possibilities for a system once it's been pushed beyond its capacity to the point of breakdown:

1. It continues to break down like the Tacoma Narrows Bridge.
2. It can go back to being the way it was, just as it does when you turn off the element before the pot starts to simmer.
3. It reorganizes itself. It transforms its structure.

When stress is good

The transformation of structure is behind the mysteries of the alchemy of cooking. It's what allows you to transform basic ingredients into amazing flavors. The trick is to avoid ongoing breakdown, while creating as much transformation as possible. That's also the key to your evolution and transformation. It's what the best healers do. They know when to push your system so you 'pop' into the next level, but they also know when not to push because your system is at risk of breaking down too much. Knowing when to push and not to push is referred to in the shamanic system as 'intervention points'. These are moments when the possibility for evolutionary transformation is at its peak.

Prigogine figured out what causes different results to occur. Essentially, he realized the difference is all in the process of dissipating the energy. The energy of stress breaks down the old structure. If there's insufficient breakdown, the system just goes back to the way it was. At the same time, it takes energy to reorganize a structure. This energy for reorganization comes from residual energy within the system itself. If there's too little residual energy in the system once breakdown is complete, the system isn't able to reorganize. So it continues to break down.

That's why simmering your stew is a good thing to do. If you don't heat the food enough, you won't break it down at all. Food cooked slowly below 42^0 C is essentially still 'raw'. If you cook it too much or boil it madly, it'll overcook. Simmering food enables the alchemy of transformation to take place, keeping it at just the right 'stress' level until the ingredients transform. The difference between you and your mother's famous spaghetti bolognese is that food can't fight back. You can.

When we resist the breakdown of our old structure or reality, we're actually using up our internal or residual energy. If this continues, we're at risk of not having enough energy to do the job of reorganizing. If that happens, we're on the road to a possible breakdown.

This is an essential process for anyone interested in transformation to understand. It's critical for professional healers. One of the most important things I teach my students is how to recognize when their clients are 'simmering' nicely. And when the heat needs to be turned down or up to keep them there until they 'pop' into transformation. That pop is the moment when our system restructures. Without a thorough understanding of this principle, a healer may be at risk of causing unknown harm to their clients.

It's important to leave a system in a better state than you found it. At the very least, employ the farm gate principle of 'leave it as you found it'. This is critically important. It's why intermittent stress makes you stronger, while persistent and unrelenting stress will kill you. Even spiritual stress.

Jodie came to see me when her nest was empty and she finally had time for herself. She'd jumped, elbows and all, into her spiritual quest. She'd done yoga and sweat lodges, found her mantra and meditated. Gone on vision quests and spoken with her inner child. Gestalted her mother and done a dozen vision boards. She'd talked through hours of therapy, exploring her emotional wounds. She was a wreck.

When I saw Jodie she was close to a nervous breakdown. Her pot had gone beyond simmer and was boiling over. She wanted to know what new thing she had to uncover in order to heal. I told her I wasn't going to do that. Her energy looked like a Fabergé egg that'd been dropped way too many times. There were hairline cracks everywhere, a sure sign that her energetic system had been breaking down way past the point where it could reorganize itself. 'You need to finish integrating the work you've already done before you start anything new,' I told her.

One of the advantages of fractal perception is that you have a literal 'map' of what the person's energy looks like in its optimal state, the state in which their energy is all aligned to their fractal or to Who They Truly Are. Working with her coherent resonance and fractal structure, I assisted Jodie to complete the long-delayed transformations. As her system reorganized, the cracks disappeared. All her energy returned. She was able to finally gain the benefit of all the insights and clearing she'd been doing. Then she felt great.

Stress that goes on and on never gives your system a chance to stop breaking down and reorganize. That's why unremitting stress will kill you. With intermittent stress, your system has a chance to recover and reorganize. That's all exercise is after all: deliberately stressing your system with periods of rest in between so you can recover.

Pheidippides, the first guy to run a marathon, shows what happens with unrelenting stress. He'd already run to Sparta to ask for help, when the Persians landed at Marathon. He ran about 240 km (150 miles) in two days, then after the battle he ran another 40 km (25 miles) from the battlefield back to Athens, to tell the Athenians that the Greeks had won. He cried 'We win!' then promptly collapsed and died.

These days, marathon runners know they need to work up to the feat or they risk their bodies breaking down in a similar way. By working up towards our goal, allowing the body to reorganize along the way, we can adapt to running further and further. When a body breaks down a little but rebounds to what it was before, that's change. When a body breaks down a little and takes the opportunity to loosen the old structure and reorganize, that's transformation. It's why personal growth or healing doesn't go in a straight line.

Your left brain would probably prefer transformation to go in a straight line. It would certainly be easier to predict and understand. But the nature of transformation means that's never going to be the case. That's why your right brain or intuition is better at navigating transformation.

If we take a look at what kind of line transformation does go in, it'll help your left brain to be more comfortable.

. . . .

The growth graph
A few graphs

· ·

There are few things left brains like more than a good graph. Those below have the benefit of working for both your left and right brain. They give details of change and transformation (for your left brain), while showing you the patterns of each (for your right brain).

Remember that Prigogine showed us that change is a difference we can return from, but there's no return from transformation. It's irreversible. Change can be likened to a linear relationship. You do something, you get a response. If you do twice as much of it, you get twice as much response. You keep plodding along in that direction and it just keeps on keeping on in that way.

Many patients think that's how medical drugs and supplements work,

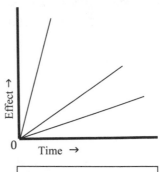

Straight line graphs mean linear relationships.

but biology doesn't go in a straight line. That's what got my mum into trouble one particular day. She'd come up to have lunch with me which was lovely. But when we got back to my place, she thought she was going to pass out which wasn't so lovely. I did some chiropractic stuff that normally rebalances the system but it didn't help.

Then I remembered that at lunch she'd told me she'd been taking therapeutic doses of magnesium. Your muscles need that mineral to relax and, because of high blood pressure, she'd been taking it to get her heart and arterial muscle to relax. She'd said it was helping, which was great. So she'd doubled her dose.

As we talked, it became clear it wasn't the first time she'd had a fainting spell. 'How long have you been having these fainting episodes?' I asked.

'Three weeks,' Mum said.

'And how long have you been on the double dose of magnesium?'
'Three weeks.'

The point is that the body doesn't work in straight lines. No biological systems do. Natural systems adapt. They're feedback systems, so you don't get twice as much benefit when you put in twice as much of anything. You might get less of a result or you might get more. With natural systems, the response is more like an exponential curve.

When you take medication, your system adapts. It tries to keep to 'business as usual' despite the drugs. So if you take more, it doesn't necessarily have twice the effect. It may have much less. That's a negative exponential curve. With some things, it goes the other way and there can be a larger effect. That's when we get into transformation territory. That's when your system crosses the threshold into the next level. That's a growth curve.

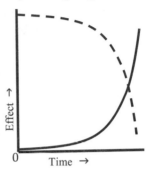

Growth is a positive exponential curve (unbroken line), while drug responses usually have a negative exponential curve. (dashed line).

The smooth-looking curve might make you think that growth happens all very evenly, but I'm sure your experience is nothing like that. The exponential curve of growth is a **trend** line, without the details of everyday life.

True growth is not change, it's transformation. That means growth involves periods of stress, where things are bouncing around, interspersed with moments of reorganizing, when we 'jump' to the next level. We need to build up the necessary energy before we can 'pop' through to the next level.

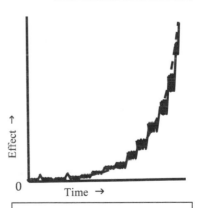

The exponential growth curve is an approximation of the stepped series of transformation.

The more energy we have to start with, the more inherent or residual energy there is in our system. That means the more we can allow ourselves to break down, before we need to pull everything back into a new structure. So the more we've already grown, the bigger our next step will be.

We can feel our systems as they begin to break down. It's how we feel the jump approaching. I see this all the time with clients. It's as if we play about with change knowing it's kind of safe, because if we don't like it, we can always change back. After a while the changes approach critical mass. One more step and it's transformation time.

That's when clients begin to get antsy. I call it 'threshold behavior'. It's as if they get stuck in the doorway of the next shift. Every time they take a step into the next room, they immediately draw back. It's simply another manifestation of fear of the unknown.

Sometimes transformation is referred to as the 'law of unintended consequences', because no one can be exactly sure how things will be once they're reorganized. Transformation always moves you into a new pattern. Your intuition is a huge assistance here. Intuition has the capacity to peer beyond the threshold and perceive the new pattern.

This is one of the benefits of having a really strong intuition. Once you've transformed your intuition, your capacity to handle transformation becomes a lot greater.

. . . .

Intuitive power
Energetic fitness
. . . .

Transformation occurs on all levels and in all your aspects, including your intuition. If you feel your intuition is weak, fragile or unreliable, then it needs a bit of transforming. Intuition requires an expenditure of energy in order to work. It also takes time to transform into an intuitive powerhouse. You can liken this to building up intuitive fitness. The process is similar to the process of getting physically fit.

The medical definition of fitness is 'the ability to recover from stress'. You can be fit and recover from stress on all levels. With emotional fitness, you recover from upset to return to a state of peace and love. With mental fitness, you recover from confusion and return to clarity. With physical fitness, you recover from exertion to feel strong and zippy once again. With spiritual or energetic fitness, you recover from moving into different resonances and come back to your own. This requires energetic strength and flexibility.

Physically, you increase your flexibility by stretching and your strength by lifting weights or doing push-ups. Energetically, you stretch by switching from one resonance to another, then shifting back to your own. You've already learned that by tuning into the resonance of other things, you shift into their resonance. Remember to do so with both frequency and amplitude. By then returning to your own resonance, you ensure you come back to your resting point. You can also do energetic push-ups by moving your EM space about, just as you move your whole body when doing physical weights or push-ups.

When you learned to balance your up and down energetic flows, you used the principles of **focus** and **intention**. You learned to do this originally by using a visualization. Then by practicing with the energy ball, you increased your awareness and sense of energy. You learned to feel the flow of energy up and down your spine. Now you can apply that awareness to your space.

Remember, your space is your EM field. Fields are cool things. Different achievements in science, from general relativity to combining the weak and strong nuclear forces, were achieved by looking at everything as different fields. Fields are a bit like balloons. Push on one side and the effect is felt on the other side, because the whole field is connected.

Your energy is similarly connected to the whole of Who You Truly Are and not just through your nervous system. The more conscious you are of being connected on all levels, the stronger your awareness and energy become. If you'd like to get 'energetically ripped', do the next exercise for a few minutes each day.

. . . .

SPACE PUSH-UPS

- Visualize your space as a balloon all around you. It's probably more egg-shaped than spherical, but whatever shape feels good to you, visualize it now.
- Focus on its edge, the skin of the balloon. Then focus on all of it at once.
- Intend for it to be half its size. Ensure it halved in all directions: above your head and below your feet, at the front and back, to the left and right.
- Having successfully halved your space, stop for a moment. Your energy is now compacted into a much smaller volume. How does that feel?
- Now do the other half of the push-up. Focus again on the edge of your energetic space and intend for it to be twice its original size. Check all the directions.
- How does it feel to have your energy spread out like that?
- You've just done one energetic push-up. Do a few more, but stop if you begin to feel tired. When you finish, remember to reset your space to its normal size.

. . . .

The two sides of this exercise can feel very different. Reducing your space can feel as if you're sucking in your metaphysical tummy as hard as you can go, just as you might with your physical tummy when some hot thing walks by. No one likes having their energy reduced and nor should you, but the 'tight tummy' feeling isn't from loss of energy. Reducing your space compacts your energy, rather than draining it. Being able to increase the density of your field or space can be helpful at times, when you're under pressure or feeling bombarded. A denser space is a stronger space.

Expanding your field enables you to hold a larger space. This is helpful when you need to be connected more broadly, such as when you're giving a speech, teaching or working with a large group. Being able to 'hold space' that's big enough to include everyone in your energy field enables more people to connect directly to you and to what you want to communicate.

Using space push-ups increases your energetic control and strength. If you do them often enough you'll get energetically fit. That's especially important for anyone doing regular energetic work or using their intuition. It means that when you navigate that board meeting intuitively or do a full day of healing, you'll become invigorated rather than drained. This is especially true when you're able to do what you do in a coordinated way, physically and metaphysically.

Synchronized flows

Energetic coordination takes a developed focus. Like many things, we tend to unconsciously do metaphysically what we've been doing physically for years. When we look at something with our physical eyes, we have a 2D (two-dimensional) focus. When you look at a box, a house or a piece of furniture, all you see is the surface of the object. Energetically, however, things are different. Energetically, you can connect with **all** of an object—at least you can if you focus on all of it with the **intention** of doing so. My students get sick of hearing me say: *It's all focus and intention.* But this is true, so I'm going to continue saying it.

Your results improve with a stronger intention. But just like a laser, your most effective results come from having a precise and all-encompassing focus. That means your focus has to evolve from 2D to at least 3D. Think about it this way: if it's all focus and intention, the more sophisticated or all-encompassing your focus becomes, and the more powerful your energy and intuition become. String theory tells us there are probably eleven dimensions. So if you're going to consciously connect with all of the universe, you're going to need a focus that works in more than two dimensions.

When you look at an object like an apple or flower, you'll focus on what you see with your physical eyes. That's just the exterior surface, what most of us would draw. Your metaphysical vision needs to go further. Energetically, you can connect to or focus on the **entirety** of an object—its inside as well as all of its outside and EM field. But first you have to develop a focus that can hold all that.

. . . .

DEPTH FOCUS

- Pick an object and study it closely. Look at it from all sides: top, bottom, left, right, back and front. Consider its inside as well. If appropriate, cut it open.

- Now close your eyes. Build the object in your mind, until the image is complete.

- Open your eyes and compare what was in your mind to the object itself. Are they the same?

. . . .

As your focus evolves, you'll be able to hold a complete 3D image of an object in your mind. Keep practicing. You'll get there. The 'depth focus' exercise has many benefits, not least of which is having another way to practice being fully present with an object.

By applying the same 3D focus to your own space, you'll improve your control. That makes it easier to get 'energetically ripped'. When you have a 3D focus and can do space push-ups with ease, you may wish to challenge yourself further. Remember the hologram? Our holographic universe is infinite in space, yet has an edge to it just like a fractal. That means it's possible for you to shift your space to being an infinite, holographic space. In spiritual terms, it's said we're all gods and goddesses. The characteristics of the divine are all the omnis: omnipresent, omnipotent, omniscient, omnificent, omni-directional, and so on. Omni is an old Latin word that means 'all'. So omnipotent means 'all powerful' while omnipresent means 'present in all times and places'.

Assuming your true nature is divine, then if you want to become Who You Truly Are you need to practice those same divine states. By learning to hold a holographic or infinite space, you're practicing the first omni: omnipresence. Omnipresence is simply a left-brained word for the right-brained spiritual state of feeling connected to all things, also known as cosmic or higher consciousness. By consciously expanding your electromagnetic space to the edges of our universe, you'll feel a sense of connection to all things. That's a profound state which gives your intuition a deep well of support and information to draw from.

Focus and intention will get you there, though this needs a little more energy than anything you've done before. Simply focus on the infinite and intend for your space to be that. Simple, but not easy. It's simple because it's genuinely just a matter of focus and intention, something every Fractology student learns to do. But it's not easy because shifting to holographic space often does their heads in, as it's so far out of ordinary experience for most of us. Often it requires some direct personal guidance to achieve this state. But if you get sufficiently energetically fit, it's quite doable.

Furthermore, if you keep working on your energy ball until your awareness of energy grows stronger, then your ability to focus on your space will also get stronger. Strong enough to be able to shift to a holographic space.

Please remember this is all part of getting fit and it takes time. Attempting to shift to a holographic space all in one go is similar to running a marathon, when you haven't been on a run in years. That could overstress your system, and I'd prefer it if you didn't do that. But just in case you do, let's talk about psychic or energetic first aid.

. . . .

Overloading your system
Psychic first aid

. . . .

Going holographic is a fundamental shift. It gives you the space to stop operating as a linear, physically-bound human and to start operating with non-linear EM consciousness. It's a huge jump. There's no need to rush it. If you just do a few space push-ups every day you'll get there. If you do rush it, you can exhaust your energy. You may even risk overstressing your energetic system. It's the metaphysical equivalent of ending up with lactic legs.

When you overexercise energetically, it's your nervous system you end up exhausting. You use up all the glucose in your brain cells. You also deplete your neurotransmitters. Most especially, you deplete your brain of the neurotransmitter noradrenaline, which helps your brain cells process faster. Noradrenaline appears to be the primary neurotransmitter involved in intuition. It can take you days to recover from lactic acidosis, if you don't do something to help your muscles. It can take up to two or even three weeks to recover from the 'brain fugue' of overexhausting your energy. However, if you use appropriate psychic first aid for overexercising metaphysically, you'll recover much faster.

. . . .

PSYCHIC FIRST AID

This is most effective when applied within twenty minutes of metaphysical exercise.

- Replace the glucose in your brain cells with some sugar. Chocolate works well.

- Rebuild your noradrenaline levels with caffeine. Caffeine doesn't give you adrenaline but it blocks its breakdown, enabling you to hoard whatever your brain has left and making it easier for you to restore normal levels.

That's it ... having coffee and chocolate cake within twenty minutes of completing your psychic processes. Now you finally have an excuse!!

. . . .

THIRD TRIANGLE

. . . .

Sovereignty

Once you've built yourself a stable platform, with a strong energetic core and energetic fitness, you have the strength to be truly effective. As you're now more connected to Who You Truly Are, you're ready to begin realizing your true power.

Your ability to do, create and effect change in the world for yourself and those around you is your power. You do this by creating or by co-creating. When you create, you're using all your energy to effect necessary changes. You're manifesting from your own essence and energy alone. That makes it an inherently independent process. It's extremely rewarding and a profound learning experience on many levels. You'll get to know a lot about yourself and the things that inspire you.

If your manifestations are delayed, you'll learn about where you're blocked. When they do manifest, you'll learn about your capacity to receive. You'll gain awareness and understanding of what works and what doesn't work in your creative process. It's all quite wonderful. Ultimately, it's a great way to expand your self-awareness, but it can also be completely exhausting. To create, you have to use your energy to hold the focus, draw energy together and activate necessary thoughts and intentions. Then you have to hold all of that in place in a world full of distractions.

You'll often feel like you have to force it. It's a bit like plodding up an endless mountain. You scramble across broken soil and around rocks, taking just one more step and one more step. You can rest from time to time, but you'll have to get going again because no one else can climb the mountain for you. Having to force things is exhausting, but that's the price of creation.

Co-creation is **so much easier**. The only problem is, you can't co-create without learning how to create first. You have to do your bit in the process.

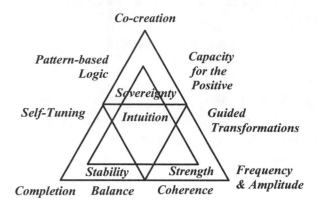

Once you learn how to co-create, you'll begin to manifest in increasingly elegant and efficient ways.

Co-creation is an interdependent process. That means you're not only using your energy, but the energy of everything that's involved. In other words, when you co-create you do so in alignment with the universe. You're still creating from your essence but you're now doing it from within the creative flow of the universe, which is what makes it all so much easier.

Centuries ago, it was believed that kings and queens embodied a sacred bond between the people and the land. They ensured the harvests were bountiful, the rains fell gently at the perfect time and that peace and plenty abounded. If this bond was violated the land suffered, then famine and plague ensued.

This is why the third triangle is that of sovereignty. When you co-create, you embody the bond between your essence and the universe. You're sovereign of your own world.

Step Seven

By completing your cycles, understanding your own intuitive process, keeping yourself balanced and knowing your own resonance, you created a solid and stable intuitive foundation. From there, you built the strength and capacity of your intuition through increasing the volume and coherence of your resonance. You also learned to work with frequency and amplitude and to apply all you've learned with confidence and certainty to the process of transformation.

You're now ready to move into true intuitive mastery. Step Seven takes you deeper into the understanding of pattern-based logic and its application to the hologram of the creation in which we live. This knowledge creates intuitive mastery.

. . . .

Pattern logic and integrity
The leopard's spots

. . . .

Just for a moment, think of someone or something you trust. Focus on being with them. Observe how you feel. Being able to truly trust someone brings with it a sense of ease, deep peace, security and openness. It means there's someone you can rely on in your world. You don't need to question or wonder what they're going to do, because you already know. This gives you freedom to relax around them, because your questions have already been answered.

Now focus on yourself. Do you get those same feelings? Do you trust yourself in the same way?

One of the biggest costs of the right-wrong or co-dependent way of thinking is that it turns that same spotlight on yourself. It's an inherently cruel spotlight, that leaves broken trust in its wake. If you think in terms of right and wrong, it's a box you inevitably won't fit into all the time. This forces you into a choice between two options. The first is making the rules right and yourself wrong, because they don't align with your pattern, and that creates internal conflict. The second is making yourself right and the rules wrong, which lands you in conflict with society, your family or whoever made the rules. Then you have to deal with all that external invalidation.

Thinking in terms of right-wrong means we'll never escape from invalidation. It's always there, internally or externally. That doesn't just apply to you, but to every single person who's doing their best to operate in such a system. It puts all of us into constant, pressured choices and compromises our integrity. All too often, the end result is a heap of invalidation. Additionally, in a right-wrong system you're always at risk of placing a higher value on the rules than on your own integrity. And that makes it very hard to trust yourself.

You can't change Who You Truly Are, nor can you change your fractal pattern to suit the right-wrong rules. Your spots are your spots. They don't change. From a spiritual point of view, you chose your fractal to be the pattern of your consciousness when you came into creation. You can't change it now. It's inherently aligned to fulfilling your purpose. From a scientific point of view, your fractal was formed within your neurology from the unique set of conditions of your conception, pregnancy and birth.

Attempting to force your pattern into a different shape is only going to cause you grief. You need to accept, acknowledge and work with it. Then you'll come to a deeper level of self-trust and understanding than you've previously known.

Take Ray for instance. He was a nice guy; that was his problem. He wanted to do the right thing so badly he'd twisted himself up into all sorts of right-wrong shapes. Despite pretty constant invalidation from many quarters he kept on going, but his second divorce woke him up to the fact that his life wasn't working. He was pretty depressed when he came to see me. Doing 'right' had left him miserable, his kids stressed and his ex-wives angry, but he didn't know how to do things differently.

It took lots of soul seat work, but as clarity of his own integrity grew, Ray let go of right and wrong. He learned to assess what he was doing according to his alignment with his integrity, rather than any set of right-wrong rules. His depression lifted, as his sense of personal fulfillment grew. From that point, his awareness of other people's integrity also began to grow. He was then able to truly help his kids, by showing them how to operate from their integrity instead of right-wrong. Seeing them start to blossom gave him back a lot of confidence. It also gave him the means to communicate more effectively with his ex-wives, as he was no longer concerned about who was right and who was wrong. He stayed focused on what it took to create a good life for everyone. By learning to appreciate his own patterns and focus on his integrity, he healed himself and his whole family.

The art of interdependence is the art of working with each person's integrity pattern. You could say it's the particular arrangement of each person's spots. Each fractal holds a different context, a different alignment. Each person's alignment holds true for their integrity. Our fractal is our spots, a pattern we can't change. We can only live in alignment with it or not. Your fractal pattern is powerful and fundamental. Like all fractals, it links you directly to the universe itself. Fractals are just one tool but at the same time are another complete tool set. Let's open the fractal box now and see what else it contains.

. . . .

Keys to integrity
One of these things is not like the others ...

Holograms have a fractal structure. That's why we end up with lots of smaller images of the original when we smash them, instead of a jigsaw puzzle. As holograms have a fractal structure and our universe is a hologram, it means we're living in one giant fractal. A giant, pattern-based reality. How exciting is that?

For a working relationship with fractals, there are four major characteristics to wrap your head around:

1. Fractals are composed of an infinite border to a finite space, or an infinite border containing nothing at all.
2. Fractals contain infinite detail.
3. Fractals are self-similar.
4. Fractals are self-referencing.

Let's look at this in more detail. The underlying structure to your energy is a fractal, like the universe itself. This means your energy is vaster than you know, yet all flows from the same essence. The four characteristics of fractals are actually relatively simple, if you take each one in turn. You already know the first one. Remember the Sierpinski triangle? You can create the Sierpinski carpet by following a similar rule, taking out the central triangle, but this time you're using a square instead. Keep taking out the middle square and you end up with something that looks like it was woven in Persia.

Just like the Sierpinski triangle, the carpet shows an infinite border enclosing a finite space. Our world is the same. While it **seems** solid, the more closely we look into everything the more it's all made up of empty space. Remember the Sierpinski sponge which we talked about earlier? It does the same thing in 3D. So again, you end up with an infinite border enclosing nothing but space. Nothing but empty space, as you look closer and closer. There'll always be moth-eaten details or missing cubes. As science looks more deeply into matter, it finds more and more of nothing, which reinforces all those spiritual truths about the world being an illusion.

It's a bit frustrating for physicists, as they keep looking for **the** fundamental particle. Yet the cleverer they get and the more powerful our technology becomes, the more empty space they find. There's more and more empty space, the further they see into matter. Put simply, everything around us is more space than anything. So different string lengths and vibrating speeds end up as different particles. In your own world, you could equate this to your limitations being an illusion as they're made up of nothing at all, while your possibilities are endless.

The second fractal characteristic of infinite detail you also know, though you may not have joined those particular dots just yet. You know that if you look at the branching pattern of a tree, then take a small piece of it like a twig or leaf, you'll see even more detail, whether it's the branching of the leaves or the branching of the veins in the leaf.

A fractal is a pattern that's repeated infinitely so, of course, if you take bits of the pattern and zoom in you're going to get more detail, and see the same recurring pattern. Put 'Mandelbrot zoom' into a YouTube search to watch the infinite detail of this famous fractal roll past. This infinite detail plays out in the quest to understand our universe. At first it was thought that everything was made of atoms, but as physicists looked closer, they discovered more detail. Atoms are now known to be made of electrons, protons and neutrons. More detail then gives us mesons. A meson is actually two quarks. Quarks are really strings ... you get the picture. With all that detail, it's easy for your left brain to get confused, as it remembers each fact or figure separately.

However, the universe and its fractal are infinite. That means no matter how many facts and figures you learn, there's always going to be more. Sooner or later, your left brain will get overwhelmed. This is where your right brain comes in, as your right brain doesn't need to remember all that stuff. It just remembers the pattern, to know what sort of tree you're looking at. Your right brain doesn't work with individual details, but with the **alignment** that gives each detail its meaning. That alignment is consistent, no matter which level of the fractal you're working with, assuming it's the same fractal.

That's what our important five Power Pentagon Principles we examined earlier do: acknowledgment, completion, focus, intention and integrity. They're the tools for creating and holding this same alignment—the true pattern of things. By acknowledging your patterns, you get to complete your cycles and so gain more energy. This work helps to activate and strengthen your fractal. By using your focus and intention, you rebalance your energy and tune yourself up to your own 'radio station' or soul seat resonance. The alignment to your own essence goes a long way to healing and strengthening your fractal. It also enables you to express your own unique pattern in every area of your life.

The more you are and do things as a direct expression of your own essence, the more you'll be in alignment to your own fractal. That's what integrity is. Integrity is the result of things being in alignment with themselves, with their fractal pattern. When the fractal is intact, it gives rise to the next two characteristics: self-similarity and self-referencing.

Self-similar means that every part of the pattern is like every other part. Or 'as above, so below', the spiritual truism mentioned earlier. It's another way of saying the same thing. So while your lungs don't look like your big toe, remember we're talking about the **underlying** structure here. A leaf doesn't look like the bark of a tree trunk, but again they're both part of a tree's pattern. When you develop fractal perception, you'll realize that on that level they're the same. They carry the same resonance.

The more that every area and every moment in your life carries your soul seat resonance, the more you'll express this same self similarity. Being in a state of self-similarity is the opposite to a state of stress. Think about it. When you're stressed, you don't feel like talking to anyone, do you? That's why it's so important to attune to your soul seat resonance.

When your body is stressed, all the different parts of your system, all your different organs and cells, stop communicating with each other. It's as if your liver no longer talks to your gall bladder and your gall bladder no longer talks to your bowel, so your whole digestion gets out of whack. Or your heart stops talking to your kidneys and your bone marrow, so your blood pressure and circulating iron are no longer what they need to be. When your system releases the stress, all your different parts can talk to each other again and become aligned with each other.

Self-similarity is the state of ultimate alignment. We often refer to this state as one of life satisfaction, but it's self-similarity that underlies it. Take Frank, who I first met after someone had smashed into his car. He had a few chiropractic injuries that needed attention, but I could see there was more going on. His health was generally good, but I could perceive that his fractal was distorted in some areas of his life. As I worked on resolving the trauma to his body, I talked to him about other life stresses. After he was physically better, he came back to see me because of my additional observations.

I taught him about his soul seat and helped him examine the rest of his life. He soon realized he was miserable in his job, that he'd only been doing it because it was what his dad had done. Forcing himself to follow someone else's pattern was distorting his fractal and undermining his happiness. He ended up having some life-changing conversations with his wife, who was also unhappy. She was being offered huge opportunities for promotion at her work, but felt she had to turn them down to be at home with their young kids, though it was everything she'd always wanted.

With what Frank had learned, they both gained clarity about living according to their own patterns and resonance. Their own essence. They agreed that Frank should give up his work and look after the kids, while she should take the promotion. What was important was the alignment of their integrity, not the conventions of society. Frank realigned his life to create greater integrity for himself, which enabled his family to do the same. He's now far happier and the family has more money.

When we lose our pattern, we no longer have self-similarity in all areas of our lives, which means some areas take us away from Who We Truly Are. That's not a recipe for life satisfaction, but rather for dis-ease. If a tree has a branch broken or gets a fungus, then that part no longer looks like the rest of the pattern. While healthy, any life form remains true to its pattern.

This understanding is now being used in cancer research. Many types of cancer are time-critical. The sooner they're treated, the more chance there is of a good outcome. Unfortunately, some cancers can't be diagnosed accurately until they've progressed. But fractal analysis changes that. When cells go crazy and turn cancerous, they change their body shape or morphology. At its simplest, that means the cell walls become a different kind of crinkly. Measuring crinkles is where fractals are particularly useful. In fact, looking for a way to measure crinkles is where the understanding of fractals began.

It turns out that cells don't go crazy in a completely random way, but according to a fractal—one that's different to their own, not the one they should be following. The fractal dimension or index of each cell turns out to be very specific to the type of cancer involved. At the moment, this kind of technology is restricted to research use. But once it gets into diagnostic labs, it'll hopefully make things easier for a lot of people.

For now, consider the fact that a cancer cell is still a fractal, just not the right kind of fractal. A tree and a parasitic vine both have fractals, just as a healthy cell and a dis-eased cell both have resonances. They're just different. If you want to get your system back 'on station', back to your soul seat resonance, then use your soul seat resonance as a reference. Get your whole system to tune up to that. That's one way to restore health. Another more thorough way is to reboot the original fractal, which is where self-referencing comes in handy.

Another spiritual truism is: *The answers lie within.* That's a consequence of us really being a fractal and therefore being self referencing. Your soul seat resonance is one of those answers. Your fractal is an even more precise answer. When the pattern gets lost or distorted, it needs to get rebooted. For that to happen you need a healthy template to work from, which is always there in an intact part of your pattern. In fact the **only** place you'll find a template is another part of the same pattern, because each fractal is unique. As unique as a snowflake, remember?

No matter how much another pattern wants to help, it can't give you the same clarity as your own, innate fractal. No matter how much others want to help and give you advice, the person who knows you best is you and your soul seat resonance. This is extremely important. It goes straight to the heart of the pattern-based awareness of your right brain. Being aware of your unique pattern (your fractal) or the fractal of a client, tree or ecosystem equates to integrity-based awareness, as the pattern holds the 'map' to your integrity.

Holly was a massage therapist who I was treating for some digestive issues. One day when I was working on her I stopped and asked, 'What's going on with your elbow?' She'd never mentioned a problem to me, but I'd become aware of a distortion of her fractal, centered in that area. She showed me how she could only straighten it halfway. She'd injured it some years before and it had healed like that. 'Why didn't you tell me before?' I asked.

'I didn't think there was anything that could be done,' Holly replied. She had already had work done on her elbow and thought it was as good as it was going to get. Certainly the muscles and ligaments had healed. The elbow was no longer sore, but I could still perceive the damage to her fractal. I took twenty minutes out of her session to reboot her fractal, as it related to her elbow. Then I asked her to straighten her arm. Her eyes nearly fell out of her head as she easily straightened her elbow.

Such healing is only one of the benefits of conscious fractal perception. While this is an extremely advanced skill and difficult to teach in a book, you can take your first steps in that direction. Indeed, you're already practicing this perception on an unconscious level every time you're in nature.

. . . .

Once is a mistake, twice isn't, three times is a pattern

Developing pattern perception

∙∙∙

A couple of exercises follow, to help you start to develop pattern-based and fractal perception:

∙∙∙∙∙∙∙∙∙∙∙∙∙∙∙∙∙∙∙∙∙∙∙∙∙∙∙∙∙∙∙∙∙∙∙∙∙∙∙

RIGHT-BRAINED VIEW 1

For this exercise, you need to get yourself a special kind of broccoli called Romanesco broccoli. Find an unblemished one so you can study its structure, which is a living fractal, that grows according to the Fibonacci sequence. Each floret looks like an entire Romanesco broccoli. (You could also do this with a cauliflower, but it's not as pretty.)

Hold the broccoli and close your eyes. Tear off a piece or two then put it down, and spin it about a couple of times so you don't know which side of the broccoli is damaged.

Then open your eyes and find the damage, the part that no longer matches the rest of the fractal.

How quickly did you find the damaged spot? Compare it to the healthy fractal or undamaged part. Can you rebuild it in your mind?

∙∙∙∙∙∙∙∙∙∙∙∙∙∙∙∙∙∙∙∙∙∙∙∙∙∙∙∙∙∙∙∙∙∙∙∙∙∙∙

You found the broken bit pretty quickly, huh? It's not surprising. Your right brain evolved in nature, a fractal-rich environment. It works by recognizing patterns when they're clear and when they're broken. Both these states communicate a lot of information. When you recognize where a pattern is broken or distorted, it tells you where things have become disconnected from their integrity. That's where healing is required.

Healing is always a return to our integrity. A strengthening of our connection to Who We Truly Are. You can use the areas of the fractal that are clear and strong to guide you towards those things that facilitate the most effective healing.

When you recognize a clear strong pattern, it tells you a lot about the alignment of the integrity of that person or system, how things need to be aligned for them to be in their integrity or to realize their essence in the most robust way possible.

Each fractal is a different context. By working within the alignment of each integrity pattern or fractal, you'll greatly increase your effectiveness in any situation. The key is to learn to live life so you're always aligned to your integrity or fractal pattern. Then everything you do, every thought and feeling, will strengthen that pattern. It's like walking the same path every day. In time, the path gets so well-worn you can see it marked out on the landscape. A pattern with that kind of strength also increases the strength of your connection to Who You Truly Are.

There's a direct link between your fractal and your resonance. Think about a guitar or some other stringed instrument. When you change the length of a string, you change the frequency of the note. That's why a musician's fingers dance up and down the string. When they press on the instrument's string, they stop part of the length vibrating effectively and change its length.

Think about the relationship between length and frequency, then the link between your fractal and your resonance becomes clearer. Every fractal is made up of lots of little lines, bits or dots. If you think of each different line or length as a string that produces a different note, you can see how each different fractal means a different resonance.

That's the same principle on which string theory in physics is based. Each different length of quantum string vibrates at a different rate to produce a different quantum particle. These particles make up atoms. The atoms make up your body and the world around you. Your fractal gives all your vibrating strings an overall design pattern or alignment. That's what right-brained things do.

When you resonate with your soul seat, you're connecting directly to your innate alignment. The only difference between that and your fractal is that your fractal resonance transmits your 'radio station' throughout all time and space, whereas your soul seat resonance only vibrates in the here and now. A fractal is infinite. It has the same reach and holds the same space as the universal hologram. Your soul seat resonance doesn't extend that far. Yet it still holds a direct and very real link to your fractal resonance. Your soul seat holds the pattern of your integrity. You just want to make sure you're working with your soul seat awareness and resonance holographically, because your intuition works holographically.

In other words, your intuition is your key to those divine states we talked about earlier: omnipresence and omniscience. Your intuition speaks to you about yourself and it also tells you about your part in the fate of the entire galaxy. For that to happen, you need to understand a little more about pattern logic.

. . . .

RIGHT-BRAINED VIEW 2

For this exercise, you'll need to get out into nature. It mightn't be easy if you live in the heart of a big city. Parks are great, but they don't have as fractal-rich an environment as in the forest or bush. Wherever you find them, look at the biggest trees and study their fractal. Each tree has a trunk and branches, yet each type has its own fractal. How is one pattern different from other trees? Which trees are the same, because they have the same fractal?

Study the trees to find where their pattern has been broken (broken branches), where it's distorted (the limbs have been pushed into different shapes by the wind) and where it's confused or disrupted by other fractals (lichen vines or parasitic growths). This last can be the hardest to spot.

. . . .

Holograms have a fractal structure
When is a pattern not a fractal?

. . . .

The fractal and the hologram are both infinite. The challenge of this earthly life is its very linear nature. Yet we're supposed to connect to Who We Truly Are, to our holographic and very non-linear self. But that's not as complicated as it may appear. You can use your fractal as a template to do it.

Your fractal shows you how to align all things in your life to Who You Truly Are. In a very real sense, the only difference between Who You Truly Are and who you are today is that right now your fractal is a bit bent, broken and distorted. Who You Truly Are has the exact same fractal, but that fractal is perfect, without any distortions or breaks.

Remember the landscape in the movie *Avatar*? I mentioned earlier how it was built using fractal programming, but the fractals of those ferns and trees were perfect. They were too pristine, compared to the fractals of the trees and ferns we're used to seeing in our everyday lives. That's the same difference between your 'everyday' fractal and the perfect fractal of Who You Truly Are. In the same way, we often experience our lives as something less than perfect, because our everyday fractal isn't perfect.

Yet we don't have to create that perfection. It already exists. We just have to let go of our imperfections and live with the alignment of our perfected fractal. Every time you invalidate yourself, you bend your fractal a little further. Every time you acknowledge yourself or flow love to yourself, you help heal your fractal a little more. The more you allow yourself to be, do and have those things that res-onate with your soul seat, the stronger and clearer your fractal will become. That leads to increasing life-satisfaction.

Living according to your fractal alignment means all things are inherently 'as above, so below'. You live naturally, with an alignment that leads you to the realization of Who You Truly Are. The more you live according to the alignment of your fractal, the more you'll experience your fractal pattern (the pattern of your essence and consciousness) running through your life.

Not all patterns in your life are fractal ones. People have combined different modalities, like massage with aromatherapy, nutrition with allopathic drugs, physiotherapy with surgery or kinesiology with acupuncture, in the belief that they will give holographic results. There's no doubt that combining different therapies increases the range of any therapy, but a bigger finite range is still a long way from infinity. There's always another chance for growth and expansion.

Making patterns bigger or repeating them isn't enough to make a fractal. Remember, a fractal is made of smaller versions of itself, while a linear pattern isn't. As the rhyme *Siphonaptera* by mathematician Augustus De Morgan says:

Big fleas have little fleas upon their backs to bite 'em,
And little fleas have lesser fleas, and so ad infinitum.

It's the 'ad infinitum' you need for a fractal. Repetition of the same shape **at all levels of the pattern**. That's what creates the non-linear properties. You feel the depth of that pattern when you know what you're doing has a larger significance, such as when you meet someone in a way that has the possibility of changing many lives.

You can find many patterns made up of repetitions of the one shape, but when you magnify the pattern you don't see more detail if it's not made up of smaller versions of itself. The Egyptian flower of life is like that. On the surface it appears as if it could be a fractal, but a closer investigation reveals that it isn't. We're all holographic, as our universe is holographic. We're non-linear. So we need to learn to operate or think consciously in a non-linear, fractal way, if we're to realize our full potential.

A self-fulfilling prophecy is one way we operate in a non-linear way. Self-fulfilling prophecies are events that are created because they were predicted. They can be as simple as arguing with a friend, because you've convinced yourself they're mad at you and so you say things that bring an argument about. Or as big as changes in our world that happen due to most people's expectations. These expectations can be limiting or freeing, so they can create problems or opportunities.

Take Jake for instance. On the morning of his session he rang to tell me he couldn't come in, because he'd tried to be too much of a hero the day before. When they'd locked up the shop the keys had been left inside, so he'd vaulted over the fence to get in through the back door. He'd saved the day at the cost of a completely dislocated shoulder. He'd had to go to hospital to have the joint put back in. Now he had only about 5 percent movement in his arm and was in a lot of pain. I told him to come in if he could manage it, which he did. The damage to his joint was obvious, as was the damage to his fractal. His shoulder was very inflamed. The joint was strapped.

When I focused on his fractal, there was a large tear matching the tear to the tissues through his shoulder. Such a tear would make it hard for his system to heal and rebuild the joint according to his pattern. If it healed according to the linear pattern of the tear, it would never work the same again. That was his initial expectation. He urgently needed his fractal rebooted, to avoid any long-term damage.

Resonating someone's fractal powerfully enough 'reminds' their system of its inherent alignment. It enables our true alignment to re-establish itself. That's the primary thing involved with rebooting someone's fractal. It's what I did for Jake after I'd cleared the energy of shock and pain from his injury. By the end of the session, he had nearly 80 percent of his normal range of movement back. He returned next day for another session. As much of the pain had subsided, his system was able to increase its alignment to his fractal even further with my resonant support. That got his movement back to 95 percent. Instead of taking months for him to heal, it took days. That's the power of operating non-linearly.

I could've worked physically on his shoulder 'gently' as a chiropractor, but that would've been linear work. The hospital gave him painkillers and anti-inflammatories—another example of linear work. Linear work has the ability to assist on one level, but only fractal non-linear work has the capacity to assist on **all** levels. That's particularly important if you're dealing with issues that are deep-seated, like family or inter-generational challenges, or those that are so deep-seated in a person's EM field they must have their source in a past or parallel life.

The universe extends in all directions, as does your fractal pattern. The universe has existed, does exist and will continue to exist in different time periods than the one we're now experiencing. Your fractal pattern also exists in different time periods. String theory tells us there are other universes parallel to our own—similar in many ways, but different in others. Your fractal exists there too. The state of your fractal in those other times and places can make it harder or easier for you to realize a life in perfect alignment to your fractal in **this** life. It's all the same fractal. Everywhere your fractal exists, your resonance exists. The state of that resonance makes your 'radio station' signal more or less coherent. Stronger or weaker. It makes it easier or harder for you to become Who You Truly Are.

When working with such large issues the fractal is a tremendous help, as it allows us to connect to a much larger part of our universe. The fractal is not just a template of our integrity and health. It's also a map of our holographic universe. Just like a map of any city helps you get around those streets, the holographic or fractal map of our universe helps you navigate in consciousness around all the different levels, times, universes and other parts which make up our universe. This is one of the keys to the tremendous insight and problem-solving power of your intuition.

. . . .

How to navigate round creation
The holographic map

. . . .

As a fractal, our holographic universe contains an infinite amount of information, with infinite detail in infinite spaces. We call all these different spaces by different names: dimension, universe, parallel universe, multiverse, time, galaxy, planet, lifetime, quantum level, energetic levels, genetic levels, atomic, subatomic, and so on. For your left brain, it's too much to think about all at once. This is a problem, because Who You Truly Are is holographic. If spiritual reality is real and you exist throughout all times and places, or in at least a number of times and places, how are you going to know Who You Truly Are if all the 'you' you know is the 'you' that's here?

In other lifetimes, you'll be a different 'you'. That difference gets greater, the further from this present moment you travel in your awareness. This was the whole idea behind the movie *Sliding Doors*, where one woman's life was profoundly changed by small differences in timing. We witnessed how tiny differences expand to create big changes in where she ended up, as the story shifted from one parallel universe to another. Think about some of the small moments that have had a big effect on your life; like when you met that particular friend or solved a problem or had an unexpected experience.

When my niece turned eighteen, I took her on a whitewater rafting and camping trip. Partway down the river, our raft capsized in the middle of rapids. It was a bit hairy scary for a few moments but we were fine. Yet that moment of looking over the abyss into possible death changed the course of my niece's life. She realized life was for living. She now says it's more important to have experiences than a job. That happened only a couple of years ago, but my niece has deferred finishing her degree to get her black belt in taekwondo, work and travel. This is a sign of the realization she had on the river. Who knows where such an adventurous attitude to life will take her?

Imagine how your life would be different if you'd made such a choice early on in your life. How would your life be different now? Where would the courage to have an adventurous life have taken you? In a fractal or holographic sense, you are living that life. Perhaps not in this universe, but it's there in a different or parallel universe. As your intuition grows stronger, you can learn to tune into the energy of that life. You can bring that energy into this life, to create some of those positive, expansionary experiences for you here and now.

The more things change, the greater will be the difference between your current life and your parallel life. What if you lived in a parallel universe where the asteroid had never arrived to wipe out the dinosaurs and they eventually evolved sentience? How would 'dinosaur you' still be you? Or what if you lived on some other world, where they had more than two sexes? Or a species that bred through parthenogenesis, a form of natural cloning? What if you were in a different dimension? There's no way you'd have a three-dimensional body. So how do you get to be you, if you're 2D and completely flat or if your body extends in more directions than 3D?

How about if your awareness was limited to the quantum level, as it would be if you were just a subatomic particle? How would you experience life then? Or you operated on the level of an entire planet or galaxy? A holographic reality makes a mockery of any kind of right-wrong thinking, because there's so many different versions of you. Learning to work with differences, to use pattern-based and integrity-based logic rather than right-wrong linear logic, is essential in the hologram. There's an infinite variety of possibilities throughout the multiverse. You exist in infinite variation in all the different reaches of the hologram.

On the surface, the current version of you and the dinosaur version of you don't have anything in common. In the same way, the current you and the version of you that existed thousands of years ago in a past life won't have much in common. Yet go deeper and that changes.

When you look at a tree branch, it looks very different to a leaf. Yet they're both simply different expressions of the same pattern. Both are part of that same pattern. In the same way, all the different versions of you have the same resonance in their soul seat. All the versions of you are connected through the same fractal. Your fractal is as omnipresent as your consciousness. It exists throughout the hologram. Knowing that can help you make the most of each lifetime, so you get maximum benefit in **this** lifetime in fulfilling all of your potential. Think of the pattern of your life as like a jigsaw puzzle. The left-brain facts are like individual pieces. If you jam the pieces together any old how that won't make a clear picture. If it's going to work, you need to know how they fit together and form a pattern. That is what your pattern logic does for you.

Anna's family came from Germany originally, which gave her a dedication to her work that had taken her far in her career. But by the time she came to see me she was feeling worn down. She was so serious about everything she never allowed herself to lighten up, take time off and recharge. That's another form of imbalance. I asked her how she felt about letting herself have a bit of fun. 'I don't know how,' she said.

I drew on the power of one of her parallel lives to help her realize how. I asked, 'What would have had to change in your background, for you to know how?' She said there was a time when her parents could've joined the hippy movement, but didn't. So I asked her to tune into that life, to find the version of herself she would've been if her parents had gone through with that potential change. She was startled by how strong a sense of fun came through. That's because it wasn't just random fun—it was Anna-type fun. In that parallel version of her, fun was central to her life and it matched the same Anna-pattern. So the fun that was part of the parallel version of Anna naturally suited her in this lifetime.

Oneness is not the same as conformity. Oneness is having the same alignment as your own pattern and makes each part of your fractal help expand you in the here and now. All the different expressions of you in all those different parts and levels of existence need to align to your one fractal pattern. This is what gives coherence and cohesion to your existence. It's what connects all those different parts and versions of you. All of these different existences of your consciousness, all the different expressions of your EM field, have one thing in common. They all have the same fractal pattern. They all hold the same resonance as your soul seat.

If you believe you're nothing more than your body, then when it eventually stops functioning you believe you'll also stop. On the other hand, if you learn to recognize your resonance as Who You Truly Are, you'll know your existence will continue. You don't stop simply because one expression of that resonance stops. Your resonance continues. With a clear awareness of your resonance, you can make the spiritual journey in confidence. With that as your foundation, you'll realize Oneness with the whole of creation.

Oneness isn't something you're ever going to manage if you operate from a linear, left-brained or right-wrong perspective. Your left brain will be overwhelmed by all the data and won't allow you to connect to those things you assess as 'wrong'. On the other hand, when you operate from a pattern-based or integrity-based perspective, you can focus on the pattern of your integrity. That gives you a template to align your connection to all that is, as well as increase your connection to Who You Truly Are.

Remember that our left-brain world is confined to the finite reaches of what we observe, while our right-brain, spiritual or intuitive world is one of infinite reach and grandeur. It's so vast that our three-dimensional brains can't hope to comprehend it, but we **can** comprehend its intrinsic pattern that's the same on all levels. So while you may seem different in different parts of the hologram, there's more to your story. Your cells may look different to your arms and legs. Your atoms may look different to your cells. There's a pretty good chance you won't look the same in your other lifetimes, whether in parallel universes or this one. However in all the reaches of the hologram, your fractal remains the same.

Each different life and each different look is simply a different expression of your fractal. Remember that each snowflake is a different expression of a six-pointed fractal. The better you get at being able to 'get a grip' on the amplitude and frequency of each resonance, the more you'll be able to read the energy of each point of the hologram. This is important, as it holds the key to understanding the hologram. It enables you to 'translate' between your left and right brains. The fractal is a literal map of the hologram. Each resonance gives you the details of that map, such as where you are in the hologram and what's required to apply the five principles in the context of where you are.

Josephine is a skilled kinesiologist, who uses her skills to complete past-life issues. She rang me one day for advice, as she was having difficulty helping a client resolve a situation with her father. Her client, Jessy, reported a number of different incidents involving her father which all tested 'true'; yet when asked when they'd happened, Jessy said 'now' for each one, which also tested 'true'. They were all happening now, even the one that involved a horse and carriage! Josephine was understandably confused.

I had a quick look at Jessy's fractal, knowing parallel universes can be quite different from our own (with their own time line or part of the time-net). I suggested that Josephine ask Jessy, 'How many universes are you operating in at present?' The answer was, of course, the same number as the incidents she was working to resolve. With a clear understanding of the part of the hologram she was working with, Josephine was able to help Jessy to a positive resolution. That's what your right brain can do. Connect to the **whole** of the fractal or find the part of the pattern that's relevant to the issue at hand.

As the fractal is your holographic map, it gives you the ability to work anywhere in the hologram. Using the fractal map with accuracy and precision is a highly-advanced skill, requiring mastery on many levels: holding a holographic space; perceiving the patterns and structures present on every level; and sorting those into linear and fractal patterns at the same time. By grasping this concept, you're opening a door in your mind to a more expansive experience of life with deeper significance—a way to understand how Oneness changes the alignment and effectiveness of your own life.

What you've learned is how to resonate your own soul seat resonance, which in turn enables you to tune yourself and create more coherence in your energy. Resonating your soul seat also increases your personal power and integrity. Whatever increases your soul seat resonance increases your integrity, as well as strengthening your fractal and understanding what doesn't do so. The good news is that your fractal resonance strengthens your integrity on all levels of your existence—everywhere throughout the hologram at once. That's why holding a holographic or infinite space is essential. It enables you to heal in all times and places. A fractal resonance is holographic. Without the ability to hold a holographic space, not just a really big one, the characteristic fractal vibration won't occur.

The truth is that being able to heal everywhere at once is part of your true nature. You can do it already. In fact you've probably done it in those moments when extreme circumstances enabled you to do extraordinary things. Like grannies lifting the car off a toddler. The difference between what you can do now and what you can do with a conscious fractal perception is the ability to do more amazing things more consistently. Shifting your space or your EM field from the here and now (or from a linear space to a holographic space) is simple, but not easy. It's an extension of the space push-ups exercise you did.

In order to do this next exercise, let's get clear about what infinity is—clear enough so that you can focus on an infinite space. Here is a simple method. Many require guidance and support the first few times they do this exercise, in order to do it successfully. But persevere. This is truly a leap into the infinite.

. . . .

FROM LINEAR TO HOLOGRAPHIC SPACE

- Focus on your space.
- Focus on what it is to be infinite.
- Intend for your space to be infinite.

Yes, I know it seems too simple, but your consciousness is already infinite. You're just helping your mind to catch up.

. . . .

The first time you do shift your space to a holographic one, you may feel very ungrounded. It's such an 'out there' experience that it's hard to stay 'down here'. It's not unusual for you to lose holographic space as soon as you attempt to move your body. It takes considerable practice to hold a holographic space and do anything at the same time. But it's worth putting in the practice, as you'll be fully connected to the hologram and then be able to do things anywhere within the hologram.

You can go into your past and change your personal history. You can learn from your future self, to make your path in life easier. You can work directly on our collective consciousness or the planet itself, to assist with the challenges of our times—at least on an energetic level. With this kind of capacity, your ability to create is going to grow. So you're going to want to make sure what you're creating is truly positive.

. . . .

Step Eight

In the first triangle, you created a solid intuitive foundation from completing your cycles, understanding your own intuitive process, keeping yourself balanced and knowing your own resonance. In the second triangle, you built the strength and capacity of your intuition through increasing the volume and coherence of your resonance. You also learned to work with both frequency and amplitude and to apply all you've learned with confidence and certainty to the process of transformation.

Now in the third and final triangle, you're making progress towards true intuitive mastery. You now have an understanding of pattern-based logic and how it applies to the hologram of the creation in which we live. Your capacity to maintain and strengthen your own integrity is greater than ever.

In Step Eight, you'll learn how to extend this in two ways. Firstly, you'll learn how to increase your capacity for the positive. You need to know how to work with ever-increasing levels of positive energy while maintaining your own resonance, so you can reach your true potential. Secondly, you'll learn how to use your growing awareness to maintain and strengthen the integrity of others. This is a powerful key to true interdependency. It means you'll be able to create positive energy for others as well as yourself. It also gives you another means of increasing your own awareness and your capacity to co-create.

• •

The universe is entangled
Breaking the light barrier

. . . .

Have you ever had your intuition speak clearly to you? Whether it's a conscious and consistent skill or not, you have already used your intuition. Everyone does, but for most it's a haphazard process. When your gut speaks to you then you remember, whether you listen to it or not. It might've been that time you had a feeling you were meant to be somewhere out of the ordinary, so you went through with your feeling and met your partner. Or the time you were hunting for collectibles and pulled up to a certain garage sale, where you found a personal treasure. Or the time you just had to call someone and it was just as well you did. Your left brain can't understand such things, yet they happen more frequently than you realize.

Intuition saves and transforms lives. It's evidence of how we all sense more of the EM field than our physical senses allow. It's also evidence that we're truly One. Each of us has a divine and resonant nature, in which we're One with all things.

In physics, the evidence for Oneness comes through quantum entanglement. That's when pairs or groups of particles become One. So the state of one in a pair or group is simultaneously translated to the others (so the sum total of all their states remains the same). If one of a pair or group changes anything like position, momentum, spin or polarization, the others immediately shift so the original value is maintained. Particles are connected, no matter how far apart they are.

Mind you, the distances involved in these experiments weren't great until recently. In June 2017, the Chinese used a laser on a satellite to produce entangled photons, then sent them both 1200 kilometers apart. The use of coherent light meant the distance at which quantum entanglement was occurring was ten times further than the previous record. Before then, they'd used optic fiber and the resulting interference distorted the resonance too much for entanglement to hold for any real distance.

Intuition is part of what we experience because the whole uni-verse is entangled. We're all One. It can be a powerful experience in your life, benefiting those you love, your career, your creativity and anything else. It supports you in creating what you want. But did you really create it?

Did you really create that?

Think about something you've created in your life: your home, your car, a wonderful meal or, classically, that perfect parking space. Did you really create that?

This planet's not an easy one to be on; all too often we feel alone and unsupported. Yet think about that perfect park for a moment. You could only manifest that park with the support of others. You needed the cooperation of the person who'd parked there before you, as well as all those who decided to park elsewhere. And more. What about the people who made the road? Created the pavement? The shop or office building you wanted to visit? For that matter, what about those who made your car? Who dug up the iron to make the steel? Manufactured the rubber, leather and glass? Processed the pet-rochemicals to make the diesel, gas or petrol your car runs off? Or those who work the power station to recharge your car if it's electric? There's a whole host of people, a veritable army, who co-created that one little satisfying moment with you.

Everything in your life is a co-creation. You're co-creating your life with a whole army of people. Whether you're conscious of their input or not, they're all there supporting you. And that's just on the human level. In a very real sense, you're co-creating your physical wellbeing with all the thousands of bacteria your body contains.

Every consciousness that touches any of your manifestations at any point has an influence on the end result. So your alignment to your intention needs to allow for the intentions of other people. Think of driving. Your intention is to get to your destination on time. The way you get there, how easily you move through the traffic and possibly even the route you take, is influenced by other drivers. If you align your energies to allow for their influence, for the alignment of the world around you, you'll create ever so much more easily.

Just as other people's creations impact on yours, your alignment impacts on the creations of others. You are consciously or unconsciously participating in the manifestations of others. Always. With those you know personally. this is easy to understand. But your EM field is much wider than that. What you do in this highly-interconnected, entangled world touches people you may never meet. Indeed in a holographic world, you can co-create with all things through your EM field. With the universe itself. You could say you're entangled with the universe.

Just as you need to choose **what** you want to create, it's important to choose **how** you co-create. Co-creation is an exchange. It's in the nature of that exchange that the quality of your co-creation is determined.

. . . .

Three types of exchange
It's all in the exchange
· ·

All of your relationships, all your co-creations, are based on exchange. An exchange means you get something in return for something given. You do it all the time. Every time you breathe, you're exchanging carbon dioxide for oxygen. If that exchange is too uneven you're at risk of passing out or suffocating, because your breath needs to be balanced. Remember 'balance' is how we sum up health. There are exchanges of energy, services and money. It might look like helping out a friend, taking time to show a stranger the way, listening or simply smiling. If we look at the energy in each exchange, we can divide all exchanges into three basic types; in every transaction we're either out of exchange, in exchange or have a mutually expansive exchange.

Put more energy in than you get out and you'll be drained. That's called being 'out of exchange' and it is the mark of a co-dependent relationship. It's unfortunate, but in co-dependency everyone feels they're always giving more than they get, which is why they're resentful all the time. Being out of exchange sucks. It makes every step you take harder than the last, because there's less energy than before. If you're experiencing pain and struggle, you're involved with this type of exchange at some point. Changing that helps you move into independency.

As we get to know ourselves better, we understand more of what we want. We gain new levels of self-respect and no longer agree to bad deals. We refuse to be out of exchange, regardless of whether the exchange is spiritual, mental, emotional, physical or even financial. We learn how to win for ourselves, at least a little bit. So we get more in our exchanges, enough so that we're now getting fair value. When you're out of exchange, it feels like one step forward, two steps back. That changes once you get a fair exchange. When you're no longer being drained, you make better headway. Being in exchange helps you maintain yourself and your life, though you still need to find more energy for each step upwards.

Things only get easier and more enjoyable once you master the art of mutually expansive exchanges. This is the essence of interdependency. Such exchange benefits all concerned. It supports each person becoming more of Who They Truly Are. This is true co-creation. In interdependent relationships, everyone receives what they need or want for the next step in their path. Energy increases for everyone involved, making mutually expansive exchanges the key to a life of ease and grace. With each step, there's more energy than before. True co-creation has its challenges and is essential for growing through joy and inspiration.

The universe is always and only interdependent. Mutual expansion is the only type of exchange it uses. At the heart of each galaxy there's a big black hole, which gives gravitational shape and form to all the dust and particles spewed out by white holes. The exchange between these two is what creates all the variation and life within each galaxy. Perhaps mutual expansion is why the universe is getting bigger at an increasing rate?

If we're to take our place in the hologram, then learning how to co-create with the universe is essential. This means learning how to work with mutually expansive exchange. The more we co-create and the more mutually expansive exchanges we have, the more energy and abundance we end up with. It might sound odd, but that creates a problem. Especially if you don't know how to handle abundance.

. . . .

Getting used to the good stuff
Stepping towards expansion

Unfortunately, we live on a planet where the vast majority of people are co-dependent. They're out of exchange most of the time and cranky as a consequence. Most of our societies are constructed along co-dependent lines; from our education system to our legal system, from mainstream medicine to religion. Most social constructs are essentially dominator/control hierarchies, where someone else gets to tell you what to do. Indeed, the challenge and opportunity of our times comes from the efforts the collective consciousness is making towards transforming from co-dependency to interdependency.

Think back to when you left a co-dependent relationship, or watched a friend do it. Remember all the drama? Like all drama, there's one driving force behind it. It starts when someone's feeling way too drained to carry on. Instinctively, all they want at that point is to get more energy. That's the unconscious purpose of all that drama—to get energy from someone else. And of course, you end up drained, looking for more energy yourself. That's the basis of the whole co-dependent relationship.

No one likes being drained. But what do we do instead? When all we know is co-dependency, when we've practiced it for years without thinking about it, the only options appear to be with others in co-dependency or to be by ourselves. For most of us, interdependency is out of our experience.

So how are we going to learn something we've never known? Something that's possibly even out of our reality? Learning to do something we don't even recognize may appear tough to the point of impossibility. As with anything else in life, we draw on our experiences to help us create. Without experience of them, creating interdependent relationships is difficult to impossible.

While people aren't reliably interdependent, fortunately the universe is. The universe operates interdependently, always and only.

Knowing that gives us what we need: a means to practice mutually expansive exchange. With practice, you will learn to recognize mutual expansion and interdependent people.

The first part of growth is releasing the negative, so fear and pain no longer control you. The second and much more fun part is all about receiving the positive. That's when you build your capacity for joy and happiness, love and health, abundance and inspiration, and all the wonderful things that Who You Truly Are is capable of co-creating. Practicing mutual expansion also helps you increase your capacity for the positive.

You'd think it'd be easy to receive the good stuff, but if it's unfamiliar, it's easy to feel overwhelmed. Having more energy coursing through your system than you're used to can feel intense. Yet it's the only way to gain the abundance in life you want and deserve. This exercise helps you increase your capacity for the positive. It's a simple extension of an earlier exercise. By taking it to this next level, you consciously expand your energy.

. . . .

EXPANDING THE LOVE AND SUPPORT
FROM UNIVERSE 1

- Focus on the love and support flowing to you from the universe in this and every moment.
- Allow it in. You don't have to do anything to get this energy, you just have to stop blocking it. Just relax and let it flow in.
- When you feel the love and support, flow appreciation for it back to the universe.

When you flow appreciation back to the universe, what happens to the love and support flowing to you?

. . . .

I've done this exercise with hundreds of people, both individually and in groups. Everyone has felt the love and support flowing to them increase in some way, once they flow back appreciation. For some it feels like the flow widens out, so they receive it throughout their system—in their belly, eyes and throat. Others feel themselves lighten, as the love and support flows more easily with less resistance. Still others feel the intensity increase, as the flow grows stronger. It doesn't matter how you feel the love and support increase. That's between you, the universe and your own neurology.

What's important is that the love and support does increase, in response to the appreciation you flow back to the universe. That's one round of a mutually expansive exchange. Now all you have to do is more rounds. Lots more rounds. Keep increasing the flow more and more, until you reach your capacity for that day.

It's just like any exercise, so you'll want to pace yourself. The first few times you do this, it's enough to simply get used to all the love and support flowing into your system. For many people, simply expanding their energy a little bit is enough to start with. It's especially important if your energy channels haven't been exercised much, so they're the width of a straw. You can't have a fire hydrant's worth of energy pouring through you without the channels to cope with it. That could short circuit your system; then you'll need more than psychic first aid!

. . . .

EXPANDING THE LOVE AND SUPPORT FROM UNIVERSE 2

- Focus on the love and support flowing to you from the universe, in this and every moment.

- Allow it in. Stop blocking it out. Just relax and let it flow in.

- Flow appreciation for the love and support back to the universe.

- When you feel the love and support flowing to you increase, flow appreciation back to the universe for this increase. You will then notice it increase again.

- Keep doing this, allowing in the increasing love and support and flowing back increasing appreciation, until you reach your capacity for that moment.

. . . .

The challenge of the positive gain side of growth or healing is how to keep yourself balanced and integrated, while expanding the energy in your system. Developing your intuition isn't like being in college. You can't forget what you learned in first year when you go into the next. You'll use every skill in *The Soul's Brain* for as long as you're using your intuition—for the rest of your life—as you continue to explore and express the ongoing expansion of the expression of your unique fractal pattern.

Fractology can often look complex but it isn't. It's just that there are fifty or sixty simple things going on at once because a Fractology practitioner is using the Power Pentagon Principles holographically. These principles, together with all you're learning in *The Soul's Brain*, keep you growing in grace and ease. In other words, they help to keep your energy balanced. Tuning yourself to your soul seat gives you stability and lets you expand even more.

If you accept the energy as it increases, no matter how intense it gets, you'll give yourself the opportunity to expand further. Yes, it can feel overwhelming at first, until you do the third part of the exercise.

. . . .

EXPANDING THE LOVE AND SUPPORT
FROM UNIVERSE 3

- Allow in the love and support flowing to you from the universe, in this and every moment.

- Flow appreciation for the love and support back to the universe.

- Feel the love and support flowing to you increase, then flow back more appreciation to the universe for this increase. Then it will increase again. Keep doing this, until you reach your capacity.

- Now focus on your soul seat resonance. Set your intention that all the extra energy in your space will tune itself up to your resonance.

. . . .

We get overwhelmed by a whole lot of new positive energy, because it isn't at our resonance. It's 'off station'. This isn't some dark plot. It's just that the wonderfully positive energy is at universal resonance, rather than your own. You have your own fractal. The universe has a different fractal. That means the universe's resonance is different to yours. And as it has a powerful signal it feels overwhelming, even though it's positive.

Tune up the new energy to your own resonance and it'll feel great. Then the energy will integrate into your system. As the ease and grace of mutual expansion becomes more familiar, your system will learn to automatically retune new energy to your own resonance, as it comes into your space.

This is a simple exercise but it's pivotal. It'll ground your reality into an interdependent one. It'll teach you how to create mutually expansive exchanges and create ever-increasing levels of energy for yourself. It's key to growing with ease and grace. It's love in action. When you love someone you want to see them flourish. Mutual expansion gives you the means to flourish in such a way that you assist others to flourish too. You can do this with the universe. And you can do it with other people, once you learn what their resonance is.

Operating optimally
Love is easy

. . . .

When clients and students first experience mutually expansive exchange, their response is usually along the lines of 'that's too easy'. They're used to working hard to get energy or anything else, like panning for tiny specks of gold or knitting Tom Baker's scarf, one stitch at a time.

Love and respect complement one another. Certainly we have to work to gain respect because it's a yang thing, based on what we do. We earn respect through the value we create by our doingness. If you don't have to earn respect, we believe it's charity, not respect. Love, on the other hand, is a yin thing. It's based on our beingness. It's the value you have simply because you are. The very nature of your essence decrees it. Your value is beyond price, for your soul is unique. If you have to earn love, it's a negotiation or manipulation—not love.

That's why it's important for you to **not to do anything** about the love flowing to you from the universe. If you do anything other than allow it in, even try to draw it in, it won't be love. All you have to do is relax, which of course is why it's so easy.

Love is like spiritual manure. You want to spread it around to make things grow. Love is our desire for something to flourish. It's the juice of creation. Look at your life. What flourishes in your space? Whatever it is you love it, whether you're conscious of that or not.

Self-love means supporting your own flourishing. Empowering your energy through mutual expansion with the universe is a great way to support yourself to flourish, especially when you tune up all that new energy to your own resonance. In the same way, expressing love to others means supporting them to flourish, to be in their resonance and integrity. That's what you're doing when you flow appreciation to anyone, including the universe. Appreciation is a rich form of acknowledgment and validation. By flowing appreciation or acceptance to others, you assist them to strengthen their connection to their integrity, to Who They Truly Are. Appreciation is an expression of love.

Even more powerful than appreciation is supporting someone's resonance. Of course, the first step here is awareness. Just as your soul seat shows you your resonance, someone else's soul seat can show you their resonance. The clearer your resonance is, the easier this process becomes. It's the difference between driving with a clean or muddy windscreen. If your resonance has a lot of noise, getting a clear focus is difficult. The clearer your energy becomes, the more mud you scrape off and the easier it is to see. If you're finding it a challenge to tune yourself up, I suggest you leave the next exercise until you find it easier. And one more thing … remember that the more disturbed your soul seat is, the deeper you have to focus to connect to the clear, calm space.

When you focus on someone else's soul seat, it's easier if it's bright, clear and shiny. Unfortunately, that only happens if they've done a lot of work on themselves. Most of the time, you have to go very deep to get past the accumulated disturbances from years of compromise and being out of integrity. Regardless of where the other person is in their relationship with themselves, you can use this next exercise to assist them.

All we can ever truly do for another Being is make it harder or easier for them to make a particular choice. We can't make choices for them. Only they can do that. But we can make it as easy as possible for them to choose to be in their integrity, and as hard as possible for them to be out of it.

. . . .

OTHER SOUL SEAT AWARENESS

- Focus on the soul seat of the other, with the intention to connect to the clear, calm space deep inside. Connect to it, regardless of how deep you need to go.

- Once there, focus on the resonance in that space. Connect to it in the same way you connect to yours, as a vibration or feeling.

- It'll be a different resonance. Do your best to lock in their frequency and amplitude for the clearest resonance.

- Once tuned to their resonance, you can perceive what supports their resonance.

- When you've finished, perform a soul seat attunement on yourself, to ensure you don't keep their resonance in your space.

· ·

We make it easier for others to be in their integrity by shining the light of clarity on the consequences of their choices, especially on the personal connection or disconnection that they're creating for themselves. The way I put this to my students and clients is: *The job is to remember Who Others Truly Are until they begin to remember for themselves.*

Interdependency is a process of mutual expansion, so if you want to operate interdependently that's what your job is as well. Supporting someone else's integrity or soul seat resonance isn't just an act of love for the other, it's also an act of self-love. It helps the other person flourish, so it's easy to understand how it's an act of love for the other. But why self-love?

Have you ever had to push and push to make something happen? To use every ounce of your will and energy to force a reluctant creation through to manifestation, especially when working with others? It's exhausting. That's the trouble with putting pressure on other people's integrity, even if they're not conscious of it. Whenever anyone steps out of their integrity, they step into soul pain. You've been using your awareness of your own soul pain to develop your soul seat compass. Soul pain lies in the direction you don't want to go, while soul ease lies in the direction of your integrity.

Even if integrity is out of someone's awareness, they don't like being out of exchange. It makes them resentful. There's nothing big enough to compensate any of us for losing even the tiniest piece of ourselves. If you're not aware of other people's integrity or resonance, you're constantly running the risk of pushing them out of exchange. That builds resistance over time, forcing you to push harder and harder to get any results. It's a bit like dragging one of those enormous blocks of stone to build a pyramid. Every foot takes more and more effort, as the stone digs deeper into the sand.

If you ignore other people's resonances or integrities, you'll dig yourself deeper into their resistances. But you can avoid that, just as you can pour water on sand. That's a trick the ancient Egyptians used. Pyramid stones weigh between 2½–15 tons and there are millions of them. Each stone was dragged through the sand on a simple sled, just a couple of upturned running boards. When Egyptologists first saw the wall painting above, they thought the libations being poured in front of the statue were purely ceremonial. That's what happens when you separate the right and left brain. You expect the spiritual to have no practical purpose, and the practical not to be spiritual.

Many societies in ancient times understood that practicality and spirituality are complementary. In the same way, your left brain complements your right brain and vice versa. That accounts for sayings like: *Cleanliness is next to godliness.* Both hygiene and spirituality aid wellbeing. The Egyptians were pouring libations, but they also knew that pouring the right amount of water on the sand almost halved the resistance. This was recently confirmed by a physics study at the University of Amsterdam. If you've ever walked on the beach you know this yourself; walking on damp sand is easier than walking on the dry stuff.

Over the years, I've had many discussions with executives and other corporate types who believe that spiritual beliefs have no practical value, because they operate the left brain without the right brain. Yet these same people are often highly stressed from having to constantly force their projects along. When they learn awareness of other people's resonance and how to work with it, much of the resistance they were struggling with disappears. Whether for spiritual or practical reasons, being aware of another's integrity works for all of us. It makes things easier, just as it did for the Egyptians.

'Balance' sums up health. The word to sum up exchange is 'optimization'. When we work optimally, we don't create resistance on our path. We create ease and grace through mutually expansive exchange. Soul seat resonance is a significant tool for awareness of your own path and integrity, as well as the integrity of others. It makes mutual expansion much easier to create. It decreases the cost of or resistance to anything we want to co-create. And it also increases the benefit of anything we want to co-create, by making the growth in our personal learning and awareness much easier.

. . . .

You're either with us or against us— or off doing your own thing
Through the looking glass

. . . .

The opposite of mutual expansion is domination and control. In the past, these have been winning strategies. Most of the royal and noble houses began with robber barons and warlords. The whole colonial era was based on domination. War was a way of enforcing control. Over the last couple of centuries, there have been various efforts to move towards cooperation. It's working to some degree. Certainly statistics show that there are now more people at peace than ever before, despite what you hear in the media. However, the problem remains. Domination has worked for such a long time many people can't see it changing. But domination only works in one-valley worlds.

Back in the days of robber barons and warlords, being the biggest, scariest, toughest guy across a few miles of territory got you a good life. But when more and more valleys get connected, that strategy falls apart. Take cane toads. They're a scourge on the Australian landscape. Introduced from Hawaii to control a native cane beetle, they preferred to dominate the entire landscape. One female can lay tens of thousands of eggs, and they can grow to the size of a small dog, eating frogs, pet food and small mammals.

Control measures like barrier fences and capturing adults hasn't stopped cane toads marching across Australia. Their aggression has changed the environment. Without a change in viewpoint, their domination would no doubt continue. Their aggression doesn't stop at other species but also includes their own. Tadpoles are drawn to the pheromones given off by the eggs of other cane toads. They are their favorite feast. From an aggressive, domination point of view, eating other cane toad eggs makes sense. It cuts down on competition for food. It ensures their genes dominate the area. Without outside intervention, without interdependent connections, it's a strategy that works.

Looking at wider patterns has enabled scientists to find a way to control them. Significantly, it's through turning the toad's own aggression. Baits are loaded with cane toad toxin to lure tadpoles into traps by their thousands. This will hopefully be enough to disrupt the cane toad lifecycle, returning a healthy balance to the environment.

Whenever we force a result without taking into account the resonance and integrity of others, we're using domination and control. We're behaving like cane toads. In energetic terms, this involves projecting our own resonance strongly enough to disrupt other people's 'radio stations'. In time, every time, there'll be pushback. For mutual expansion, we need to be aware of the resonance of others. To avoid resistance and make things easier for ourselves, we have to take our first step towards conscious co-creation.

Personal context

Each of us is a different aspect of the divine. We each have a different fractal pattern to our consciousness, which gives us our unique resonance. When we walk our true paths, our resonances get stronger. That's great but it's also tricky, because everyone has a different resonance. That's why conformity never works. You can't squash everyone into the same box or onto the same 'radio station'. Yet that's what right-wrong thinking attempts to do. How do we learn to operate so we don't create resistance? How do we operate so **everyone** gets to be in their integrity, even though that integrity is different for every person?

This is where thinking of each fractal, each resonance, as a different context is helpful. A context aligns our thoughts, actions and energy. There's a bay window in my clinic. I like to look out one of its side windows on Catherine Street (yes, I know) and see the long row of beautiful trees lining the street. If I look through the middle window instead, I see the crenelations of the old building across the street. The other side window looks out on a narrow brick and cement laneway that runs between our two buildings. There are three completely different views from the same window, because each side holds a different alignment.

In the same way, when we connect to a different fractal, a different resonance, it gives us a different alignment. We all learn from alignments or contexts different from our own, just as we see more by looking out different windows. Each of us embodies a different context of the infinite hologram. Our energies flow through co-creation with different alignments. Each of us can learn and grow through experiencing the alignments of others. Connecting with others is a challenge and an opportunity.

Each of our different resonances is strengthened or weakened by different things. We risk losing our own signals when we connect with others' resonances, resulting in a loss of both energy and integrity. Yet by stepping in and out of the resonances of other people you will continue to learn. Firstly, you get to observe life from a new perspective. That'll always show you new and surprising things. Secondly, you learn how to get comfortable with difference. Another's resonance is a box of endless experiences which can enrich your own life. Thirdly, when you connect back to your own resonance you'll notice it more clearly. Remember, we learn through contrast. So by connecting to the resonances of others, then back to your own, you get to compare and contrast your resonance with theirs

This next exercise gives you a taste of just how rich, inspiring and empowering it can be to appreciate the integrity of others. I suggest you give yourself a meaningful experience, by choosing something you'd like to learn or experience. If (like me) you have no musical skills, you may want to experience having some. Or if there's a problem you've been working on, you may want to focus on the resonance of someone with skill in that area.

There's an old book, *Stranger in a Strange Land*, by Robert Heinlein. It tells the story of a young boy orphaned on Mars, brought up by the locals, then sent back to earth to observe humans. Of course, the boy observes earth and humanity from a Martian perspective. There's lots of local knowledge he doesn't have, but he gains quickly because he knows how to absorb new skills directly and intuitively. Put another way, the boy knows how to step completely into someone else's resonance.

There have been times when my students have been stuck working on a case study or some exercise, when I wasn't physically present. So they shifted to my resonance then 'knew' how to proceed. You can do this. Say you're working on creating a business in which you have little experience. You can shift into the resonance of someone who does know. Or the resonance of a great artist or writer or whatever skill you're after. It can greatly shorten any learning curve. As always, this is a matter of focus and intention. It helps if you know the other person, or if they're physically present, as it helps anchor your focus. But it's not completely necessary.

. . . .

OTHER SOUL SEAT LEARNING

- Set an intention for what you'd like to learn or experience. The clearer your focus and the stronger your intention, the better. Think of someone skilled in this area.

- Go into your soul seat resonance. Focus on your intention from your own context. Notice how your intention aligns in your space.

- Now focus on the soul seat resonance of the other. For a clearer experience, remember to lock in their frequency and amplitude.

- Focus once again on your intention, while in the other's resonance. Notice how the alignment feels different. What does their perspective show you about your intention? Are there different ideas or realizations connected with their resonance?

- When you've finished, perform a soul seat attunement on yourself, to ensure you return to your own resonance.

. . . .

What did you learn from holding the other's soul seat resonance? Have you seen or learned things you wouldn't have thought of from your own space? Keeping your resonance in an increasingly coherent state is key. Without that, other people's resonances can feel disruptive, even threatening. Consciously retuning to your own resonance after having been out of it becomes easier. It's your natural 'default' state. Your ability to return to your integrity and resonance will only get stronger.

At first, you'll hold either your resonance or the resonance of another. Then, as you develop true interdependency, you'll learn to hold both at the same time. When you can do that, your awareness has reached critical mass, because your awareness itself will generate more awareness through what you observe. That's the final step of your nine-step journey towards intuitive mastery. Having co-creation as a simple and obvious lifestyle choice for you is the sign of your intuitive mastery.

. . . .

Step Nine

The first triangle creates intuitive stability through completing your cycles, understanding your own intuitive process, staying balanced and knowing your own resonance. The second triangle generates intuitive strength by increasing the volume and coherence of your resonance, working with both frequency and amplitude, as well as applying all of that to the process of transformation. The third and final triangle gives you intuitive sovereignty—the ability to decide what happens in your own world and space.

Sovereignty is the power of true intuitive mastery, which comes through pattern-based logic and its application to the hologram of creation. True intuitive mastery requires an ever-expanding capacity for the positive in yourself and co-creation with others.

In Step Nine, you'll gain an understanding of the power and mechanics of co-creation, in such a way that it becomes a simple life-style choice from this point on. Co-creation or interdependency as a life-style choice means you'll never again have a problem you can't solve.

. . . .

You can't have your cake and eat it too (unless you buy two cakes)
Energetic deliciousness

. . . .

When I was young my mother used to say: *You can't have your cake and eat it too*. I'm sure that was common wisdom, but I always found it confusing. It took me until I was seventeen to figure it out. Then the next time she said it I replied, 'Don't be ridiculous. All I have to do is buy two cakes.' Okay, I was being an obnoxious teenager, but the point stands.

Many years later, I told a client that story. She got the idea immediately. 'Yes,' she said, 'or I could buy the whole bakery!' That is when I realized I needed a bigger vision.

Our two eyes and their single focus influence our thinking. Working with energy is all about focus and intention. In order to have your cake and eat it too, you need to focus on **both** simultaneously. That's a bit like juggling two balls.

You'll have the same problem when working with two different resonances. Holding two foci is impossible. Our neurology just isn't made that way. It's like trying to watch two different seagulls at the same time. You can't maintain a steady focus on either, so your eyes keep flicking from one to the other.

Give this exercise a go to experience what I mean:

. . . .

DUAL SOUL SEAT RESONANCE

• Focus on your soul seat resonance, as you've learned to do.

• Now focus on the soul seat resonance of another, as you've also learned to do.

- Focus on both resonances at once. Attempt to hold both reson- ances in your space with equal clarity and strength. Notice how easy or difficult that is.

- Are both clear and steady in your mind? Or are you flipping from one to the other?

. . . .

Focusing on two things at once is extremely difficult. Your eyes can't do it, not really. You can focus clearly on one and attempt to keep the other in your peripheral vision, but that makes it a bit fuzzy. You can't have crystal-clear vision of two things simultaneously, and your physical focus creates the template for your mental focus. That's a problem.

I solved the problem posed by Mum with two cakes. But how did I get there? Like most things, there's a left-brain and a right-brain way. The right-brain way is simpler, but not always so in business or when you have to 'show your working', like your mathematics homework. Then the left-brain way is also helpful. It will give you a clear understanding of the thinking involved, so let's start there.

. . . .

Why a problem is a problem
Problem solving
· ·

What's a problem? I'm sure you can think of lots of examples. Like your parents not getting your life choices, your neighbor's dog constantly barking, the state of your kids' bedrooms or your tendency to bloat. Those are personal problems. Bigger, less personal examples are road congestion in the big cities, pollution, the economic divide and the education system. Even bigger issues include the state of the Great Barrier Reef and climate change, unrest in the Middle East and immigration.

When you look at problems, sometimes even personal problems, it's easy to feel as if there's nothing you can do. The structure of a problem—what makes a problem a problem—is the cause of most of that. Understanding this structure helps both sides of your brain deal with problems.

A problem is created by two equal and opposing thoughts, desires, goals or intentions. These forces drive against each other, creating the stuck situation you recognize as a problem. When looking at a problem, we tend to focus on the 'energy ridge'—the stuff stuck in between. Trying to move that never works, unless you deal with the two forces creating it,.

Remember that time you had a cramp? Felt horrible, didn't it? That's a physical problem. The muscle fibers contract like mad, while you're desperately trying to get them to relax. The more you try to relax the more it cramps, as you're opposing what the muscle's doing. The fastest (admittedly paradoxical) way to stop a cramp is to tell the muscle to contract even harder. After a second or two the muscle, now unopposed, settles down.

That's the key to handling a problem: releasing the energy that's piled up between the two opposing forces. Your left brain has four ways to do this, though some work better than others. These four ways are denial, compromise, completion and resolution.

Unfortunately, the first method is favoured by many politicians, with such statements as: *I did not have sexual relations with that woman.* It's denial, plain and simple. It doesn't so much release the pent-up up energy as seek to distract from it. Here's a purely hypothetical example. Imagine that in one lifetime you found your one true love, your soul mate. There was such a profound depth of connection and love between you that, when you fell ill with the plague, instead of abandoning you to your fate your love stayed and nursed you back to health. With love and nurturing care you survived, so naturally you thought, 'I can't live without love.'

That thought lodged deep in your subconscious, driving you desperately to find a relationship in your next life. You grabbed onto the first person to come along. Tragically, this time it was someone who loved your money more than you. Soon after your wedding, you lay dying of poison. You realized your spouse had killed you to get your money then marry his/her lover. So you had another powerful thought: 'Love kills me.'

Now you had a problem. In your next lifetime, your desperation to be in a relationship was matched by your terror of being in a relationship. It's all so fraught and difficult you decided to forget about relationships and pursue a career instead. That's denial.

Replacing two problem-bound goals with a third, unconnected one enables us to ignore any unresolved tension. We use that third goal to distract ourselves from the problem. It's not unlike politicians talking about immigration issues to distract people from the problems at home. Denial doesn't handle the problem. Rather, it's choosing to go unconscious around it.

In our right-wrong world, many people are great believers in the second way of handling conflict or a problem—compromise.

Here is another thing my mum used to say: *Half a loaf of bread is better than none.* This recipe for compromise described as a 'solution that makes everyone equally unhappy' is anything but, because it's linked to right-wrong or co-dependent thinking. It attempts to decide which goal is right—to be in a relationship or to be out of one. The 'right' goal is pursued while the other is ignored. Pursuing one goal

stretches the energy ridge further and further, until it snaps back like
an overstretched elastic band. This often results in someone flipping
from one extreme to the other and back again. In our hypothetical
example, that means you'll end up jumping into relationships and
jumping out again just as quickly, only to jump back in when you
feel alone once more.

Compromise is based on the belief that you can't have it all. Who
You Truly Are knows that's not true. Check it in your soul seat. You'll
realize the only solution that truly satisfies **is** to have it all, because
your soul only knows abundance. Your soul operates like the universe itself. Always and only interdependently, not co-dependently.
If your soul wants a whole loaf, it'll never be happy with half and
will resent being told that's enough.

I discussed earlier how acknowledging and completing your cycles
stabilizes your energy. Acknowledgment can sometimes do the same
thing for your problems. This is the third way to handle them. If you
acknowledge **both** goals, it's possible you may complete one. Perhaps
one was your mum's idea rather than yours. Once you've acknowledged and completed a 'false' goal, you're free to pursue the other one.

In our hypothetical example, you may realize the thought 'love
kills me' wasn't about real love at all. Hence you may complete that
side of the problem. Checking your goals within your soul seat can
assist in recognizing and releasing false goals, the ones that don't truly
serve you. Releasing false goals resolves problems, strengthening our
energy and independence.

Yet sometimes no matter how much we acknowledge our goals,
we still want both halves of the loaf. Wanting both sides of your brain
to work together is like that. No matter how much you acknowledge
your right brain is talking gibberish or your left brain is being anal,
you'll want a whole brain.

Taking on false goals is one of the greatest drains on your energy.
You might take them on to make other people happy or to do what
you believe is right. Yet if you check the goal with your soul seat
awareness, you'll find your soul seat compass reacting negatively. This
tells you it's not a goal that serves you. Tuning yourself up to your

resonance through your soul seat attunement ensures you are being Who You Truly Are. It means you have integrity in who you're being. Making sure your goals strengthen your soul seat through your soul seat awareness ensures you are being Who You Truly Are. It means you have integrity in what you're doing.

Sometimes you'll have conflicting goals or want to go in two different directions. Yet when you check your soul seat, they're both in your integrity. When giving up either conflicting goal is **out** of integrity, you have a real problem. That calls for the quintessential skill of the interdependent, the creation of true resolution. That's the fourth way to handle a problem.

Resolution is how you realize all it takes is two cakes, if you want to have one and eat it too. It's the ability to ride two horses at once, see both sides of the coin, or get to have the whole loaf. Whichever analogy floats your boat, if you want to manifest your most expansive life then it's an essential skill.

If we solve problems with a right-wrong approach, we have to make a decision by eliminating the options we believe are wrong. This means that over time we'll end up with fewer and fewer options. Our lives will be narrower and more inflexible. With resolution, that changes. With resolution, you'll never get stuck in a problem again. Resolution enables you to go way past right-wrong. It brings you to a perspective where difference is nothing to be feared and chased out of your one-valley.

With resolution, the conflict of difference becomes the energy which helps you create a new option. Then every decision you make will give you more options and your life will become more expansive, with more freedom and flexibility. Resolution embraces differences for the enrichment it brings to your life.

. . . .

Why a problem is not a problem
When everything's right

. . . .

Resolution is an essential interdependent skill, but how do we create it? Carl Jung gave us a clue when he said: *Problems are never solved, they're simply outgrown.* Jung was referring to the sorts of problems that seem huge yet diminish over time, like arguments with your brother or sister over who got to play with a treasured toy, or fights with your friends over your first love. As the seasons pass, those problems dwindle until they mean nothing. However just waiting around until you outgrow a problem isn't very appealing.

Problems also fade when we gain a bigger view of life. So to achieve resolution we need to grow our vision, until it's big enough to incorporate both original goals. Just like seeing a secret picture hidden among all the dots, resolution can be frustrating until you get the hang of it. Then it's so easy it appears natural. Just as seeing the hidden picture requires you to look with a soft focus, resolution requires you to soften any thoughts of right and wrong. Resolution requires you to **accept both goals are right**.

That's the first necessary step. It's easier to do when both goals check out in your soul seat. Once we accept both goals, we don't waste energy trying to decide which is wrong. Once again our soul seat assists us, because if we know both are in our integrity, they must both be right somehow. So instead of asking, 'Can I do this?' we focus on both and ask, '**How** can I do both of these together?' When you get the knack of finding that answer, you'll have resolution down pat. Until then, your left brain can follow the four-step process below.

. . . .

STEPS TO RESOLUTION

1. Acknowledge both goals. This is 'what' you want.
2. Acknowledge both purposes. This is 'why' you want it.
3. Create a bigger purpose that aligns both purposes.
4. Using your bigger purpose, create a bigger goal that aligns both goals.

. . . .

Let's examine each step in the kind of detail your left brain likes. Acknowledging both goals focuses your mind effectively. Initially, most people focus on the 'what'. Each goal or intention is 'what you want'. If you're resolving an issue between yourself and someone else, then it's what you want and what the other person wants. The trouble with 'what' is that it doesn't give you any room to maneuver. It's hard, if not impossible, to create resolution when you're looking at a specific issue, because it's so fixed.

In our hypothetical example, our goals are (i) to create a relationship and (ii) to remain single. On the surface of it, they're irreconcilable, so you may be tempted to give up. That's why you need a bigger picture. The easiest way to get a bigger picture is to shift your focus to the **purpose** of each goal. **Why** you want that goal or **what** you believe achieving that goal will do for you. Purpose is always bigger or deeper than the goal itself. Once you acknowledge why you want something, new options open up. You'll realize there are many ways to achieve the same purpose.

Our hypothetical goals have the purpose of (i) creating a relationship, so we can survive and (ii) staying single, so we're not killed. You'll notice there's already alignment on this level. That's actually pretty common. It's one more reason you'll want to switch from a goal-based perspective to a purpose-based one. In my experience, most people really want similar things. They're just too busy arguing about what they want to notice. On the purpose level, alignment is much easier to create. Once you have some alignment, it's even easier to create more. The bigger the purpose the better. Yes, there are times when size does matter.

How would you feel if you had a lollipop and I took it away and gave you a similar but smaller one? Not too happy, right? But what if I gave you a similar and **bigger** lollipop? In a holographic universe, there's always a way to have **everything** you want, not just a bit of it. You could say that the version of you who has everything already exists. Just like Who You Truly Are already exists. You just have to connect to that version of yourself, which is where your soul seat comes in. Resolving things so you can have everything is another step closer to Who You Truly Are.

With our hypothetical purposes of surviving and not being killed, there's some clear alignment. Completing that alignment grows our purpose, which becomes to expand or enhance our life. Resolution, co-creation and mutual expansion are hallmarks of interdependency. It's a choice for positive growth. It's the only choice Who You Truly Are will agree with, because it's choosing abundance.

The fourth and final step is to use our bigger purpose to find a tangible goal that enables us to achieve both of our previously conflicting goals. With our bigger, aligned purpose to expand our life it's clear. The new goal is to create a **relationship which expands our life**. This is a 'bigger' kind of love. Resolution is most often a quality decision, rather than a quantity decision. As is often the case, it's not **what** we do but **how** we do it. It's not about us doing the **right** thing so much as doing **our** thing. Our bigger resolution goal can be a growth in quality and/or quantity.

Here's another classic example. Two friends with different cravings meet for dinner. One's hankering for Indian, the other for Chinese. Due to travel arrangements, they've only one night to satisfy their cravings. This is a problem. If they go into denial, they'll eat Thai instead. If they're doing compromise, they'll decide which of them gets to choose. Acknowledgment won't work in this case, as they both know what they want. So it's resolution or dissatisfaction. How would you resolve this?

They could go somewhere that serves both. They could get takeaway and meet somewhere to eat. They could find a fusion restaurant with the kind of spice palette they both like. They could do a kind of degustation, with an entrée at one restaurant and main at the other. As long as they're both having fun, a great catch-up and are happy with what they do (their purpose) it's all good.

If compromise is a solution, it makes everyone equally unhappy. Resolution is a solution that makes everyone happier than they thought possible. I'm constantly impressed and amazed at the resolutions people find. They can feel incredibly stuck only to expand into everything they want, as soon as they decide there **is** a way. It's fascinating how quickly they find it.

Bernie came to me for an ongoing back problem. Her life was good. She loved her husband and two kids, but was going out of her mind at home. She wanted to be there for her kids but needed to do more with her life. Her emotional stress over feeling limited in her life was a big factor in her spinal issues, but she couldn't get a full-time job without losing her 'kid time'. When we worked on her stress and limitations, she realized her resolution—a flexible, part-time, stimulating job she could do in school hours. What Bernie created went one better. She was able to do additional hours during term to build up flexitime, so she didn't have to work over the school holidays. She got to go back to work earlier than she thought possible and still be a full-time mum.

Gary had almost the opposite issue. He was working long hours in a job where he had all the responsibilities yet none of the advantages of being his own boss. He was running the whole show. But with no capital, he didn't feel capable of going out on his own. He resolved the money issue with some clever negotiating and was soon his own boss. Like all new businesses, it took a little while to get going, but Gary's never looked back. He's now supplying a wide clientele with his artisan products. Through resolution, you can always find a way to achieve all you desire, leaving you free to live life with curiosity and a sense of fun, rather than impending doom.

The more you practice resolution, the more skilled at it you get. Then your outlook naturally grows in positivity. You'll even come to trust the positive. Not with blind faith, but because you know you have the skill to turn a possible negative into a definite positive. Resolution is a skill that takes win:win from a nice concept to a powerful strategy for winning with elegance.

The above resolutions were created by the four-step left-brain approach you've just learned. So what about your right brain? How do you create resolution with your intuition? Does interdependency exist on both sides of your brain?

. . . .

Interdependency is a harmonic structure
The sound in between

O f course, interdependency exists on both sides of your brain—as well as between both sides. Interdependency is how the whole universe operates, including your brain. Resolution enables both sides of your brain to work together as a seamless whole, despite their differences. Your left brain focuses on tiny details, while your right brain contemplates the big picture. Your left brain uses the details of the last process to achieve resolution. Your right brain uses one more characteristic, one more pattern of EM energy, to do the same thing. Harmonics.

Harmony isn't some airy-fairy cosmic concept or any kind of metaphor. It's very real. Left brain real. When two instruments play a note in perfect harmony, a third note 'appears' in the space. That third note can be recorded, its frequency and amplitude analyzed in an oscilloscope. I often refer to this third note as the 'bridging harmonic', as it enables both original notes to relate to each other in a pleasing way. That energetic bridge aligns them into a chord of music, which is richer than a single note yet retains the original alignment.

How does it do such an elegant thing?

A harmonic series is a collection of different EM waves that are harmonic. They exist because each wavelength in the series is a multiple of the first or fundamental wave. Divide the wavelength of the fundamental note by two and you have the second harmonic. Divide it by three and you have the third harmonic, and so on. That's why the nodes line up.

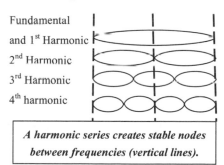

A harmonic series creates stable nodes between frequencies (vertical lines).

If you look at any EM wave, there are points where it crosses the 'horizon' or the plane that it's traveling through. These points are called 'nodes'. If you look at a harmonic series, you'll notice one very significant thing about the nodes. They tend to line up with each other. That happens because of their mathematical relationship.

It's interesting that the word 'integrity' comes from the word integer, meaning whole number. When we have integrity, we're whole in ourselves. We're living in alignment to our own pattern. When we operate interdependently, we operate to support our own integrity while being mindful of the integrity of the other. Harmonics are created through the relationships of whole numbers to the original frequency.

That wholeness is what enables the nodes of each frequency to find a point of alignment with its harmonics. Energetically, it feels like a still point in all that moving energy. The alignment of these still points creates a stable relationship between different waves or resonances. That's the pleasing sound we call 'harmonic'.

However the importance of harmonics goes way beyond esthetics and the power of a great riff. Remember that earlier you tried to focus on both your soul seat resonance and someone else's? And how you just flipped from one to the other? Left-brain resolution equates to right-brain harmonics. They're both ways of resolving two points into one, whether the two points come from a problem or two different resonances.

Harmonics are the key to a life of ease, grace and alignment. Here's how you find them:

. . . .

SOUL SEAT HARMONICS

- Focus on your soul seat resonance, as you've learned to do already.
- Now focus on the soul seat resonance of another, as you've also learned to do.

- Now focus on both resonances at once with the intention to find the harmonic. When you set that intention, you'll find your focus moving. Allow it to do so. It'll move to a different resonance from the two underlying ones. The frequency may be above or below the other two, though most often it's in between.

- Once you find the harmonic, focus on it with the intention to resonate it. Notice how holding the harmonic resonance affects the two underlying resonances.

. . . .

Holding the harmonic means you're focused on just one resonance, rather than the two underlying or base resonances. This is much easier, just as it's easier for your eyes to focus on one thing at a time. The harmonic allows **both** base resonances to have free play while adding another layer of richness, just as a chord in music is so much richer than one note. When you work with the harmonic, you're working interdependently. I've practiced finding the interdependent path so often it's now faster and easier for me to do this with my right brain (harmonics) than with my left (resolution). It has become as natural as breathing, yet working with both has advantages.

The harmonic gives me the focus, but I need to translate it into words when communicating it to others. The more stable my energy, the easier it is for me to find the still points or harmonics and match the resonance of that to words. The more you find the still point in the energy and match it to words, the more impactful your intuition will be. You'll be clearer about what your intuition is communicating to you, and you'll be able to communicate your intuitive insights more clearly to others.

. . . .

Inner stillness comes with harmonics
Standing stillness

. . . .

Harmonics are another reason why it's so important to get your energy stable before you do anything else. When your energy gets really stable your EM field also stabilizes, which means your energy waves are held by your space. This turns them from a traveling wave into a standing wave. A traveling wave is like those you see in the ocean, where the crests and troughs of the waves move along. That means the nodal points also move, which makes it hard to spot or align them. With a standing wave, the nodes don't move position. In between the nodes the crests go up and down, changing into troughs and back again.

Traveling waves are great for transmitting energy, but they're not so good at keeping it. A traveling wave loses a lot of energy through friction. In a standing wave, the alignment of the nodal points doesn't waste energy in that way. That's why there's a relationship between stable energy and standing waves. With the nodes holding a stable position there's no friction. So creating harmonics is much easier, as the nodes or still points are easier to spot and align. So stability is yet another reason to keep working on your soul seat. When it gets stable enough, your energy will also take on the characteristics of a standing wave, making it easier for you to align your harmonics.

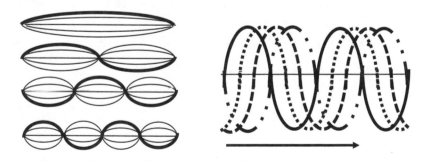

With standing waves (left), nodes or still points are clear. With traveling waves (right) crests and troughs move, making the nodes or still points difficult to locate.

Creating harmonics even has benefits at work. Ever heard of synergy in business? It's when a team produces much more than each individual could alone, so the whole is greater than the sum of its parts. This is spoken about as if it's modern-day magic, as no one seems to know how it's created. Yet synergy is greatly desired for its ability to produce teams with extraordinary results. I'm sorry to say it's not magic. A team with synergy is just a team that's operating interdependently from the group's harmonic. The harmonic creates a framework for mutually expansive exchanges between all team members. With interdependent mastery, producing synergy is just what you do.

You can align the still points within different energetic fields or fractal patterns to create something that holds the alignment of each person's integrity, while creating something altogether richer. There are always still points or harmonics where different fractals or patterns intersect or line up, to create these richer, more complete patterns. The pattern-based logic of your right brain can find these intersection points. It's there that resolution is found.

Such an alignment enriches our resonance with the resonances of others, without any loss in the coherence of our own signal. We can bring in the resonance of all the abundances we want in our lives, while maintaining our own strong central signal. Through the harmonic, all other signals will relate to that. In this way, each person's own alignment or integrity is maintained. There's no static or white noise.

Have you ever met someone you felt awkward or uncomfortable around? That happens when your resonances don't align. What about when you met someone and felt comfortable straightaway, as if you'd known them forever? You might think you were close in another lifetime or they remind you of someone you knew before. But the energetic truth is that their energy is harmonic with yours.

The more harmonics you hold in your own space, the more you'll attract people and connect in integrity to situations. To develop the necessary clarity for harmonic connection, we need to take our learning to the next level. We need to be able to lock in those still nodal points.

Anchoring the stillness
Resonant ballet

. . . .

Remember doing all those spins as a kid? And how dizzy it made you feel? While you spun around until you fell over, a ballerina has to do many more turns and not fall over. Collapsing is the opposite of the grace, elegance and physical poise of a ballerina. Ballerinas can do all those pirouettes because of a trick called 'spotting' and not because they're nervous system is immune to the effects of angular momentum.

Spotting is a focusing technique. The ballerina picks a specific object to return their eyes to after each revolution. It's a still point. If the spot is unfocused, uncertain or forced, it throws the ballerina off. If they don't choose their spot before they turn or worse, change it mid-turn, the pirouette can end in disaster.

That's what makes you seasick. You feel nauseous when your nervous system is shaken up. You can reduce that horrible feeling by focusing on the horizon, because it's a still and stable reference point. That stable reference point allows your nervous system to find its balance. The spot focus of a ballerina does the same thing. Still points or harmonics can do that for you, when you're working with your intuition. However finding those points is a very precise skill. You need a very precise focus to do it. It's the energetic equivalent of a ballerina spotting as she does endless pirouettes. The more exact your focus is, the better you'll do.

With a precise focus, you'll be able to hold a much larger harmonic series or range of resonances. Holding an increasing number and variety of different resonances gives interdependency its true power. Interdependency is the power to create elegant solutions and the most effective path in all situations.

So how do you get a focus as specific and stable as a ballerina? Earlier, you learned to get a grip on difference resonances. A resonant 'lock' takes this to the next level. You may find it helpful to go back and review how to get an energetic grip (see Pages **155-156**). When you do, you'll feel your mind and focus shifting around. That's your nervous system looking or scanning for the frequency and amplitude.

You could say that resonant locks are the culmination of everything you've been learning. They give you a focus that's so clear and stable it's much easier for you to hold your intention. Finding each lock is a small completion in itself, so working from one lock to the next means you're always operating with increasing energy. This makes it easier for you to maintain your own resonance and strengthen your integrity. It also makes it easier to work with harmonics. Resonant locks give you a huge intuitive advantage.

Another advantage of working with resonant locks is the clarity and certainty they generate. It's the same difference as crossing a creek on wobbly stepping stones or on completely stable ones. Each resonant lock makes that situation so much clearer and certain that everything else becomes easier. It's a paradox. You have to do quite a bit of work and practice to get to this point, but once you get to work with resonant locks everything becomes easier. Locking in the resonance in this way means you don't waste energy. You know what you know and can get on with what you need to do. It helps you make better decisions, be clearer on the outcome, and even manage the consequences of each choice you make.

One particular winter, several clients were doing their best to give me their flu. I usually just turn up the volume of my own resonance (as you learned to do earlier) and it throws the virus off. This time it was keeping the flu at bay, but I was having difficulty getting it to leave my system entirely. Admittedly, it was one of those years when the flu was so bad it was all over the news but I still wasn't having it. With that intention in mind, I sat down to focus on clearing the flu out of my system completely. In my intuitive vision, I saw the most beautiful indigo color. I thought that must be the resonance I needed to clear the virus, but it wouldn't lock in. That told me it wasn't the completion I needed. It was a puzzle. Later that day, I was in the health food store and was drawn to a cold and flu formula. I read what was in it. I probably appeared a little mad just then, as I laughed out loud when I read that one of the ingredients was wild indigo! Sure enough, when I tuned into the resonance of that herb it finally locked in. That told me what I needed.

The completion of a resonant lock creates a lot of clarity. The one with the wild indigo told me the reason why the flu was so bad that year. Most flus affect your kidney energy, but wild indigo is more for your spleen and clearing the lymphatics. Your kidneys usually deal with short-term stress, whereas your spleen works with more long-term issues. I took the wild indigo formula and increased the strength of my resonance in my spleen, then was able to clear the flu completely out of my system. I also knew how to help my clients through that winter. One resonant lock gave me the clarity to help myself and many others.

Did you ever watch the movie *Star Wars*? I mean the first one, *A New Hope*? At one point, the hero's fighting a space battle and attempting to shoot down an enemy ship. The ship's image shifts about in the targeting mechanism until he's 'locked on'. Then it's fixed in the middle of the screen. That's how finding a resonant lock feels in my mind. When you achieve a complete lock it becomes a still point in your mind, as still as any nodal point. Empathically, it's as though the resonance is spongy, but once you have a 'lock' it goes hard.

An energetic grip approximates the frequency and amplitude of a resonance. It's enough for you to connect, but not enough for the kind of specific focus you need for energetic 'spotting'. A complete lock is far more exact and specific.

For this next exercise, you'll need a few different objects like a crystal, a vase and some cutlery. You may want to use the objects from the household resonant range you used before.

. . . .

LOCKING IT IN

- Place your hand on an object and flow energy into it, intending to exactly match the energy flowing from the object. Make sure you get a grip on its frequency and amplitude.

- Now push your focus further to get a resonant lock. Focus specifically on the object's frequency. Get clearer and clearer on it until you feel it 'lock in', as though it goes 'clunk' or it's fallen into the right slot. A complete lock feels fixed.

- Having got a specific lock for the frequency, now do the same thing with the amplitude. Focus on that specifically, with the intention to get clearer and clearer on it until you feel it 'lock in'. Once again you'll feel it go 'clunk'.

- Once you've completed your lock in both frequency and amplitude, remove your hand and move your focus back to your own soul seat resonance.

- Then return once again to your object. Set your intention to lock in its resonance. Notice if you have to go through the whole process of searching for the resonance again, or if you go straight to it. A complete lock is a stable reference point, so your mind will return immediately to the 'lock point' as it now 'knows' that frequency and amplitude.

. . . .

Taking your focus away and then returning to it is a simple way of checking whether you have a true lock. Remember, a lock is a **stable** reference point. Your mind will **always** go straight back to it, if you completed it in the first place. That's quite different to your mind searching around as it 'scans' for each resonance. Working with complete resonant locks is an advanced skill, requiring a high degree of self-awareness. You'll need to pay attention to the subtle shifts caused by different EM signals in your system. It's a skill worth developing however. Once you get a handle on it, it makes everything so much easier.

When you don't lock in each resonance, the energies keep shifting around in your mind. It's as if you've got intuitive dyslexia. One of the difficulties with dyslexia is the meaning of words isn't stable. Each time you come across a word, you have to learn its meaning all over again. It's no wonder the condition makes learning tricky and difficult. Scanning for resonance each time is like looking for meaning each time as well. With resonant locks that changes. With resonant locks, you start to develop your own resonant vocabulary. It's as if each lock is a distinct word in your own energetic language.

With a complete lock on a resonance it becomes 'fixed' in your mind, so you have a stable point of reference for it. Each time you tune in, your focus returns immediately to the exact same frequency and amplitude. Equally, if you come across something else with the same resonant reference point or 'resonant word', you'll know it's the same thing. You can test this yourself. Find the resonant lock point of another object made of similar material (like a fork and knife from the same cutlery set). You'll find the resonant point is the same or very close between them. That resonant point is the resonant word for 'stainless steel'—or for 'silver', if you run to the fancy stuff.

When I work with clients, they often want to know how I know what I know. That's like asking how you know what's written on this page. You know because you've got the vocabulary. With a resonant vocabulary, you literally 'read' the resonances in a person's space, system or body. This is beyond basic sensorial language, the kind of synesthesia we all used when we first worked with our intuition. An energetic vocabulary gives your intuition clarity and specificity, which makes finding practical answers easier.

That's what Nancy needed when she came to me. She's a skilled naturopath with a busy practice, who's helped a lot of people. She was frustrated with herself, as she wasn't able to clear her own chronic fatigue. I read the resonances in her space. Then I told her she'd had glandular fever and the Epstein-Barr virus was still in her system, which she knew. I also told her the EBV had a 'buddy', which she didn't know.

Some viruses get together with another pathogen to really go to town on your system. It makes them difficult to treat. If you go after one, it'll 'hide' behind the other. Together they have a more complex resonance. There's the resonance of one bug, the resonance of the other and also the harmonic. I could feel the resonance of the other pathogen but had to dig around in my memory to find what it was, like a word you haven't used for a long time. Finally, I remembered it from my veterinarian days. It was swine erysipelas, a bacteria most pigs have. Most of the time it doesn't cause any issues, but if it gets together with another pathogen it can wreak havoc on a piggery.

I told Nancy what it was. She looked at me skeptically. Fair enough, it's not the kind of thing you'd expect. If you're living in the middle of a city, you don't generally come across pig farms. 'Where would I have gotten that from?' she asked. Once again I read her resonances and told her that it had been in her system since she was eight. She gave me that wide-eyed look people get when startled by the truth. 'That's when my aunty got pigs,' she said.

My resonant vocabulary had given her the answers she needed and with that specific knowledge, we put a program together. After a couple of months she was feeling robust again.

Developing a resonant vocabulary takes time and a lot of reading. Just as it took you reading time to grow your English vocabulary, which in turn enables you to read this book. You use a dictionary and the understanding of other words to grow your English vocabulary. In order to grow your resonant vocabulary, you'll need to grow your awareness of resonant locks. The following exercise will get you started.

. . . .

BUILDING A RESONANT VOCABULARY

- Choose an object. I suggest you start with the ones you used to lock in resonance in the previous exercise. That resonant lock is the energetic 'word' for that object, which means you have both the word and the resonant word for it.

- Now do it the other way around. Focus on the English word for the object, with the intention of locking in the resonance of that word. Notice how your mind goes to the exact same resonant lock point. So the word is the resonant lock and the lock is the resonant word.

- Do that same thing with some other objects. Some will have similar resonant words, like a knife and a fork, and others will be quite different, like a knife and a table.

- For each object, lock in the resonance then ensure that when you focus on locking in the resonance of the English word, your mind goes to the same lock point. This is what a resonant vocabulary is: the ability to know that English word is that resonance and that resonant lock is that English word.

Tip: If you do this with everything you deal with in a day, you'll soon have a sizable resonant vocabulary, one that'll help you in your everyday life. Of course, until you've been doing this for a while it means a lot of energetic 'reading'. So set yourself the task of learning (say) five new energetic words each day, which means finding five new resonant lock points each day.

. . . .

The more complete your lock, the more specifically you'll focus on each resonance, then the greater your resonant vocabulary will be. Having the skill and awareness to consistently get resonant locks transforms your intuition from a questionable resource to a reliable and consistent one. A precise and specific lock takes you to intuitive mastery. Learning to do this is just one exercise, but the clarity and certainty that building a resonant vocabulary brings to your intuition can culminate in significant changes to your life path. It's what we call a 'watershed' moment.

Watershed moments
Changing watersheds

· ·

When water falls on land it flows downhill, no questions asked. We all know that. That means if a drop of rain falls one centimeter either side of a ridge line, it could end up somewhere completely different. On one side of a ridge line, all the water ends up in the same river or pond. That whole area is one watershed. The other side of the ridge is a different watershed. Wherever there's a long line of mountains running parallel to a coast, water on one side of the range will run towards the ocean, whereas water on the other side will run inland into marshes or rivers. The tiniest shift has a huge effect on a raindrop's destiny.

We all have moments like that. These are our watershed moments, when the smallest change ends up making the biggest difference. Learning how to get an exact and specific resonant lock is like that. Before you achieve an exact and specific lock, your intuition will work in one of two ways. Either you'll expend a lot of energy gripping each resonance you come across (as if having to hold it in place), or you'll waste time and energy finding the resonance all over again every time.

To achieve a resonant lock, you start by focusing on the general resonance. Then you 'push' your focus further, until you feel it lock into the exact frequency and amplitude. At first it feels like a tiny subtle thing, yet it makes a huge difference. Push your focus, with an intention to be aware of the 'lock point'. You'll soon get to the point where it'll feel neither tiny nor subtle, but clear and obvious. To me, it feels like a definite 'clunk' in my mind. Resonant locks are not just a 'Catherine weirdness' but something everyone can do.

When I talk directly to someone and give them feedback on what they're doing, they pick it up easily. I especially have to encourage them to push their focus that little bit more, to take it to the 'lock point'. I shared with you earlier my editor Jason's experience. By focusing on how both frequency and amplitude felt to him, and how his neurology worked with each of those energy characteristics, he learned to get a specific lock. Without a resonant lock my mind is constantly scanning, shifting about to keep track of the frequency and amplitude. As soon as it's locked in, it's fixed. It becomes a stable point of reference in my mind.

Without me giving you feedback in person, it may take you a little while to get it. But you **can** do it. The more time you've spent getting to know your own neurology and how your system gives you information, the easier it'll be. You can train yourself to this level of clarity and precision with your intuition if you choose. Firstly, you need to learn to recognize how the 'lock' feels to you. Depending on your neurology that could vary. All my students learn to lock in their resonances, but it's always different. Their experience is as unique as their neurology.

Maret worked in the corporate world for many years and was nearing the end of her Fractology training while I was writing this book. In Maret's words:

> I simply had to learn to trust that what I was sensing was accurate. Through my training, I've come to trust that when I set an intention it happens. I set my focus and intention to allow whatever happens to happen. With frequency, I can feel a shift internally, as if it's going up or down a scale. Amplitude is different; it feels more like width. I can feel that narrow or widen. I keep focusing on the frequency or amplitude until I feel a little energy 'squeeze', or energy 'bounce', within. After that everything eases; it feels as though I can relax, which is what that tells me it's stabilized and locked in.

Developing the discipline to get to a resonant lock with every energy you come across isn't easy initially. Yet it makes everything so much easier, once you get the hang of it. That's true even for those who've worked with resonances for a long time. I generally teach people to tune into the frequency first, because that's easiest for most people. However, there are some who find it easier the other way around.

Do whichever is easiest for you first, as it'll stabilize the signal enough for you to get the other one and complete your lock.

The level of clarity necessary for a resonant lock may seem as though it's something you can only achieve through your mind, but that's not the case. Nicola is one of my former students and now a Fractology colleague and nurse. She operated almost entirely from her heart (or right brain) when I first met her. Now she's able to do it with either hemisphere. Nicola writes:

> *For me, locking in the resonance is an empathic sense, so I look at it from both my heart space and from my mind. When I lock in from my heart, it feels like a kind of worm hole which is radiating outwards, feeling for the specific resonance. When I find it, the edges of the worm hole stabilize and hold as I lock onto the resonance. If I go with my mind, I set the intention of which resonance I'm wanting. My mind searches for that resonance and when it finds it, it locks on. It's a bit like one of those Tupperware containers. When it's lined up properly, it just 'clicks on' and then it'll hold whatever I want it to.*

The ability to hold a lock is why this is such a watershed moment for your intuition. It's this that takes your ability to apply your intuition to a level of mastery. Jane is a Fractology practitioner and she tells us how she applies this in her yoga:

> *I like to lock in the resonance of health, wisdom and happiness. In my years of yoga, I've experienced how increasing the volume of an emotion or mindstate strengthens the outcome. To hold the frequency of each one feels more or less like two thirds of its total potential, but it's complete once it's locked in. When I add in the amplitude, the lock feels stable. Then that gives me power throughout my day.*

Remember the importance of completion? The most effective way of working intuitively is from one point of completion to the next. In a very real way, getting each energy you're dealing with to a point of resonant lock is a form of completion. It's a completion that leads to a whole other energetic language.

By locking each resonance you're working with, you'll accumulate a collection of stable reference points. You could consider each of those stable references to be an energetic word, because you can 'read' it. This is what it means to have a resonant or energetic vocabulary.

. . . .

It's all resonance
Resonant vocabulary

When you've got a group of fixed points (see left and right, and below), it's relatively easy to tell what kind of pattern creates alignment between all of them. (Circle on the left and triangle on the right.) Finding the alignment patterns is important. It enables our right brain to guide us reliably. It also shows us whether we're in alignment with our own patterns or if others are in alignment with theirs.

Remember when we're in laser alignment, we have far greater power and clarity than when we're not. Alignment and coherence go together. We can't achieve this if our resonances aren't specific still points. When we don't 'lock in' the resonance, the energy we're focusing on isn't fixed. It's rather a general field of possibilities, a region of resonance in which it may exist. If we were to draw it, rather than looking like a fixed point it would look something like a squiggle:

If each point isn't clearly defined, you end up with a group of points that look like the ones on the next page.

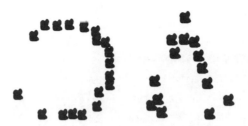

Here it's much harder to determine what the correct alignment is, despite the fact that all I've done is replace each point above with a small copy of the scribble that touches the point somewhere.

Locking in the resonance gives you a clear energetic 'word'. You don't have to look for the resonance again. Once you've locked it in properly, your mind 'recognizes' the resonance. So you now know its meaning. Developing a resonant vocabulary in this way is important, but locking in your resonances consistently does so much more.

A resonant lock gives you a clear energetic 'word'. It enables you to align that word accurately with others, to create energetic phrases and sentences. A word means something in itself, but means a whole lot more in the context of a phrase or sentence. In the same way, resonant lock points mean more when they're aligned in a pattern. If you did the last exercise and have started developing your own resonant vocabulary, you'll know what I mean. The resonant lock for 'knife' is one point, but there'll be other resonances with it depending on whether it's on the table or the floor. Or for whether the knife is being used or is part of a table setting that's waiting to be used. And also for what kind of knife it is.

All these resonances tell you something about the purpose and function of the knife, just as all the words around a noun in a sentence tell you something about it. Your right-brain patterns are like having not just individual words, but a whole book. Depending on how much of the pattern you focus on at a time, you may get a phrase, a sentence, a chapter or the whole entire book. Being able to read that book tells you about the past and the present. Significantly, it also has a lot to say about the future.

With this kind of resonant vocabulary, you can navigate the future with a great deal more confidence and certainty.

. . . .

Future **Steps**

Well done. You've completed a tremendous journey through the nine steps of intuitive mastery, but the journey doesn't stop here. The first triangle gave you intuitive stability with completion and balance. It gave you self-awareness of your own intuition and resonance. The second triangle gave you intuitive strength with a powerful and coherent resonance, through awareness of both frequency and amplitude. It increased your control over the process of transformation. The third triangle gave you pattern-based logic with an ever-growing capacity for positive expansion. You can now use that for consummate co-creation, as you grow your power through the certainty and confidence of a growing resonant vocabulary.

So what more is there to do? Use all that you've learned to create the future for yourself and others that you currently only dream of. An interdependent future, in which everyone gets to expand into their fullest potential. This is a future in which you begin to realize the brilliance of Who You Truly Are, and your life realigns itself with grace and ease to reflect that brilliance. The joy of this future will only be increased by your growing ability to assist others to create a future for themselves in which they experience the same, even though Who They Truly Are may be very different to you.

. . . .

The future exists in the hologram
Destiny or dice?

....

Looking at the current state of the world or considering the future seems pretty scary just now. The way we govern our countries has worked pretty well for the last couple of hundred years, but isn't really cutting it anymore. Climate change and the future of our planet are open questions that need bigger answers than any one of us is capable of. Our wonderful new technology has created a whole raft of new stresses. Even the way we're taught to think seems to be fashioned for an era long gone.

Star Trek called the future 'the undiscovered country'. For many of us, it feels as though those words have never been more true. It's as if we're all driving down an unknown road together, with no GPS and an uncertain map. What do we do when we come to a crossroad? Do we hesitate? Look for a street sign? Barrel ahead and just hope for the best? When the route is unclear or street signs non-existent, we may stop for a long time trying to decide which way is best. Without clarity, moving on can be an anxious process, giving you a gut wrench as you ease your foot onto the accelerator.

The further you drive without some clear sign, the less certain you become that you're heading in the right direction. The more uneasy you become. You begin to wonder if you should turn back or take a different direction. You keep scanning for landmarks. You recheck your map, as if it'll suddenly give you information that wasn't there before. You might even end up turning round, just before you get to your destination.

Life's like driving along that strange road. Naturally, we dislike uncertainty. It triggers our old fight-flight response. In fact, we dislike uncertainty so much that we grasp at anything that'll give us a hint of certainty. That's what you're looking for when you visit a clairvoyant, psychic or tarot reader.

The linear view of life is that destiny is a singular road, leading to a clear and specific conclusion. Yet we don't live in a linear world. Our universe is holographic. Within an infinite reality, an infinite number of futures exist. We have many possible paths to reach our destiny. At first glance that may appear terrifying, lacking any kind of certainty. Yet certainty still exists. Our lives are more than the throw of cosmic dice.

Linear certainty comes from 'knowing' what's right and what's wrong. Holographic certainty is a little different. The power of your intuition is in navigating towards your future and the future of the world with holographic certainty. That is the key to manifesting your future with increased confidence.

. . . .

The future is fractal
Quantum futures

. . . .

In right-wrong thinking, there's only one way to be right. Everything else is wrong. So there's only one 'right' path in life that holds your one true destiny. Not ending up there means failing completely and utterly.

Holographic reality is kinder and more fluid. In the holographic multiverse of string theory, every single reality is played out. That means every time you came to a crossroad and went one way, other versions of you took other directions. You may not be conscious of it, but some part of you is over there in another parallel universe experiencing your other options. The ones you didn't take in **this** universe. Everything that could happen does happen, though not always in this universe.

No matter what you want to achieve, no matter how lofty the destiny you wish you had, there's a version of you out there somewhere in the hologram that's done it. Give up asking, 'Can I do that?' It's a holographic nonsense, because somewhere in the hologram you already have. You don't have to become perfect, you just have to connect to your perfection. Your soul seat always comes in handy for doing that. In that same way, you don't have to create your perfect, most expansive future. It's already out there. You just have to connect to it.

Connecting to your most abundant future is a lot easier than hacking it out of the jungle, one step at a time. The only trick is making sure you connect to the future you really want, so you end up experiencing it in **this** universe. Quantum physics gives us the best clue on how to do that. Not surprisingly, the answer is in your resonance—just as it is for your intuition and also string theory.

In quantum mechanics, every possible future exists simultaneously as a probability. Every different future has its own quantum signature or resonance.

The quantum resonance of your current moment matches one of your futures. It forms a resonant feedback loop that draws that future towards your present and your present towards that particular future. This is exactly the same mechanism that spiritual tradition refers to when speaking of you manifesting your future. So you can either create your future the hard way (from the present) or the easy way (from the future). Tuning yourself into the future you're 'dialing up' from the hologram is definitely the best way to navigate through all your possible futures to the one you want.

Both you and the hologram of creation have a fractal structure. Your timeline is not one straight line but a fractal. Linear time flows straight, from past to present to future. Non-linear, fractal time resembles a net more than a line. You experience it as a time line because you experience only one strand of the net at a time, but that strand splits from and joins into others. The time-net looks like a road map, with ways splitting and converging. There are lots of different ways to get from the present to the future, as well as different versions of the past.When you're going to take a trip along a well-worn path, you plan your route from your point of departure to your destination. You know you turn right at the roundabout, take the next left, travel a distance, turn right again and there you are. However when you don't know the path, you plan it in the opposite way. You go straight to your destination on the map, then work backwards to your departure point.

Your left brain likes known details. It'll plan your route when you know it from departure to destination. Your right brain or intuition navigates the unknown. It'll connect directly to the resonance of your future and use that as your 'compass' to guide

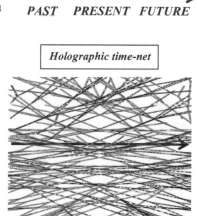

Linear time line

PAST   PRESENT FUTURE

Holographic time-net

PARALLEL   PARALLEL   PARALLEL
PAST   PRESENT   FUTURE

you there. Just as when you're driving, you'll come to crossroads in the time-net and each crossroad is a point where you have to make a choice. In my work, we call those crossroads choice points or completion points, because they're the same thing.

It's only when you complete the cycle of action that resulted from an earlier choice that you get the energy from that cycle back. Then and only then are you free to use that energy for a new choice, a new cycle. Interestingly, these points usually correspond to nodal points in your EM field. Each choice determines which strand of the time-net you'll experience. With each choice, we'll either navigate towards our chosen future or away from it. The future can be one of increased integrity with all the abundance, fulfillment and life satisfaction that goes along with it, or it can be one of decreased integrity with all the difficulty, internal conflict and stress that goes along with that.

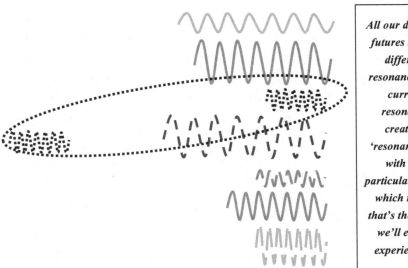

All our different futures have a different resonance. Our current resonance creates a 'resonant loop' with one particular future, which means that's the future we'll end up experiencing.

Your soul seat doesn't just help you connect to Who You Truly Are in the now. It also helps you navigate towards a brighter future, in which your resonance is clearer, stronger and richer. The hard way of creating the future is the left-brain way. You start from the present and try to hack your way step by step to the future you want.

It's much easier to manifest the future with your intuition and your right brain. Then you can connect directly to the future you want. It's already out there, waiting for you. You can lock it in just the same way you lock in any resonance.

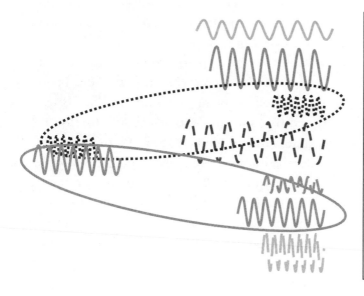

If you want to create a different future for yourself than the one you're currently headed for, you'll need to switch your resonance to that of the future you want to create.

The future is also a resonance
The future already is

. . . .

Your future already exists within the hologram as an expression of your fractal, just as your present self is an expression of your fractal. You step into your future by tapping into or connecting with that point of the hologram that holds your chosen future. Each point of the hologram has a different resonance. Each point has its own unique signature, created through the particular configuration the multiverse has in that time frame or moment. Shifting from one resonance to another creates the illusion of time. All the different frames of a movie already exist on your DVD, but your player scans over them one at a time to create a sense of flow, storyline and of time passing. You can pull up any particular scene on your DVD player, just as you can tune into any point in the hologram.

The most effective way to do this is to tune yourself to the version of you that exists in the future, effectively practicing being the you that **has** that resonance. Your future self already exists within your fractal, the pattern of your consciousness. You connect to it in the same way you connect to anything with focus and intention. Once you choose your future, focus on it with the intention to connect with your future self.

If you could have absolutely anything you wanted, what would it be? It's as if you'd found your magic wand and could just wave it, so whatever you wanted would appear.

Sometimes clients claim to not know what they want. I tell them that's not exactly true. Their left brain may not yet have all the details, but their right brain knows something of the pattern they'd like their life to follow. They want an expansive future, one that's fulfilling and full of love and satisfaction. One that's more inspired and creative, full of abundance and great health, with a lavish serving of wonderful relationships. Don't tell me you don't want that! Yet sometimes we can sabotage even the most wonderful of futures.

That's another reason why it's good to practice being 'future you'—to prevent self-sabotage.

The future is unknown. We don't even know who we'll be if we have all that good stuff. In trying to avoid fear of the unknown, we often mess things up. By practicing being your future self, at least you'll know who you'll be in the future. It'll feel more familiar and comfortable. That cuts out a lot of self-sabotage, while you create a resonant loop to draw your chosen future to you. The more you practice being your future self, the closer you'll get to that future.

. . . .

LOCKING IN THE FUTURE

- Focus on who you'll be, once you have your chosen future. Remember to use all your senses: feel it, see it, hear it, smell it and taste it. Hold this focus until you feel the shift between the current and future versions of yourself.

- Spend a few minutes every day 'being' the future you. Ways to do this include:

  - aligning your senses and how you feel to your future self.

  - letting your future self make decisions. This is often helpful, as your current self doesn't know how to create that future, but your future self has already done it.

  - tuning your resonance to your clearer, stronger, future resonance.

. . . .

Creating the future from the future, instead of the present, is the easiest way to create all your desires. It'll give you the certainty that your neurology craves, as your future becomes more familiar. Moreover, creating your future from the future avoids a lot of unnecessary angst and difficulty. You may have experienced times in your life when you've worked on creating or manifesting from the present and, instead of getting what you wanted, you created a whole lot of things you didn't want.

When you fully engage your intuition by using it to navigate your life path, you'll avoid many of those unintended consequences.

. . . .

The only thing that's constant is change
The law of unintended consequences

. . . .

Our universe is not a neat little Euclidean sphere. No matter how many epicycles we use, we won't make that simple and linear shape. Our universe is a hologram with a fractal structure. It's non-linear. It has an infinite number of details which are of interest to your left brain with its linear logic, and many non-linear patterns that only the pattern-based logic of your intuition can perceive. When we try to navigate the time-net using left-brain logic, we focus on the expected consequences of each action. But our universe is non-linear, so there's always some consequence your left brain won't expect. That's referred to as 'the law of unintended consequences'. There are **always** non-linear effects and your linear left brain can't predict them.

You need your non-linear intuition or right brain to make the most effective use of the time-net. Even when you know the path, you need to pay attention to your intuition. If your soul seat compass squawks at you, it's a warning about an unintended consequence. You don't just want to choose; you want to choose which side of your brain is doing the choosing. It's this 'hidden' choice that often has the biggest impact on your path, determining how easily and gracefully you get to walk it. If you know all about whatever it is you want, then let your left brain deal with it. When it's **within** your reality, when you know all your necessary action steps to achieve your goal, that's left-brain territory. But if you don't know the details of your dream, or if you don't have a clear idea of what it is because it's **outside** your reality, that's right-brain territory.

When the butterfly flapped its wings, it wasn't intending to create a hurricane. But the little zephyr of wind produced by its wings met up with another. That turned it into a puff, which grew into a gust. That combined with another into a breeze, then coordinated with more breeze to form a wind. It built up again and again, until the hurricane was born. The 'butterfly effect' is one big fat unintended consequence or non-linear effect. Knowing when to flap your wings to produce a hurricane, or when to hold still to avoid one, is what your intuition is for.

When you're walking along the street and find a tree planted in the middle of your path, do you step inwards to the sidewalk or outwards onto the roadway? Most of the time such a small decision doesn't make any lasting difference. A few steps further and you're in the same place, regardless of which way you go. The same goes for the butterfly. Most of the time, when it flaps its wings there's no hurricane as a result. The butterfly needs its butterfly intuition to tell it when one flap of its wings will produce huge non-linear results. You need your intuition for the same reason. Sometimes when you step around the tree one way, you bump into a stranger who changes the whole course of your life. Another time you step into the traffic and force someone to brake heavily, which may change their life in a way you'll never know.

When there's an intuitive or holographic difference, you need to pay attention to your intuition. When there are no non-linear effects to concern yourself with, you can leave it to your left brain to observe the differences in the density of foot and car traffic. Anything we do, including walking along the street, we do most effectively when we're not just doing it right foot then left foot, but when we're also engaging our intuitive right brain, then linear left brain. Your left-brain data handles the immediate details, while your right-brain intuition handles the holographic approach. Working this way gets the most out of your whole brain—your neurology. And it can open the door to your future in another more tangible way.

. . . .

Neurology and technology
Left to right and back again

. . . .

All of us, even the most science-minded or creative among us, navigate from left brain to right brain and back again. Our society or collective consciousness does it too. As one civilization followed another throughout history, the emphasis swung from the spirituality and mysticism of the right brain to the science and engineering of the left brain. Societies that balanced both, like the ancient Egyptians and Greeks, thrived. They gave a legacy to the world that affects us even today.

Those civilizations which were unbalanced in either direction tended to make little progress. The religiosity and mysticism of the Middle Ages became known as the Dark Ages, due to the suppression of the light of science. The Confucianism of ancient China honoured the details of the social construct but distrusted innovation.

Our modern world has benefited hugely from advances in science and technology. For each advance to have had practical applications, left-brain details were necessary and obvious. Yet we need to remember the right-brain inspiration that triggered each advance. Einstein's vision led to his general theory of relativity. During his dreams, Michael Barnsley solved the fractal problem necessary for streaming large amounts of data. If we're to find our way forward into a more expansive future for ourselves and the planet, we'll need to work with both sides of our brain.

In 1936, Alan Turing dreamed up his rules of logic that led to our modern computers. He was influenced by new understandings of the brain that advances in the microscope had brought about in the late nineteenth century. The word 'neuron' was only introduced in 1891. At that time, the understanding was that each neuron had an axon for sending signals, and dendrites for receiving signals. Information only flowed one way, from dendrites through the cell body to the axon, with each neuron telling the next to turn off or on.

That was the logical framework that went into your computer. All the amazing things that your computer, iPad and phone do are because of a series of 1s and 0s, where 0 means 'off' and 1 means 'on'.

Your brain does the same with neurotransmitters. Norepinephrine and dopamine turn the neurons 'on'. GABA (gamma-aminobutyric acid) turns them 'off'. This on-off approach is left-brained, right-wrong logic.

At one time, that's all we knew about the brain. That's now changing, opening the way for a more right-brained approach. Functional MRI scans show it isn't just each neuron directing the next one to get the job done, but the **total** pattern of firing. The overall alignment of active neurons has a huge impact on how you function, that goes beyond the activation of individual cells. As our understanding of the importance of alignment grows, our appreciation of the power of patterns and right-brained logic also grows.

Just as our current technology grew from left-brain on/off logic, so our future technology is likely to be inspired by our growing understanding of fractals and the alignment logic of integrity that they represent. In fact, right-brain fractal logic has already brought many benefits including fractal compression, which enables you to stream data. And the fractal analysis of your heartbeat, which shows the very earliest signs of impending heart attack. And the fractal index of cells, which can accurately diagnose specific cancers. Yet all of this great stuff is done by crunching data with the linear-logic of our current computers. Once we have fractal programming, we will get the next leap forward in technology—perhaps even a Star Trek-inspired future?

One of the science fiction gizmos I'm looking forward to is a device about the size of a large matchbox. You run it across an injury site and the injury heals immediately, even broken bones and terrifying burns. Such a thing may not be as far-fetched as you might think, and not just because a lot of sci-fi from the past is now modern-day science. Anything done systematically can, with the right technology, be done by a machine. Much of what I do in my healing practice is systematic, using the fractal logic of my right brain. Some of what

I do is similar to the fractal reconstruction of lost data, which can already be done. The essence of my work is focusing on where the client's fractal is broken or distorted, where their 'data' or self-referencing information has become lost. I reboot their original pattern, using the healthy parts of their fractal as a template.

You do the same thing when you look at a zen painting. The few brush strokes are enough for your right brain to find the fractal and 'read in' the rest of the pattern. It's the same when you look at a tree. If a branch is broken into bits, you could put it back together using the rest of the tree as a template. If you could then re-energize the branch, it would be as if nothing had ever happened. At present it takes conscious focus and intention to reboot the fractal of a living system and re-energize it. Yet once computers with pattern-based logic are created, it should be possible for a gizmo to do it.

Once the new understandings of the brain's activation patterns are incorporated into machines, we'll have computers that understand integrity. A machine can use a lot of power and create a powerful and sustained EM field, so the results will be interesting to say the least. Technology has always had an impact on our future. Fractal technology, or technology that's inherently aligned to the integrity of each system it's working with, will have a huge impact in the years to come. Yet it'll always take conscious awareness to guide the process.

. . . .

Creating with expansive exchange
The middle column

. . . .

One of the strongest patterns in any of our lives is exchange. Like all patterns, the pattern of our exchanges doesn't shift without a lot of work on our part. Transforming our exchange pattern is one of the most effective ways of creating profound shifts in the expansion of our life. Creating the future is an exchange. You put in time, effort and energy in the hope of getting what you want in life in exchange. Remember there are three types of exchange patterns: being out of exchange, in exchange and mutually expansive exchange. The way you go about your manifestation from the very beginning has a huge influence on the kind of exchange life will give you in your future.

What do you do when you start working on creating something new? If you're like most of us, you'll write a list. The clearer you are on what you want, the easier it is to focus on it. All those left-brain details help you find the point in the hologram where you have already manifested what you want, so you can tune into its resonance. However there's an issue with this method that we need to consider. The list you write is all about the 'other'. It may include details of your new relationship partner, your new job, car or house. In other words, it's something other than yourself. That means the situation is a little more complicated than it may first appear.

What your list is describing is something outside of you, which means you're starting from a co-dependent pattern. By focusing on your future in this way, you're unconsciously telling yourself, 'In order for me to have the life I want, the other (the house, car, partner, etc.) has to be like this.' That's a great way of setting yourself up for a hard time. When you only look at the external parts of your manifestation, it's easy to end up invalidating yourself. You may be tempted to give yourself a hard time whenever a day goes past with no signs of what you want; or if there's even one small thing left off your list. You may feel that happened because you don't deserve what you want or your karma's off or something. Invalidation is a heavy personal cost in energy, self-connection and personal belief. It can be so heavy it can make the victory of creating your desire a hollow one.

By also taking your internal state into consideration, you shift the balance of your exchange with the future. You can do this by writing a second list, or column, that's all about you. From a spiritual or personal growth standpoint, the benefit of achieving your goal or dream is in becoming a more expanded version of yourself. Becoming more of Who You Truly Are. Fill out your second column with details about the version of yourself you'd like your manifestation to help you become. That will move your creation from a co-dependent to an independent foundation.

Who will you be in the future? Will you be more loved and loving? More confident? More capable? More aware? More creative and inspired? More abundant? More generous? Remember, practicing being your future self is one of the most elegant and efficient ways of creating your future. So it's worthwhile giving yourself time to become as clear as you can on who you're going to be in the future. Doing this improves your exchange with the future considerably. You reduce the risk of self-sabotage, while you increase the opportunity for self-acknowledgment.

Being clear on your future self means your internal sense of whether you're on track for your desire is a lot more certain. Every day you're a little more like your future self is a day you've taken a step towards your desire. Aligning your energies in this way makes the manifestation easier. It gets you into fair exchange with your future. Focusing on the future as a process of personal evolution, that it's all about you becoming Who You Truly Are, gives you an independent perspective. If you want to go to the next step and manifest from an interdependent perspective, there's one more column you'll need.

The Other	Middle Column	Future Self
• New partner	• Mutual support	• Happier
• Compatible values	• Their passion is	• More open
• Sense of humour	inspiring to me	• More loving
• Gorgeous eyes	• They appreciate my	
• Intelligent	passion	

Example of the three columns of manifestation for a new relationship

This final column is the most interesting and powerful. The essence of interdependency is a mutually expansive exchange and that's what this third column focuses on. I call it the 'Middle Column' because that's where I write it—between the other two. For me, this makes visual sense. This list will help you make your future real to you, right now. In the middle column, write down what your 'other' is going to give you every day, to make it easier for you to expand and be the future version of yourself, as well as what you're going to give to the 'other', in order to maintain it in your life. In this way, you ensure you not only get what you want, but that it also makes your life easier, more graceful and expansive.

Many of my single clients want to manifest a partner for themselves. They tend to focus on the kind of person they want to be with, but often forget to consider the relationship itself. That's crucial. If it's a male partner they're after, they need to consider how they're going to feel when his mates are around sitting on their couch, drinking beer and farting. If it's a female partner that's desired, they need to consider how they'll feel when the state of the house becomes a higher priority and is full of the noise of conversation. Not considering this middle column is why you can do a brilliant job of manifesting the 'other' and have it just not turn out the way you want it to.

The Other	Middle Column	Future Self
• New house	• Easy to maintain	• More relaxed
• Walk-in robes	• Supportive energy	• More creative
• Spa bath	• Inspires me to write	• More abundant
• Great views		• Fitter
• Light and airy		

Example of the three columns of manifestation for a new house

That's what happened to Michelle. I'd known her a while before she built her dream home, way off the grid in the middle of the countryside. This was years before solar technology was as efficient as it is now. She built her gorgeous cottage out of local material, but it took her an hour or two of work every day to make sure all the passive and sustainable stuff worked. Initially, she loved her cottage. It was her dream after all. But as the years passed it took its toll. Her dream home started to turn into a bit of a nightmare, because she didn't think about the middle column—the level of ease the house would give her.

Veronica did a similar thing with her job. She loved what she did, but hated that she wasn't appreciated. It caused her a lot of emotional stress. She worked on manifesting a new job in which her talents would be recognized and got it. It came with a big promotion. Her new boss thought she was fabulous. Yet again, she hadn't thought about the middle column, so her new job also came with a really big workload. Being appreciated so much, she didn't want to let anyone down. She was soon working ridiculous hours. She ended up emotionally happier, but physically more stressed.

Both Michelle and Veronica manifested their desire but neither had thought of how it was going to be mutually expansive in their lives. The middle column ensures we don't just get **what** we want, but we get it **how** we want it, in a way that increases the ease, grace and abundance in our lives. In other words, we don't just get the stuff we want, but the quality of life we're seeking. Just as we're conditioned into co-dependency, rather than interdependency, we have a tendency to manifest from a co-dependent place. Focusing on the exchange, on how your desire will make your life easier and more graceful, ensures you'll manifest your future with a mutually expansive exchange. You're not so much creating it yourself, but co-creating it with the 'other'. The middle column is crucial for your manifestations to work out the way you hope.

Everything in your life is an exchange, even if you're not conscious of it. It's not just the effort and cost of getting it **into** your life, but the effort and cost of **keeping** it in your life. Take your car. You bought it, yet it's how you maintain it that determines whether it ends up a pile of junk or a classic automobile. Your health is the same. What you usually think of as maintenance is really an exchange. It's what you have to give to your car or body for them to continue to support your life. It's the **nature** of that exchange, whether you're out of exchange or whether it's more of a mutually expansive exchange, that'll decide whether your manifestations are the realization of a dream or a nightmare.

Your left brain is good for all the details of the 'other'. Your right brain will give you the intuitive connection to the future that you need for your future self and your mutually expansive exchange. The middle column is the harmonic between the 'other' and your future self. Working with all three columns, especially the middle one, gives you the scope to work with non-linear consequences. This helps ensure that your future will be all you wish for, and that you'll be supported in your journey to Who You Truly Are. Then you'll realize the full potential of your integrity or fractal pattern. And being Who You Truly Are, your life will be full of the love and joy, bliss and abundance, inspiration and creativity that is the natural state of Who You Truly Are.

. . . .

The future is interdependent
The fractal future

. . . .

It was Joseph Campbell who said: *Follow your bliss.* He understood that the source of our greatest joy was in becoming Who We Truly Are. He also said that whenever humanity goes through a transformation, it generates a new archetype or personality template in the collective consciousness. The last major archetypes to be created were the independent ones, first seen in the lone knight of the Arthurian myths. Galahad and Perceval achieved the Holy Grail by not getting distracted by relationships and staying true to the quest, their purpose.

Now the world is going through another transformation. The collective consciousness is seeking a new way of relating between people of different races, different moral constructs, different genders and different life choices. It's also seeking a new way for humanity to relate to our environment and other life forms. As yet we don't have interdependent archetypes, because the whole idea of operating interdependently is still very new to many of us.

Interdependency is a natural consequence of pattern-based thinking. Knowing your own fractal, your own resonance, enables you to develop integrity-based thinking. You can leave behind the limitations of right-wrong thinking. Having learnt to operate through the harmonic, you can now uphold your own integrity, while your life is enriched by the integrity of others.

What kind of future do you want for yourself? If you absolutely knew, you could create literally anything. With all the skills you've learned here in *The Soul's Brain*, you now have the skills to do just that. The stability of the first triangle (Steps One to Three) gave you a solid foundation to create steady progress, to ensure your future will truly serve you through the insight of your soul seat. The second triangle (Steps Four to Six), gave you the strength you need to create powerfully and with tremendous clarity, including knowledge of the process of evolutionary transformation. Through the third triangle

(Steps Seven to Nine), you've developed pattern-based logic, to navigate the future with certainty. You've learned how to use co-creation to manifest your true desires with the ease, grace and abundance of mutually expansive exchange.

You have the skills, so now all you need to do is focus on the future you want, with the clarity and specificity of a resonant lock. Begin by checking in your soul seat, to ensure that your future strengthens your resonance, to ensure that what you want is inspired by your soul, by Who You Truly Are. Then work on your three columns of manifestation, until you lock in the resonance of your future.

Tune into that resonance every day, the resonance of 'future you'. Then you'll navigate through the fractal universe to that point in the hologram where you have all you desire. Then you'll be truly complete. By acknowledging all you've achieved, you'll make it easier for you to manifest what you desire, again and again and again, expanding your cycle, your life and your world every time.

When you create your future from mutually expansive exchange, you'll create a wonderful, amazing, joyful, inspiring, loving and abundant future for yourself, while supporting all those around you to do the same. This is the true power of interdependency. The more of us who live our lives in this way, the more energy, joy, love and inspiration there will be to go around. From all you've learned, you know that's true. It's a practical reality, not just a nice idea. By reading *The Soul's Brain* and doing the exercises, you've empowered yourself to use your intuition as a reliable tool, to create the kind of life for yourself you've always dreamed about.

You know how to do this now, so get out there and live it! This is what using both sides of your brain, the linear logic of your left brain (or data) and the pattern logic of your right brain (or intuition), can deliver. This is how your whole brain is meant to work. It's how your life is meant to be. Together, the two sides of your brain form a seamless system for co-creating the future, realizing inspiration and manifesting the life of Who You Truly Are.

The future is certain because it's an interdependent fractal, and because it already exists out there waiting for you to connect to it.

. . . .

If You Want to Know More

Get Ready

The Hitchhiker's Guide to the Galaxy by Douglas Adams, Pan Books, 1979
TED Talk on *Why our IQ levels are higher than our grandparents* by James Flynn,
https://www.youtube.com/watch?v=9vpqilhW9uI
The answer to the question on pattern-based logic is:
For the latest count of exoplanet numbers, go to: https://exoplanets.nasa.gov/

Step One

Doughnut-shaped Universe bites back by Zeeya Merali, published online in *Nature*,
23 May 2008, http://www.nature.com/news/2008/080523/full/
news.2008.854.html
Birds can 'see' the Earth's magnetic field by Catherine Brahic, in *New Scientist*, 30
April 2008, https://www.newscientist.com/article/dn13811-birds-can-
see-the-earths-magnetic-field/
What causes the Earth's magnetic field? http://www.physics.org/article-questions.
asp?id=64
Frogs levitate in a strong enough magnetic field, http://www.physics.org/facts/frog-
really.asp
Antigonish by Hughes Mearns, 1899
For more information on the electromagnetic spectrum and your physical
senses, go to: https://madstone2000.wordpress.com/frequencies-and-the-
5-senses/

Step Two

Physical inactivity a leading cause of disease and disability, WHO, 4 April 2002,
http://www.who.int/mediacenter/news/releases/release23/en/
Sleep and health, http://healthysleep.med.harvard.edu/need-sleep/whats-in-it-
for-you/health
Awakening Osiris: A New Translation of the Egyptian Book of the Dead by
Normandi Ellis, Red Wheel/Weiser, 2009 [excerpt from *His Soul and His
Shadow* reprinted with permission]
A Brief History of Time by Stephen Hawking, Cambridge University Press, 1988

Ten things you might not know about antimatter by Diana Kwon, http://www.
symmetrymagazine.org/article/april-2015/ten-things-you-might-not-
know-about-antimatter

To watch how an ecosystem powerfully rebalances itself once all the elements
are in place go to *When Wolves Change Rivers* at: https://www.youtube.
com/watch?v=ysa5OBhXz-Q

For more information on the true meaning of the caduceus, go to: http://
www.dailyrounds.org/blog/only-6-of-doctors-knew-the-real-symbol-of-
medicine-staff-of-asclepius/

Step Three

Jonathan Livingston Seagull by Richard Bach, Macmillan, 1970

The Hitchhiker's Guide to the Galaxy, TV adaptation, BBC2, 1981

Step Four

Theoretical Physicist Brian Greene Thinks You Might Be a Hologram, https://www.
wired.com/2012/05/geeks-guide-brian-greene/

From Planck Data to Planck Era: Observational Tests of Holographic Cosmology by
Niayesh Afshordi, Claudio Coriano, Luigi Delle Rose, Elizabeth Gould
and Kostas Skenderis, Phys. Rev. Lett. 118, 041301, 27 January 2017

Fractal Dynamics of Heart Rate and Gait: Implications and General Conclusions,
https://www.physionet.org/tutorials/fmnc/node16.html

Step Five

Origin of the words 'camelopard' and 'giraffe' by Jakub Marian, https://jakubmarian.
com/origin-of-the-words-camelopard-and-giraffe/

The Tibetan Book of Living and Dying by Sogyal Rinpoche, Harper, San Francisco,
1992

Oprah Winfrey, interview with Esther Hicks, *Talk to Me*, XM156 Radio, April
2007

For a short video on what a watershed is go to: https://www.youtube.com/
watch?v=QOrVotzBNto

Step Six

Einstein's Pathway to Special Relativity by John D. Norton, University of
Pittsburgh, 2015

To read more about Einstein's thinking that led him to the theory of relativity, go to: http://www.pitt.edu/~jdnorton/teaching/HPS_0410/chapters_2015_Jan_1/origins_pathway/index.html

Gravitational Waves Detected 100 Years After Einstein's Prediction, News release February 11 2016, https://www.ligo.caltech.edu/news/ligo20160211

Step Seven

A Budget of Paradoxes by Augustus De Morgan, Longmans Green, London, 1872

Step Nine

According to Dyslexia International, dyslexia affects over 700 million people worldwide. Impacting on a person's ability to read, write and spell, this learning difficulty can have a knock-on effect on academic success and self-esteem. Individuals with dyslexia are affected to different degrees. This website gives a small taste of what it's like to be dyslexic: http://geon.github.io/programming/2016/03/03/dsxyliea

Future Steps

New Fractal Methods for Diagnosis of Cancer by Klonowski W., Pierzchalski M., Stepien P. and Stepien R. A., International Symposium on Biomedical Engineering and Medical Physics, 10-12 October 2012, Riga, Latvia, pp.70-73

Acknowledgments

I'd like to thank all the amazing people at Hay House for believing in this work and the workings of intuition. I'd like to especially thank the people at Hay House Australia who helped with the manuscript and all those at kn Literary Arts who started me on my writing journey, especially Chandika Devi. The biggest thanks goes to Jason Buchholz, my editor, who helped with the challenging task of condensing 30 years of work into one book. He helped me construct an accessible work that kept the message true. Special appreciation goes to my grammar guardian, Barbara Callan. A big thanks to the Friday Knights who helped grow my understanding of the power of story. The influence of my teachers, physical and spiritual, is everywhere within these pages and to them goes my deepest appreciation. And of course I want to thank all my amazing students and clients, without whose trust I'd never have reached the understandings contained within these pages and whose enthusiasm for my work has brought this book into the light of day.

About the Author

Are you searching for a more brilliant life?

From a young age Dr. Catherine Wilkins was aware of how we spend our lives caught between who we are today and Who We Truly Are. Her commitment to finding a sure path from the pressures of everyday life to the expansive joy of living our greatest potential took her through veterinary and chiropractic degrees into a deep exploration of functional neurology with its links to our energetic systems.

For nearly thirty years she's been developing and teaching her unique system, called Fractology, transforming the lives of clients and students. Renowned as a medical intuitive and holistic therapist, she's guided thousands to develop their conscious intuitive logic and balance the left and right sides of their brain. Witnessing the resulting expansion of their lives is a testament to her work.

You can access her powerful teachings to create your most brilliant life through her YouTube channel, Facebook and website, www.fractology.info.

We hope you enjoyed this Hay House book. If you'd like to receive our online catalogue featuring additional information on Hay House books and products, or if you'd like to find out more about the Hay Foundation, please contact:

Hay House Australia Pty. Ltd.,
18/36 Ralph St., Alexandria NSW 2015
Phone: +61 2 9669 4299 • *Fax:* +61 2 9669 4144
www.hayhouse.com.au

— — —

Published in the USA by: Hay House, Inc.,
P.O. Box 5100, Carlsbad, CA 92018-5100
Phone: (760) 431-7695 • *Fax:* (760) 431-6948
www.hayhouse.com® • www.hayfoundation.org

Published in the United Kingdom by:
Hay House UK, Ltd., Astley House, 33 Notting Hill Gate,
London, W11 3JQ • *Phone:* 44-203-675-2450
Fax: 44-203-675-2451 • www.hayhouse.co.uk

Published in India by: Hay House Publishers India, Muskaan Complex,
Plot No. 3, B-2, Vasant Kunj, New Delhi 110 070
Phone: 91-11-4176-1620 • *Fax:* 91-11-4176-1630
www.hayhouse.co.in

— — —

Access New Knowledge.
Anytime. Anywhere.

Learn and evolve at your own pace
with the world's leading experts.

www.hayhouseU.com